Wider World
AMERICAN EDITION

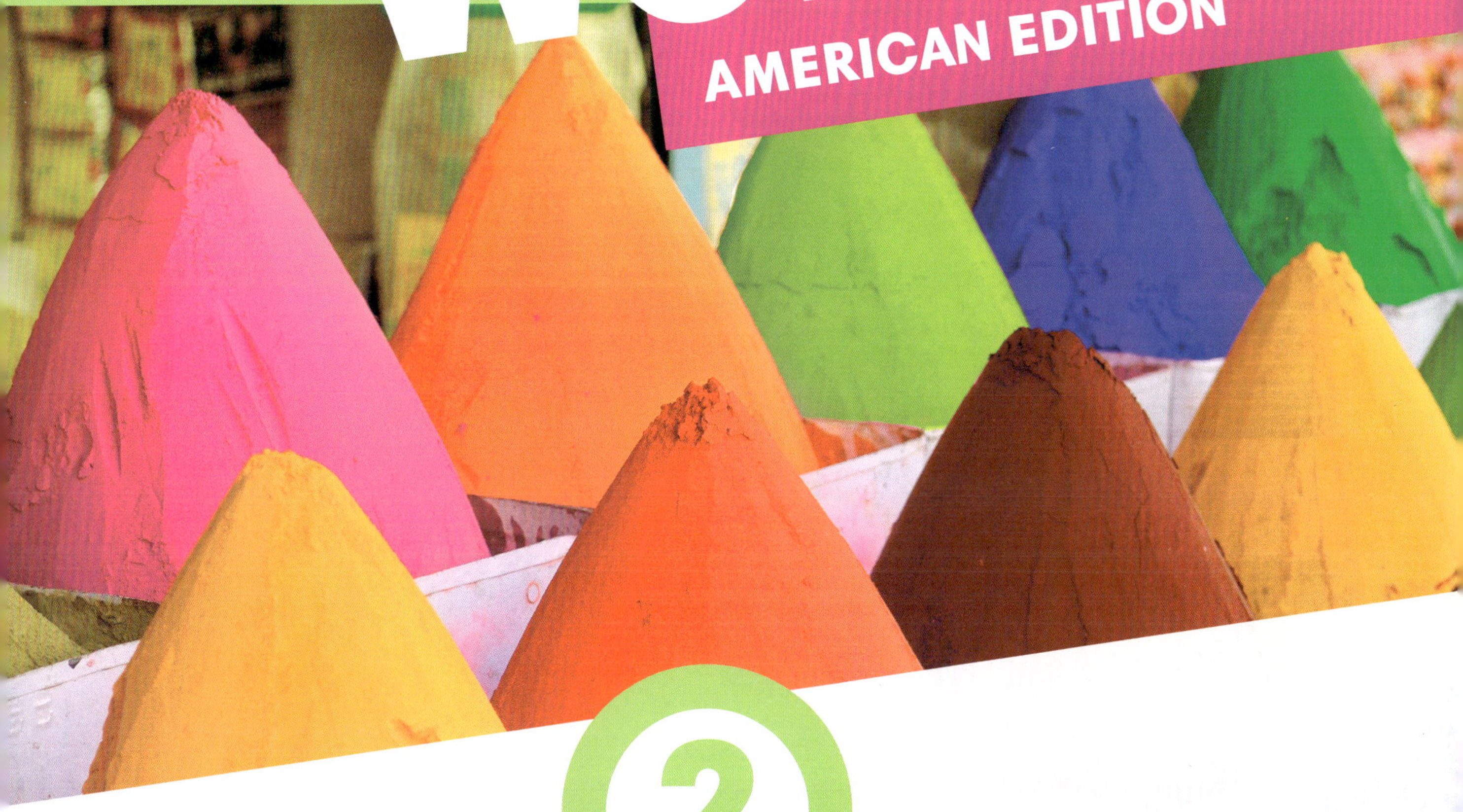

2

STUDENT'S BOOK

Bob Hastings
Stuart McKinlay

Pearson Education Limited
KAO Two, KAO Park
Hockham Way,
Harlow, Essex, CM17 9SR England
and Associated Companies throughout the world

www.english.com/widerworld

© Pearson Education Limited 2020

The right of Bob Hastings and Stuart McKinlay to be identified as authors of this work has been asserted by them in accordance with the Copyright, Designs and Patents Act, 1988.

All rights reserved. No part of this publication may be reproduced, stored in a retrieval system, or transmitted in any form or by any means, electronic, mechanical, photocopying, recording or otherwise without the prior written permission of the copyright holders.

First published 2020
ISBN: 978-1-292-30693-3

Set in Harmonia Sans
Printed in Brazil by Reproset Indústria Gráfica Ltda. - 01/2020.

Acknowledgements
The Publishers would like to thank all the teachers and students around the world who contributed to the development of *Wider World*, especially the teachers on the *Wider World* Teacher Advisory Panel: Irina Alyapysheva, CEE; Reyna Arango, Mexico; Marisa Ariza, Spain; Alfredo Bilopolski, Argentina; Isabel Blecua, Spain; Camilo Elcio de Souza, Brazil; Ingrith del Carmen Ríos Verdugo, Mexico; Edward Duval, Belgium; Norma González, Argentina; Natividad Gracia, Spain; Claribel Guzmán, Mexico; Izabela Lipińska, Poland; Fabián Loza, Mexico; Miguel Mozo, Spain; Huỳnh Th Ái Nguyên, Vietnam; Joacyr Oliveira, Brazil; Montse Priego, Spain; Gladys Rodriguez, Argentina; Lyudmila Slastnova, CEE; Izabela Stępniewska, Poland.

The Publishers would also like to thank the teachers who contributed to the *Go Getter series*, as materials from *Go Getter* Level 1 were adapted to create *Wider World* Starter Level: Anna Borek, CEE; Svetlana Chistyakova, CEE; Marina Grechanichenko, CEE; SofijaLjilakVukajolvič,CEE;EceKahraman,Turkey; Maria Soledad Saravai O'Keefe, Argentina; Bilbana Pavolvič, CEE; Jovana Popovič, CEE; Alla Sichurova, CEE; Marta Skałbania, CEE; Anna Standish, CEE; Katarzyna Szwejkowska, CEE; Renata Woldan, CEE; Ewa Wódkówska, CEE; Oksana Zinchenko, CEE.

The Publishers would also like to thank all the teachers who contributed to the develpment of *Wider World American*: Acacio Tavares, Adriana Felice Gimenes Camargo, Alessandra Franco, Ariane Belchior, Arlete de Simone, Cristiane Tulmann, Danilo Meris, Felipe José Batista Silva, Gil Carla Leite do Nascimento, Iara Toledo de Assis Batista, Ivy Caroline Farias Vieira, Kelly Cardoso, Liliane Reis Soares da Cruz, Marcia Aparecida Auricchio, Maria Isabel Rossignolli, Maria Luiza Corbisier, Renan Cyrino Mansur, Sávio Câmara Leite, Sueli Valente da Silva Caparroz, Vainer Eduardo Pedra. The publishers would like to thank the editors and authors, Rhiannon Sarah Ball and Viviane Kirmeliene who contributed to the adaptation of *Wider World American*.

Photo Acknowledgements
The Publishers would like to thank the following for their kind permission to reproduce their photographs:

123RF.com: alinamd 164, Cathy Yeulet 7, 7, Jose Manuel Gelpi Diaz 7, jovannig 164, neonshot 25, Nicholas Piccillo 50, Sergey Soldatov 102, sjenner13 70, texelart 134; **Alamy Stock Photo:** Chad Ehlers 41, epa european pressphoto agency b.v. 41, fStop Images GmbH 11, Hemis 1, 117, INTERFOTO 73, Jacky Chapman 42, Jeff Greenberg 125, Jochen Tack 41, Mike Kemp 54, NG Images 103, Prisma Bildagentur AG 3, Rosanne Tackaberry 130, scenicireland.com/Christopher Hill Photographic 80, WENN Ltd 103; **BBC Worldwide Learning:** 91, 93, 95; **brando.com:** 30, 30, 30; **Corbis:** 70, Bettmann 33, Global Look / Serguei Fomine 81; **Fotolia:** Adrian Hillman 125, Aleksey Ipatov 85, Alexander Erdbeer 21, Anastasia Bobrova 135, andreusK 20, 21, Andrey Armyagov 125, baiajaku 65, Brian Jackson 35, destina 62, engy1 10, Eric Isselée 29, Grafvision 152, haveseen 164, J And S Photography 21, Kenishirotie 120, ktsdesign 72, LoloStock 152, Lucian Milasan 167, michaeljung 70, micromaniac86 159, Minerva Studio 70, Monkey Business 120, monticelllo 152, Mortazza 152, olgasalt 159, pixelliebe 142, pongans68 97, Popova Olga 120, sborisov 164, shock 120, smspsy 152, Stefano Garau 120, tonda55 134, UMB-O 125, valeo5 29, WavebreakmediaMicro 146, Wrangler 125, yanukit 21, zoryanchik 152; **Getty Images:** Alexandra's Sunset Photography 12, Andrea Pistolesi 11, Bartosz Hadyniak 94, Bloomberg / Vladimir Weiss 103, Dan Kitwood 154, Fred Bavendam 104, Fuse 125, Inti St Clair 16, Julie Thurston 100, LOOK-foto/ Don Fuchs 97, Patrick Boudinet 96, The LIFE Picture Collection/Grey Villet 63, ullstein bild 81; **MIXA Co. Ltd:** 120; **Pearson Education Ltd:** Jon Barlow 6, 7, 8, 9, 10, 14, 17, 20, 24, 26, 30, 32, 36, 40, 44, 46, 50, 52, 56, 60, 64, 66, 70, 74, 76, 80, 86, Studio 8 6, 8, 12, 14, 22, 24, 32, 34, 42, 44, 52, 54, 62, 64, 71, 72, 74, 82, 84; **PhotoDisc:** 10, 20, 30, 40, 50, 60, 70, 80; **Press Association Images (PA Photos):** AP Photo/Shizuo Kambayashi 103, PA Archive/Andrew Milligan 99; **Shutterstock.com:** 37, 158, Abraksis 115, Africa Studio 57, Alexey Boldin 134, Allgord 50, Andreas G. Karelias 158, Andrey_Popov 31, 134, apple2499 21, ayakovlevcom 90, bjul 164, BlueSkyImage 16, 26, 36, 46, 56, 66, 76, 86, bokan 158, Bradley Blackburn 20, Castleski 57, Cheryl Casey. 152, Chris DeRidder 152, Cookie Studio 57, cynoclub 21, D and D Photo Sudbury 93, Daria Rybakova 21, Dean Drobot 11, design56 120, Dmitry Kalinovsky 30, 134, dotshock 120, Dragon Images 17, 27, 37, 47, 57, 67, 77, 87, effective stock photos 20, EpicStockMedia 85, Eric Isselee 21, 21, 25, fizkes 158, FRDMR 21, Georgejmclittle 116, Iakov Filimonov 10, irin-k 20, 21, Jaclyn Schreiner 93, Jiri Pavlik 120, Jon Bilous 45, 45, Kamira 101, Kamonrat 93, Keith Muratori 70, Kenneth Sponsler 60, Kevin Eaves 164, kongsky 99, Kzenon 158, Larich 82, Iuri 164, Macrovector 15, Marie C Fields 152, michaelheim 57, Michel Cecconi 97, Milica Nistoran 33, mirrormere 164, Monika Wisniewska 158, MyImages - Micha 98, Neil Burton 104, nimon 8, Oleg Zabielin 85, Oleksiy Mark 31, 134, Patryk Kosmider 21, 21, paul prescott 75, 99, pavalena 75, paytai 93, Pete Saloutos 120, phol_66 71, photomaster 20, PlusONE 40, PopTika 17, PORTRAIT IMAGES ASIA BY NONWARIT 53, PriceM 30, 134, rbrown10 23, RetroClipArt 83, Rich Carey 104, Rido 53, Robert Wroblewski 116, Rocksweeper 85, Saikorn 30, Sergey Peterman 13, 23, 43, 53, 63, 73, 83, sirtravelalot 120, ssuaphotos 125, StockLite 15, 25, 35, 45, 55, 65, 75, 85, studioVin 120, Sudowoodo 73, suns07butterfly 20, T-Design 158, TalyaPhoto 71, Tero Vesalainen 31, TierneyMJ 30, Tracy Starr 92, Utekhina Anna 25, Valentina_S 20, VanderWolf Images 20, Vangert 25, vblinov 21, Voysla 47, withGod 125, Yakobchuk Viacheslav 31, Yalana 11, Yana Zubkova 81, Yuriy Vlasenko 30, 134; **Superstock:** Citizen Of The Planet 11; **The Kobal Collection:** Film Four / Pathe / Sutton-Hibbert, Jeremy 166

Cover Images: *Front:* **Alamy Stock Photo:** Hemis

All other images © Pearson Education

Level 2 SB
Illustration Acknowledgements
Nicolas Aznarez (Sylvie Poggio) p. 34; Tim Bradford (Illustration Ltd) p.55; John Lund (Beehive Illustration) p. 25, 34, 47; Maria Serrano Canovas (Plum Pudding) p.13, 22, 41, 51, 60, 61.

Level 2 WB
Illustration Acknowledgements
Laura Arias (Beehive Illustration) p. 147, 152; Tim Bradford (Illustration Ltd) p.142; John Lund (Beehive Illustration) p. 132, 140, 153; Maria Serrano Canovas (Plum Pudding) p.121, 146.

Every effort has been made to trace the copyright holders and we apologize in advance for any unintentional omissions. We would be pleased to insert the appropriate acknowledgement in any subsequent edition of this publication.

MISTO
Papel produzido a partir de fontes responsáveis
FSC® C103535

See the Wider picture

Spice shop, Karnataka, India

The colourful piles of powder at the front of the shop are not spices but paint or dye. This is used to dye fabrics for saris, the beautiful costumes worn by Indian women.

Do you know what the powders are made of?

CONTENTS

WELCOME UNIT Welcome to Chesterton		W.1 Time for introductions Family members; possessive adjectives; possessive 's; free-time activities pp. 6–7		
	VOCABULARY	**GRAMMAR**	**READING and VOCABULARY**	**GRAMMAR**
UNIT 1 Time for culture	Talk about cultural activities and likes and dislikes pp. 10–11	Use the Simple Present and adverbs of frequency to talk about habits and routines • Simple Present • Adverbs of frequency p. 12	Predict the topic of an article from its headings and talk about age groups p. 13	Talk about what usually happens and what is happening around now • Simple Present and Present Continuous p. 14
UNIT 2 Animal magic	Talk about animals pp. 20–21	Use *was* and *were* to talk about the past • Simple Past: *was/were* p. 22	Find specific information in a book chapter and talk about personality and behavior p. 23	Use the Simple Past of regular verbs to talk about the past • Simple Past: regular verbs p. 24
UNIT 3 New technology	Talk about technology pp. 30–31	Use the Simple Past of irregular verbs to talk about the past • Simple Past: irregular verbs p. 32	Include missing sentences in texts and talk about using technology p. 33	Use relative clauses to be specific about people, things, and places • Relative clauses p. 34
UNIT 4 My home, my town	Talk about things in the house pp. 40–41	Use adverbs of manner to describe how people do things • Adverbs of manner p. 42	Make inferences from a narrative and describe places p. 43	Talk about permission and obligation • Modal verbs: *can*, *have to*, *must* p. 44
UNIT 5 Take care	Talk about the body, injuries, and keeping fit pp. 50–51	Talk about quantities and amounts of food • Quantifiers p. 52	Find specific information in an online advice column and talk about sleeping habits p. 53	Talk about an event in the past and what was happening around it • Past Continuous and Simple Past p. 54
UNIT 6 Shopping around	Talk about stores and what they sell pp. 60–61	Compare things • Comparatives and superlatives of adjectives p. 62	Find specific information in a magazine article and talk about shopping malls p. 63	Talk about intentions and arrangements • *Going to* and the Present Continuous p. 64
UNIT 7 Learning to work	Talk about people and their jobs pp. 70–71	Use *will* to talk about future predictions • *Will* for future predictions p. 72	Infer the author's purpose in a blog post and talk about jobs p. 73	Use the First Conditional to talk about possible consequences in the future • First Conditional p. 74
UNIT 8 Close to nature	Talk about landscapes, natural features, and countries pp. 80–81	Use the Present Perfect to talk about past experiences • Present Perfect – all forms p. 82	Use the context to understand a personal story and talk about personal experiences p. 83	Use the Present Perfect to talk about recent events • Present Perfect with *already*, *just*, and *yet* p. 84

STUDENT ACTIVITIES pp. 116–117   IRREGULAR VERBS p. 118   SELF-ASSESSMENT ANSWER KEY p. 170   GRAMMAR TIME ANSWER KEY p. 171

				WORKBOOK
W.2 Time at home! Possessions; *there is/are* with *some/any, can't/can*'t for ability; skills and abilities pp. 8-9				pp. 120–121
LISTENING and VOCABULARY	SPEAKING	WRITING	REVIEW	EXTRAS
Identify specific information in a conversation and talk about media habits p. 15	Buy a ticket at the movies p. 16	Write an "About me" section on a webpage p. 17	WORDLIST p. 18 VOCABULARY IN ACTION p. 18 SELF-CHECK p. 19	BBC CULTURE 1 Why do we dance? ▶ *Young Dancer Competition* pp. 90–91 GRAMMAR TIME pp. 106-107 WORKBOOK pp. 122-127
Identify specific information in a conversation and talk about pets p. 25	Make and respond to apologies p. 26	Write a personal account of an event p. 27	WORDLIST p. 28 VOCABULARY IN ACTION p. 28 SELF-CHECK p. 29	BBC CULTURE 2 Why do parrots talk? ▶ *Wild at heart* pp. 92–93 GRAMMAR TIME p. 108 WORKBOOK pp. 128-133
Identify specific information in a conversation and talk about websites p. 35	Put events in order when talking about the past p. 36	Write a blog post about advantages and disadvantages of using a cell phone p. 37	WORDLIST p. 38 VOCABULARY IN ACTION p. 38 SELF-CHECK p. 39	BBC CULTURE 3 Is there wi-fi in the Sahara? ▶ *The digital revolution* pp. 94–95 GRAMMAR TIME p. 109 WORKBOOK pp. 134-139
Identify specific information in a conversation and talk about my town p. 45	Ask for, give, and receive advice p. 46	Write a comment in a forum post p. 47	WORDLIST p. 48 VOCABULARY IN ACTION p. 48 SELF-CHECK p. 49	BBC CULTURE 4 Why are there houses on stilts? ▶ *I want my own room!* pp. 96–97 GRAMMAR TIME pp. 110-111 WORKBOOK pp. 140-145
Identify specific information in a conversation and talk about illnesses p. 55	Talk about feeling sick and give advice p. 56	Write an instant message conversation about a health problem p. 57	WORDLIST p. 58 VOCABULARY IN ACTION p. 58 SELF-CHECK p. 59	BBC CULTURE 5 Is chess a sport? ▶ *Unusual sports* pp. 98–99 GRAMMAR TIME pp. 111-112 WORKBOOK pp. 146-151
Identify specific information in conversations and talk about money p. 65	Go shopping for clothes and other things p. 66	Write notes and messages to make arrangements p. 67	WORDLIST p. 68 VOCABULARY IN ACTION p. 68 SELF-CHECK p. 69	BBC CULTURE 6 Where can you buy a town? ▶ *City shopping* pp. 100–101 GRAMMAR TIME pp. 112-113 WORKBOOK pp. 152-157
Identify specific information in a conversation and talk about education p. 75	Talk about probability p. 76	Write a personal statement p. 77	WORDLIST p. 78 VOCABULARY IN ACTION p. 78 SELF-CHECK p. 79	BBC CULTURE 7 Will robots do our jobs? ▶ *The amazing Henn Na Hotel* pp. 102–103 GRAMMAR TIME pp. 113-114 WORKBOOK pp. 158-163
Identify specific information in personal accounts and talk about outdoor activities p. 85	Ask for, give, and refuse permission p. 86	Write a fictional story p. 87	WORDLIST p. 88 VOCABULARY IN ACTION p. 88 SELF-CHECK p. 89	BBC CULTURE 8 How many fish … ? ▶ *Can you count fish in the sea?* pp. 104–105 GRAMMAR TIME pp. 114-115 WORKBOOK pp. 164-169

W

W.1 TIME FOR INTRODUCTIONS

Welcome to Chesterton

VOCABULARY
Family members | Months and dates |
Free-time activities | Sports |
Possessions |
School subjects | Skills and abilities

GRAMMAR
Possessive adjectives | Possessive *'s* |
There *is/are* with *some* and *any* |
Can/can't for ability

1 Mia   2 ___   3 ___   4 ___

1 🔊 **1.02** Read the text. Label the pictures with the correct names.

Dave   Mia   Ruby   Lee

> This is Lee Marshall. He's fifteen and he's from Chesterton, a small town near Chicago. He's in 10th grade at Chesterton High and he's really into music. Lee has a sister, Ruby – she's thirteen. He doesn't have a brother. Lee's dad, Dave, is an artist. His mom's name is Mia and she's a police officer. She's from a big family in Jamaica. Lee's family also has some pets – a cat and two guinea pigs. Their cat's name is Elvis. The guinea pigs' names are One and Two.

2 Mark the sentences true (T) or false (F). In pairs, correct the false sentences.

1 [F] Lee's last name is Smith.
       Lee's last name is Marshall.
2 [ ] Chesterton is in the USA.
3 [ ] Ruby is Lee's cousin.
4 [ ] Lee's dad doesn't work.
5 [ ] Lee's mom is Spanish.

3 🔊 **1.03** **I KNOW!** In pairs, listen and check if you understand the words below. Can you add more words?

Vocabulary — Family members

aunt   cousin   grandfather   mother   parents   sister   son   wife
grandmother/grandma

4 Look at Lee's family tree and Grammar A box. Write the names. Complete the sentences with the correct possessive adjectives.

Grammar A	Possessive adjectives				
I	you	he	she	we	they
my	your	his	her	our	their

1 _Mia_
   I have a husband – _his_ name is Dave.

2 _____
   I have a sister – ____ name is Ruby.

3 _____
   I have a brother and a sister – ____ brother's name is Bob.

4 _____
   Jack and I have three children – ____ names are Bob, Sue, and Mia.

5 Add apostrophes (') to the sentences about Lee's family.

Grammar B	Possessive 's
Singular	my sister's laptop, Lee's sister
Regular plural	my parents' car
Irregular plural	the children's mother
Two words	Lee's dad's bike, Dave and Gloria's house

Lee's sister's name is Ruby. His dads name is Dave. Mia is Daves wife. Sue is the childrens aunt. Bob is Lee and Rubys uncle.

6 1.04 Listen and read the text. When is Amy's birthday?

>> This is Amy Arnold, Lee's best friend.
She's fifteen and she also goes to Chesterton High. Amy's birthday is on November 15. Amy is very good with computers and her hobbies are playing video games, surfing the internet, taking pictures, swimming, and, in summer, cycling. She also does judo two evenings a week.

7 1.05 Write and say the dates in full. Listen and check.

We write: **November 15**	**Watch OUT!**
We say: **November fifteenth**	

1 1/21 = _January twenty-first_
2 10/12 = _____
3 2/15 = _____
4 7/22 = _____
5 5/4 = _____

8 Read the text about Amy again. Underline her hobbies and interests.

9 1.06 Listen and check if you understand the words below. What other free-time activities can you think of? Talk in pairs.

Vocabulary	Free-time activities

doing nothing   going to the movies
going cycling/running/swimming
listening to music   playing video games
playing basketball/soccer/volleyball
reading books   surfing the internet
taking pictures   visiting relatives
watching TV/movies/online videos

10 In pairs, talk about your family and your favorite free-time activities. Then share what you learned with the rest of the class.

Marta's parents' names are Dan and Lea. She doesn't have a sister, but she has a dog. Marta's favorite hobby is listening to music.

Welcome! 7

W.2 TIME AT HOME!

1 🔊 **1.07** Listen and read the text about Amy's bedroom. Mark the sentences true (T) or false (F).

> Amy's house is on a quiet street in Chesterton, pretty far from downtown. There aren't any stores, but it's near Amy's school. Amy's bedroom isn't very big, but it's her favorite place in the house. There's a bed, a chair, a closet, and a big mirror. There is a table, but the bed is Amy's favorite place to work! Amy's room is very messy. There are always some clothes on the floor … and there are often arguments about this between Amy and her parents!

1. [T] Amy's hometown is Chesterton.
2. [ ] Amy's family's house is downtown.
3. [ ] It isn't far from the school.
4. [ ] Amy's bedroom is small.
5. [ ] Amy doesn't have a desk.

2 🔊 **1.08** Listen and check if you understand the words below. In pairs, underline the things you can see in the picture.

Vocabulary	Possessions

backpack   bike   book   camera   cell phone
dictionary   guitar   earphones   helmet
keys   laptop   pencil case   picture
poster   sneakers   sports bag   sunglasses
tablet   TV   video game   watch

3 In pairs, use the Vocabulary box to tell your classmate three things you have/don't have/ would like to have.

I have a bike. I don't have a poster. I'd like to have a guitar.

4 Study Grammar A box. Complete the sentences about Amy's room.

Grammar A	There is/are with some/any
	Singular	Plural
+	There's (there is) a bed.	There are some clothes.
−	There isn't a desk.	There aren't any stores.
?	Is there a chair?	Are there any books?

1. There __is__ a chair in Amy's room.
2. There _____ a TV.
3. There _____ two posters on the wall.
4. There _____ _____ desk.
5. There _____ _____ camera.
6. There _____ books.

5 Use *there is/are* to write five sentences about your bedroom. Compare with a classmate's.

1. *There are two posters in my bedroom.*
2. _____
3. _____
4. _____
5. _____
6. _____

6 In pairs, ask and answer questions about your bedrooms. Use the items from the Vocabulary box or your own ideas.

A: *Are there any pictures on the wall?*
B: *Yes, there are. / No, there aren't.*
A: *Is there a desk?*
B: *Yes, there is. / No, there isn't.*

7 Write about the street where you live. Then share your text with a classmate.

My house is on a quiet street pretty far from downtown.

8 🔊 **1.09** Listen and read the text. Is Krystal a good student? How do you know that?

a Yes
b No
c It doesn't say

Krystal Ang is fifteen years old. She has a little sister, Lisa, and a dog called Daisy. Krystal is very artistic – she has extra art classes and she can draw very well. She's kind of musical, too – she can play the piano, but she can't sing! Amy and Lee are her friends, but she's at a different school. She's a very hard-working student and she has extra Spanish classes after school on Mondays and Thursdays. Her favorite subjects are Spanish and history. Krystal sometimes has problems with math, but she always gets good grades. She's not very athletic, but she can play tennis pretty well.

9 🔊 **1.10** **I KNOW!** In pairs, match school subjects 1-6 to pictures A–F. Listen and check. Can you think of any more subjects? Talk to a classmate.

1 [B] geography
2 [ ] music
3 [ ] chemistry
4 [ ] English
5 [ ] biology
6 [ ] computer science

A   B   C

D   E   F

10 Read the text again and answer the questions.

1 What are Krystal's favorite subjects?
_____
2 What are your favorite subjects?
_____

11 Study Grammar B box. Complete the sentences with *can* or *can't*.

Grammar B	Can/can't for ability
+	**–**
I **can** cook.	I **can't** sing.
She **can** draw.	She **can't** drive.
?	
Can you sing?	Yes, I **can**. / No, I **can't**.
Can he speak English?	Yes, he **can**. / No, he **can't**.

1 We can speak French, but we _**can't**_ speak Russian.
2 I'm afraid of water because I _____ swim.
3 My brother can't play the guitar, but he _____ play the piano.
4 I _____ help you – I _____ speak Italian. Sorry!
5 What an awful song! The singer _____ sing!

12 🔊 **1.11** In pairs, listen and check if you understand the verbs and phrases below.

Vocabulary	Skills and abilities

act   cook   dance   drive a car
play the guitar/piano   repair a computer
speak English/Spanish   swim

13 🔊 **1.12** Listen to Amy and underline the things in the Vocabulary box that she can do.

14 In pairs, say which things in the Vocabulary box you can and can't do.
I can't speak Spanish, but I can speak English. And you?

15 In pairs, ask and answer the questions.
Can you …

1 study with music?
2 sleep in a chair?
3 run more than two kilometers?
4 do your homework on a bus/in bed?
5 draw people's faces?
6 shoot a basketball?
7 bake a cake?
8 say "hello" in French or Chinese?
9 read music?
10 play chess?
11 ski?

A: *Can you… ?*   B: *Yes, I can./No, I can't.*

16 Tell the class about five things your classmate can do and two things he/she can't. Use his/her answers in Activities 14 and 15 to help you.

Welcome! 9

1

Time for culture

VOCABULARY
Culture | People | Cultural activities | Likes and dislikes | Age groups | News and entertainment

GRAMMAR
Simple Present | Adverbs of frequency | Simple Present and Present Continuous

Grammar:
He's awesome!
Look at the picture. Amy is not happy with Lee. Why not?

Speaking:
At the movies
Look at the picture. What are Lee and Amy talking about?

1.1 VOCABULARY   Culture
I can talk about cultural activities and likes and dislikes.

Art 1   Reading 2

1 🔊 **1.13** What can you see in the pictures? In pairs, match pictures 1–6 to phrases a–f. Listen and check.

a ☐ Is the concert very long?
b ☐ It isn't easy to learn the steps.
c ☐ I like stories with a happy ending.
d ☐ Look at the camera … say "cheese"!
e [1] I like the colors in that painting, but what is it?
f ☐ The actors in this movie are terrible!

2 🔊 **1.14** Study Vocabulary A box. Listen and repeat the words.

Vocabulary A	People		
art	artist	cinema	actor, director
writing	writer	dance	dancer
photography	photographer	music	musician

3 In pairs, make true sentences with the phrases below and the words in Vocabulary A.

I'm a good …   I'm not a bad …   I'm not a great …

A: *I think I'm a good actor. What about you?*
B: *No, I'm not a great actor, but I'm not a bad …*

4 🔊 **1.15** **I KNOW!** Study Vocabulary B box. Add the words below to the correct category. Listen and check. Can you add more words?

~~action movies~~   hip-hop   horror movies   rock   short stories   techno   violin

Vocabulary B   **Cultural activities**

Types of movies: cartoons comedies documentaries fantasy movies romantic movies science fiction (sci-fi) movies [1] *action movies* [2] _____

Things to read: comic books novels graphic novels [3] _____
Types of dance: ballet flamenco salsa [4] _____
Musical instruments: drums guitar piano [5] _____
Types of music: classical music hip-hop pop traditional [6] _____ [7] _____

Photography 3   Dance 4   Cinema 5

5 🔊 **1.16** Study the Speaking box. Listen and circle the correct option.

> **Speaking** — **Likes and dislikes**
>
> I'm (really)/ *not really* interested in modern art.
> I *love / hate* reading horror stories.
> I *really like / don't like* taking selfies.
> I *love / hate* dancing salsa.
> I'm *into / not into* classical music.
> I *like / don't like* acting much.
>
> After these phrases you can use a verb + *-ing* or a noun.

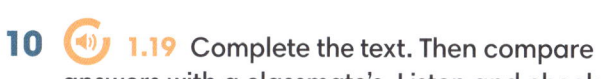

Music 6

6 🔊 **1.17** Listen and circle the option that sounds more expressive.

Speak UP!

1 ↑ (a) ☐ b   3 ☐ a ☐ b
2 ☐ a ☐ b   4 ☐ a ☐ b

7 🔊 **1.17** Listen again. Does their intonation go up 🔼 or down 🔽? Draw the correct arrow in the boxes.

8 🔊 **1.18** **WORD FRIENDS** Complete the sentences with the words below. Listen and check.

> acting ~~dancing~~ drawing listening
> playing reading taking watching

1 I like _dancing_ samba.
2 I hate _____ to techno.
3 I'm interested in _____ the guitar.
4 I love _____ pictures.
5 I'm not into _____ in plays or movies.
6 I really like _____ pictures.
7 I'm into _____ comic books.
8 I don't like _____ horror movies much.

9 In pairs, change the sentences in Activity 8 to make them true for you. Practice using expressive intonation.

10 🔊 **1.19** Complete the text. Then compare answers with a classmate's. Listen and check.

> mikeblog.com
>
> **I'm Mike**
>
> I like [1] _listening_ to classical music. I have a violin, but I'm not a [2] _____ musician, so I can't play it very well. I'm shy, so I hate dancing and [3] _____ in plays, but I'm really [4] _____ photography – I have a good camera and I love [5] _____ pictures. I'm not a bad photographer. I'm [6] _____ in art, too. I don't like painting much, but I really like drawing [7] _____ and I love [8] _____ graphic novels and watching sci-fi movies. What about you?

11 In groups, talk about your likes and dislikes. Use Activities 9 and 10 and the Speaking box to help you. Which classmate has similar likes and dislikes to you?

And YOU

A: *Are you into music?*
B: *Yes, I am. I love rock music. I play the guitar. I'm a musician. What about you?*

Unit 1

1.2 GRAMMAR | Simple Present | Adverbs of frequency

I can use the Simple Present and adverbs of frequency to talk about habits and routines.

1 🔊 **1.20** Listen and read Rose's blog. How are Rose and Violet different?

my sister and me

Feb. 10 4:56

We look the same, but we don't like the same things! Violet studies classical music, but I study art. She reads novels and poems, but I don't read much. And she often watches TV, but I never watch TV – it doesn't interest me. Violet writes poems. I write messages on my cell phone. I love hip-hop. She says that hip-hop annoys her. But do we argue or do we spend time together? We always spend time together, of course! We like different things, but we are still best friends!

added by Rose   Tweet 13   Like 2

2 Study the Grammar box and circle the correct words to complete the rule. Then underline examples of the Simple Present in the blog post in Activity 1.

Grammar	Simple Present
+	−
I love hip-hop. She writes poems. She often goes out. She studies art.	I don't watch TV. She doesn't like music.
?	Short Answers
Does she like music? Do we look the same? What do you like? Where does he study?	No, she doesn't. Yes, we do.

Adverbs of frequency (*always, usually, often, sometimes, never*) go *before / after* the verb, but *before / after* to be.

GRAMMAR TIME > PAGE 106

3 Use the prompts to write questions. Then answer them using adverbs of frequency. Compare answers with a classmate's.

1 you / write poems?
   Do you write poems?
   Yes, I do. I sometimes write poems.

2 your mother / read novels?
   _____
   _____

3 your teacher / draw pictures on the board?
   _____
   _____

4 you and your friends / go dancing?
   _____
   _____

5 your cousins / listen to classical music?
   _____
   _____

4 🔊 **1.21** Complete the interview with the correct form of the verbs in parentheses. Listen and check.

Q: ¹ _Do you go_ (go) to the movies a lot?

A: Well, I ² _____ (live) in a village, so I ³ _____ (not go) to the movies very often. My brother usually ⁴ _____ (watch) movies online, but I ⁵ _____ (prefer) playing video games.

Q: Who ⁶ _____ (be) the best player?

A: Dylan! He ⁷ _____ (not win) every game, but he usually ⁸ _____ (get) the highest scores.

Q: When ⁹ _____ (play) video games?

A: We ¹⁰ _____ (not play) on school days, so we ¹¹ _____ (play) a lot on weekends!

5 In pairs, use the phrases below and adverbs of frequency to ask and answer questions about what you do in your free time. Tell the class about you and your classmate.

watch action movies   read movie reviews
listen to rap music   read comic books   take pictures
make crafts   play board games   walk in the country

I often listen to rap music, but Jo prefers pop.

Unit 1

1.3 READING and VOCABULARY — A magazine article

I can predict the topic of an article from its headings and talk about age groups.

1 **CLASS VOTE** How much TV do you usually watch before/after school?

- ☐ I never watch TV.
- ☐ Less than one hour.
- ☐ One–two hours.
- ☐ More than two hours.

2 Read the title of the magazine article and look at the picture. What kind of person is a "couch potato"? Circle the correct answer.

a A person who eats potato chips in front of the TV.
b A person who spends a lot of time sitting and watching TV.

Where are all the couch potatoes?

By Ann Taylor

1 **d** Parents and teachers say that teenagers are "couch potatoes" and spend all their time in front of silly TV shows. But is it true that young people really watch a lot of TV?

2 ☐ The results of a recent survey show that people in the UK typically watch twenty-seven and a half hours of TV every week – almost four hours a day! But there is some surprising news – young people don't watch as much TV as adults. For example, middle-aged adults (aged forty-five to sixty-five) watch about five hours a day. But young people aged twelve to seventeen watch about two and a half hours a day. And an older person watches about six hours a day!

3 ☐ Studies in countries such as the USA and Australia suggest the same: kids today spend less time in front of the TV than young people in the 1980s.

4 ☐ Teenagers today don't often sit with their families on the living room couch. So where are they? Do they spend all their free time outdoors, away from the TV? The simple answer is no, they don't. They're still watching series and movies – around thirty-one hours a week! So, what's different now? Well, now they're online! Watching series and movies on streaming apps installed on cell phones and tablets is now one of the most popular free-time activities for teenagers. The couch potato is alive and well – he's just back in his bedroom.

3 Read the headings of different sections of the magazine article. In pairs, predict what each section is about and take notes in your notebook.

a A global change
b Surprising statistics
c TV is cool again
d Too much TV?
e A new obsession

Reading tip

Before reading a magazine article, read the headings and try to predict the topic of each section. This will help you better understand the text.

4 🔊 **1.22** Read the magazine article. Match headings a-e in Activity 3 to paragraphs 1-4. There is one extra heading. Listen and check.

5 🔊 **1.23** Look at the Vocabulary box. Listen and repeat the words. How do you say them in your language?

Vocabulary — Age groups

adults   kids   middle-aged (people)
older people   teenagers

6 In your notebook, write sentences about the people below, using the words in the Vocabulary box.

1 Jon and Cara are sixteen. *They're teenagers.*
2 Wendy is eight and Peter is five.
3 Julio and his wife are seventy-nine.
4 Emma and Don aren't children.
5 Oscar and Helena are both fifty-two.

7 Read the magazine article again. Mark the sentences ✓ (right), ✗ (wrong), or ? (doesn't say).

1 ✓ Parents and teachers agree that teenagers watch too much TV.
2 ☐ Middle-aged people watch more TV than teenagers.
3 ☐ Older people watch TV six hours a week.
4 ☐ Teenagers don't watch TV because they prefer to be outdoors.
5 ☐ Teenagers in the USA and in Australia usually have a TV in their bedroom.

8 The survey in the magazine article shows that adults watch a lot of TV. In groups, talk about how much TV you and your family watch.

I don't watch TV very often, but my sister watches TV every night.

Unit 1   13

1.4 GRAMMAR   Simple Present and Present Continuous

I can talk about what usually happens and what is happening around now.

1 🔊 **1.24** Listen and read the dialogue. Then answer the questions in your notebook.

1. What does Lee usually do on Wednesdays?
   He usually plays the guitar with his band.
2. What is he doing today?
3. Is Lee a fan of Bro?

HE'S AWESOME!

Lee: Hey, Amy. Do you want to hear my new song?
Amy: But it's Wednesday! You usually play with your band on Wednesdays.
Lee: I know, but today Luke and Peter are traveling, so I'm practicing in my bedroom.
Amy: OK, but there is a live Bro show online soon. He doesn't often do live shows, but he's playing music from his new album today.
Lee: To be honest, I don't really like …
Amy: Ssh, it's starting now! Oh, he isn't playing his new music, he's playing "My perfect girl." It's my favorite song!
Lee: Does he write his songs?
Amy: Yes, he always writes his songs and plays his instruments. And in his free time he helps sick animals. He's perfect!
Lee: Yeah, right …

To be honest, … Yeah, right …	**OUT of class**

2 Study the Grammar box. Complete with *Simple Present* and *Present Continuous*. Underline examples of the structures in the dialogue in Activity 1.

Grammar	Simple Present and Present Continuous

I usually play guitar with my friends.
It isn't raining now.
My friends are traveling this week.

We use the _____ for facts and routines.
For things happening at the moment of speaking, we use the _____ .

GRAMMAR TIME ▶ PAGE 107

3 Circle the correct option.

1. We *study* / (*are studying*) ancient history this semester.
2. Leo *saves* / *is saving* his money to go to a concert.
3. Sam is only two, so he *doesn't go* / *isn't going* to school.
4. How often *do you play* / *are you playing* video games?
5. You *don't watch* / *aren't watching* this TV show. Can I change the channel?
6. Look! The baby *uses* / *is using* your cell phone!

4 In your notebook, write sentences with *but* to describe Paula's usual life and what's happening now.

Paula usually goes to bed late, but tonight she's going to bed early.

Usually	Now
go to bed late	tonight / early
watch online videos	today / listen / a podcast
not read novels	a great book at the moment
wear jeans	today / go / a party / so a dress

5 🔊 **1.25** Complete the text with the correct form of the words in parentheses. Use the Simple Present or the Present Continuous. Listen and check.

RUSSELL, OHIO

I ¹ _live_ (live) in a rural area, so I usually
² _____ (go) hiking on weekends. But this week
I ³ _____ (visit) my aunt and uncle in New York.
They ⁴ _____ (have) an apartment in the city.
Today I ⁵ _____ (do) something different.
I ⁶ _____ (ride) the subway to go to a Broadway show. It ⁷ _____ (rain) at the moment, but
I ⁸ _____ (be) happy!

6 Work in pairs. Look at Activity 4 again and make sentences about you.

I always go to bed early, but tonight I'm staying up late to watch the new episode of my favorite series!

1.5 LISTENING and VOCABULARY   Types of media

I can identify specific information in a conversation and talk about media habits.

1 **CLASS VOTE** Read the questions in the survey and then ask and answer them in pairs. Share your answers with the class. What is the most popular type of media in your class?

Newspapers   The radio   The TV   The internet

What type of media do you use:

1 to listen to new music?
2 to watch music videos?
3 to find news about your favorite celebrity?
4 to find sports results?
5 to see what's on at the movie theater?
6 to find information for school projects?
7 to read the news?
8 to check the weather forecast?

2 🔊 1.26 Read the survey again. Then listen and match speakers A–E to questions 1–8. There are three extra questions.

A 7   B ☐   C ☐   D ☐   E ☐

3 🔊 1.27 Look at the Vocabulary box and listen to the words. In which type of media from the survey can you find these things? Sometimes more than one answer is possible.

Vocabulary	News and entertainment

blog/vlog   call-in show   documentary   game show
game/movie reviews   message board   news
news headlines   online videos   reality show
talk show   TV series   weather forecast

4 Use the Vocabulary box to complete the sentences.

1 My dad loves watching ___game shows___. He usually shouts out the answers at the TV!
2 The group's _____ is a place on the internet for fans to meet and write about the group.
3 My favorite _____ is on TV on Mondays. I think the actors are awesome!
4 I don't often read _____ because my friends tell me which games to buy.
5 My sister often sends me links to funny _____ with cats on the internet.

5 In pairs, take turns to name an example of the types of media in the Vocabulary box.

A: *The Voice.*   B: *That's a reality show.*

6 🔊 1.28 Listen and match speakers 1–4 to the type of radio show they like (a–e). There is one extra answer.

1 ☐ Cara   a news
2 a Cara's dad   b Pop Top 20
3 ☐ Rob, Cara's   c sports
     brother   d call-in shows
4 ☐ Cara's mom   e rock music

7 Complete the sentences to make them true for you. Use the Vocabulary box to help you. Then compare with a classmate's.

And YOU

1 I often read these magazines/books by these authors: _____.
2 My three favorite websites are _____, _____, and _____.
3 My favorite radio station is _____. I usually listen to it when I _____.
4 My favorite types of TV shows are _____ and _____. I always watch _____.

8 Tell the class about your classmate's answers.

Unit 1   15

1.6 SPEAKING — At the movies

I can buy a ticket at the movies.

1 **CLASS VOTE** Look at the movie theater showtimes and say what types of movies are on. Which ones would you like to see?

A: *I think True Love is a romantic comedy. I'd like to see it.*

B: *Me too!*

Amy:	So, what's on?
Lee:	The new Tom Lewis movie, *True Love*. It starts in ten minutes.
Amy:	No way! I want to see *ZooWorld*.
Lee:	I don't like fantasy movies. They're boring.
Amy:	Oh, come on, please.
Lee:	Oh, OK.
Later…	
Amy:	Can I have two tickets for *ZooWorld*, please?
Attendant:	Sure, which screening?
Amy:	The 6:30.
Attendant:	I'm sorry, it's sold out … Oh, no, hold on! There are two seats.
Amy:	Great!
Attendant:	But they're in the front row.
Lee:	Oh, I don't want to sit in the front row!
Amy:	OK … I'd like two for *True Love* at 6:15, please.
Attendant:	Row seven. Is that OK?
Amy:	Yes, thanks. How much is that?
Attendant:	That's twelve fifty, please.
Lee:	Here you are.
Attendant:	Thank you. Enjoy the movie!
Amy:	Thank you …

OUT of class
No way! Come on, please! Hold on!

2 🔊 1.29 Listen and read. Answer the questions.

1 Which movie do Lee and Amy go to see? *True Love.*

2 What time does it start? _____

3 How much is each ticket? _____

3 🔊 1.30 Study the Speaking box. Complete the dialogue below with one word in each blank. Then listen and check.

Speaking — At the movies

You need to say:
- What's on?
- Can I have two tickets for *ZooWorld*, please?
- I'd like two tickets for *True Love*, please.
- The 8:15 screening.
- How much is that?
- Here you are.

You need to understand:
- Which screening?
- I'm sorry, it's sold out.
- There are two seats in the front row.
- Row seven. Is that OK?
- That's twelve fifty, please.

Krystal:	Can I have two ¹ _tickets_ for *True Love*, please?
Attendant:	Which ² _____?
Krystal:	The 8:15 screening.
Attendant:	Here you are … two tickets in ³ _____ five.
Krystal:	How ⁴ _____ is that?
Attendant:	That's twelve fifty, ⁵ _____.
Krystal:	⁶ _____ you are.
Attendant:	⁷ _____ you, enjoy the movie.

4 In pairs, buy tickets for a movie from Activity 1. Use the Speaking box to help you. Then switch roles.

1.7 WRITING An "About me" section

I can write an "About me" section on a webpage.

1 **CLASS VOTE** Do you have a personal webpage or blog? If so, what do you write about?

Lee Marshall
Chesterton, near Chicago, the USA

About me

1. My name is Lee Marshall and I'm fifteen. I live with my parents and my sister, Ruby, in Chesterton, near Chicago. I'm in 10th grade at Chesterton High. My favorite subjects are music, art, and English.

2. I like books and movies, but my big passion is music. My favorite band is Arcade Fire – they're from Canada and they're awesome! In my free time, I sing and play the guitar.

3. Chicago is a great place for music lovers like me. There are more than 200 places to listen to live music! I recommend the National Jazz Museum, too. You can learn about music there.

4. I make music on my laptop every day and I sometimes write songs. Click on the media player to listen to them and tell me what you think!

1 ▶	NO WAY! 3:20	BUY	
2 ▶	COME ON, PLEASE! 4:05	BUY	
3 ▶	NOT RIGHT NOW 3:55	BUY	
4 ▶	CHESTERTON BLUES 3:33	BUY	

2 In pairs, look at Lee's webpage. Read the sentences and check (✓) the sentence that isn't true.
1. There is a picture of Lee on the webpage.
2. You can listen to some of Lee's songs.
3. You can look at Lee's picture gallery.
4. There is personal information about Lee.

3 Study the Writing box and compare sections 1–4 to the sections in the text in Activity 1.

Writing An "About me" section

1. **Personal details**
   - My name is …
   - I'm … years old.
   - I live with … in …
   - I'm in … grade at …

2. **Interests/Hobbies**
   - I like/I'm into/I'm crazy about …
   - My big passion is …
   - My favorite … is …
   - In my free time …

3. **About my town**
   - My town is a great place for …
   - There is/There are …
   - I recommend …/You can …

4. **Routines**
   - I often/sometimes/usually …
   - I … once a week/every day.

4 Write an "About me" section for your personal webpage.

Writing Time

1. **Find ideas**
   Look at the Writing box. Think of how the sentences would be true for you.

2. **Draft**
   In your notebook, write a draft of an "About me" text. Look at Lee's text to help you.

3. **Share**
   Share your text with a student for feedback. Listen to his/her opinion and suggestions. Check the spelling and grammar.

4. **Check and write**
   Make any necessary changes to your text. Do you use a variety of phrases and different expressions? Write the final version of your text.

WORDLIST Culture | Media

act [v]
acting [n]
action movie [n]
actor [n]
adult [n]
art [n]
artist [n]
ballet [n]
blog [n]
board game [n]
call-in show [n]
camera [n]
cartoon [n]
celebrity [n]
cinema [n]
classical music [n]
comedy [n]
comic books [n]
concert [n]
couch potato [n]
craft [n]
dance [v]
dancer [n]
dancing [n]
director [n]
documentary [n]
drawing [n]
drums [n]
fantasy movie [n]
flamenco [n]
game show [n]
graphic novel [n]
guitar [n]
hip-hop [n]
hobby [n]
horror movie [n]
interests [n]

kid [n]
media [n]
magazine [n]
message board [n]
middle-aged [adj]
modern art [n]
game review [n]
music [n]
musician [n]
nationality [n]
news [n]
news headlines [n]
novel [n]
older person [n]
online video [n]
painting [n]
passion [n]
photographer [n]
photography [n]
piano [n]
picture [n]
play [n]
poem [n]
pop [n]
poster [n]
radio station [n]
rap [n]
reading [n]
reality show [n]
rock [n]
romantic movie [n]
row [n]
salsa [n]
science fiction (sci-fi) movie [n]
screening [n]
seat [n]
short story [n]

showtime [n]
sing [v]
sold out [adj]
sports pages [n]
story [n]
survey [n]
talk show [n]
techno [n]
teenager [n]
the movies [n]
ticket [n]
traditional [adj]
TV series [n]
violin [n]
weather forecast [n]
writer [n]
writing [n]

WORD FRIENDS

act in plays/movies
be into something
be crazy about something
check sports results/the weather forecast/the news
couch potato
dance flamenco
find information
go dancing
happy ending
learn the (dance) steps
listen to (dance) music/hip-hop
make videos
play the guitar
read comic books/movie reviews
see what's on (at the movies)
take pictures/selfies
watch online videos

VOCABULARY IN ACTION

1 In your notebook, write words for each category. Use the Wordlist.
  1 eight types of movies: *horror movies, ...*
  2 eight types of radio/TV shows:
  3 seven things you can read:
  4 five types of music:

2 In pairs, say which three things you prefer in each category in Activity 1.
I prefer horror movies, comedies, and ...

3 Complete the Word Friends. In pairs, say if the sentences are true for you.
  1 I'm really __into__ poems.
  2 I never _____ selfies.
  3 I'm crazy _____ game shows.
  4 I hate movies with _____ endings.
  5 I _____ the weather forecast every day.

4 Complete the sentences with the correct form of the words in bold.
  1 Banksy is a famous British __artist__. **ART**
  2 My sister's a great _____ – she can play four instruments. **MUSIC**
  3 Who is your favorite movie _____? **ACT**
  4 I want to be a _____ when I leave school. **PHOTOGRAPH**

5 🔊 1.31 **PRONUNCIATION** Listen to the underlined vowel(s) in each word. In your notebook, write the word in the correct column.

~~guitar~~   m*e*dia   m*i*ddle-aged   r*ea*ding
s*ea*t   s*i*ng   t*ee*nagers   v*i*deo

1 /iː/	2 /ɪ/
	guitar

6 🔊 1.31 **PRONUNCIATION** Listen again, check, and repeat.

SELF-CHECK

1 Write the correct word for each definition.
1. This person makes movies and tells actors what to do. d _i r e c t o r_
2. It's something you like doing in your free time. h _ _ _ _ _ _
3. It's a big picture or drawing. p _ _ _ _ _ _
4. It's a good idea to read one before you see a movie. r _ _ _ _ _ _ _
5. This person is aged from thirteen to nineteen. t _ _ _ _ _ _ _ _

2 Complete the Word Friends in the text. Then ask and answer the questions in pairs.

✽ **the media and your parents**

Do your parents:
1. listen to the radio? When? Which shows do they prefer?
2. watch the ¹n _ews_____ on TV? At what time?
3. check the weather ²f_____ every day?
4. watch documentaries on TV? What about ³s_____, ⁴t_____ shows, ⁵g_____ shows, ⁶r_____ shows?
5. buy newspapers or ⁷m_____? Which sections do they read first?

SUBMIT ▸

3 Complete the poem with the words below. There are two extra words.

act ~~go~~ make play potato sing story take watch write

I want to ¹ _go_____ dancing and ² _____ the guitar
And then ³ _____ a song with my favorite pop star.
I want to ⁴ _____ a poem and ⁵ _____ in a play
And ⁶ _____ some pictures of a beautiful ballet.
I don't want to ⁷ _____ movies on TV all day
Or be a couch ⁸ _____, no way!

4 Complete the sentences with the Simple Present or the Present Continuous form of the verbs in parentheses.
1. Beyoncé _lives_____ (live) in the USA. This week she _____ (stay) at her apartment in England.
2. Jo always _____ (go) to dance classes after school, but he _____ (not go) today.
3. No, I _____ (never/watch) online videos. I'm _____ (listen to) music right now.
4. We _____ (watch) a romantic movie right now. My friends _____ (not enjoy) science fiction movies.

5 In your notebook, write questions for the answers in Activity 4.
1. Where … ? _Where does Beyoncé live?_
2. When … ?
3. … online videos?
4. What kind of … ?

6 In pairs, use the words in A and B to write five sentences about a friend or a classmate in your notebook. Then write about something different they are doing this week.

A: always often sometimes usually never once/twice/three times a …

B: act go listen paint play read watch

Lucas always listens to rap music, but today he's listening to classical music!

7 Work in pairs. Student A, ask your classmate these questions and buy two tickets to see a movie. Student B, look at page 117.

Student A
- What's on?
- What time …?
- … seats / row 7?
- How much …?
- … two tickets / please?

8 🔊 1.32 Listen, then listen again and write down what you hear.

_____
_____
_____
_____

SELF-ASSESSMENT Think about this unit. What did you learn? What do you need help with? **WORKBOOK** p. 127

2

2.1 VOCABULARY Animals
I can talk about animals.

Animal magic

VOCABULARY
Animals | Animal body parts
Personality | Taking care of pets

GRAMMAR
Simple Past: *was/were*
Simple Past: regular verbs

Grammar:
Taking care of Daisy
Look at the picture. What happened to Lee?

Speaking:
I don't know how it happened!
Look at the picture. What are Lee and Krystal talking about?

1 1.33 In pairs, match the animals to the words in Vocabulary A box. Then listen and repeat.

Vocabulary A	Animals
Pets:	G parrot ☐ rabbit ☐ tortoise
Farm animals:	☐ chicken ☐ cow ☐ donkey
Wild animals:	☐ bear ☐ chimp ☐ elephant ☐ giraffe
	☐ kangaroo ☐ tiger ☐ zebra
Insects:	☐ bee ☐ butterfly ☐ fly

2 1.34 **I KNOW!** In your notebook, add the animals below to the correct category in Vocabulary A box. Listen and check. Then listen again and repeat the words.

ant   cat   dolphin   duck   monkey   shark   sheep   snake   spider

3 In groups, think of two or more animals for each category below. Then compare with another group.
1 We can ride these animals. *horse, …*
2 These animals sleep in the winter.
3 People keep these animals for meat.
4 These animals are good at climbing.
5 People use the skin of these animals for clothes or shoes.
6 These animals are good at running.
7 These animals are very dangerous.
8 These animals have sharp teeth and eat meat.

20 Unit 2

4 🔊 **1.35** Look at Vocabulary B box. Listen and repeat the words. How do you say them in your language?

Vocabulary B	Animal body parts

claw   feather   fur   mouth   tail   wing

5 🔊 **1.36** Look at the pictures and decide which animal you think it is. Circle the correct words. Listen and check.

The feathers of
a parrot / (a duck).

The claws of
a chicken / a parrot.

The wing of a fly /
a bee.

The tail of a donkey /
a monkey.

6 In pairs, mark the sentences true (T) or false (F). Check your answers on page 116. Which fact do you find surprising?

True or False?

1. ☐ Polar bears have white fur, but black skin.
2. ☐ A flamingo's feathers are pink because it eats a special kind of plankton.
3. ☐ Tigers have stripes on their fur, but not on their skin.
4. ☐ Bees can beat their wings 200 times a second.
5. ☐ Elephants have a special call that means, "Danger: Humans!"
6. ☐ The tail of a giraffe can grow to over 2.5 meters.

7 In pairs, ask and answer the questions. Use the words from the Vocabulary boxes to help you.

- What's your favorite wild animal? Why do you like it? Can you describe it?
- Which dangerous wild animals live in your country? Can you describe them?

My favorite wild animal is … because it is cute/smart/fascinating/funny … It has fur and claws …

Unit 2   21

2.2 GRAMMAR Simple Past: was/were

I can use *was* and *were* to talk about the past.

1 🔊 1.37 What can you see in the picture? Listen and read. What does Kyle say about his brother and sister?

Zadie: You weren't at home yesterday.
Kyle: I was out.
Zadie: I know that! Were you at the mall?
Kyle: No, I wasn't.
Zadie: Where were you?
Kyle: We were at the zoo.
Zadie: You were at the zoo! Why?
Kyle: It was the twins' birthday.
Zadie: Really? Was it fun?
Kyle: Yes, it was. It was awesome! There was a great café and there were lots of interesting animals.
Zadie: Were the kids excited?
Kyle: Excited? They weren't excited, they were crazy! The chimps were shocked!

2 Study the Grammar box and complete the rule. Then underline examples of *was/were* in the dialogue in Activity 1.

Grammar	Simple Past: was/were
+	**−**
I was out. We were at the zoo.	I wasn't at the mall. We weren't at home.
?	
Were you at home? Was it boring? Were you happy? Where were they?	Yes, I was./No, I wasn't. Yes, it was./No, it wasn't. Yes, we were./No, we weren't.

there is (isn't) → there was (wasn't)
there are (aren't) → there were (weren't)

Time expressions: *last night/weekend, yesterday, this morning, two days ago, at ten o'clock*

Was and *were* are the past forms of the verb _____.

GRAMMAR TIME > PAGE 108

3 🔊 1.38 Complete the dialogue with *was, were, wasn't,* or *weren't*. Listen and check.

Kyle: Where ¹ _were_ you yesterday, Zadie?
Zadie: I ² _____ with Mel. We ³ _____ at the stores.
Kyle: ⁴ _____ you at the mall downtown?
Zadie: Yes, we ⁵ _____.
Kyle: ⁶ _____ it busy?
Zadie: No, it ⁷ _____. There ⁸ _____ any people there because the stores ⁹ _____ closed. It ¹⁰ _____ a holiday. There ¹¹ _____ only one store open, a convenience store!

4 Use the words below and the correct form of *there was/were* to write sentences about the picture in Activity 1.

> chimps   not many people   old lion   giraffe
> not any bears   small monkeys
> penguins   gift shop

1 *There were three chimps in a cage.*
2 _____
3 _____
4 _____
5 _____
6 _____
7 _____
8 _____

5 Complete the chart with the places below. In pairs, guess your classmate's answers. Then say where you were at each time.

> **AT** home   school   a friend's   a party   a snack bar
>   the movies   the zoo   an aquarium   a concert
> **IN** a pet store   the classroom   a park   a store

Where	When
	an hour ago
	last weekend
	yesterday at 7 p.m.
	in the summer

A: *Were you at the zoo last weekend?*
B: *No, I wasn't.*
A: *Where were you?*
B: *I was at home!*

22 Unit 2

2.3 READING and VOCABULARY — A book chapter

I can find specific information in a book chapter and talk about personality and behavior.

1 Read quickly the chapter from a book. Who do you think the book is for?
a parents
b animal lovers
c zoo keepers

2 🔊 1.39 Listen and read the text. Mark the sentences ✓ (right), ✗ (wrong), or ? (doesn't say).
1 ✗ It's impossible to love adolescent dogs.
2 ☐ Young dogs often change their behavior.
3 ☐ All young elephants live with their families.
4 ☐ Teenage elephants sometimes kill other elephants.
5 ☐ Young sea otters always follow their parents' example.
6 ☐ Dangerous situations can teach a young animal a lot.

Reading tip

If you don't know the meaning of a specific word in a text, try to identify it from the context before checking it in a dictionary.

3 🔊 1.40 Find the words below in the text. Listen and repeat the words. Then match the words to the characteristics in sentences 1–5.

Vocabulary — Personality

adventurous   aggressive   forgetful
impulsive   lovable

1 Grandpa often loses his glasses.
   forgetful
2 Harry often buys things he doesn't need.
   _____
3 The Smiths love traveling to exotic, dangerous places. _____
4 Male rabbits often fight when they live together. _____
5 My puppy is friendly, fun, and cute. _____

4 In pairs, ask and answer the questions.   **And YOU?**
1 What do your parents or teachers criticize you for?
2 Do you agree with their opinion?

Chapter 2: Those difficult teenage years

Let me tell you a story. When Sally was an adolescent, she was noisy. She was adventurous, lovable, and sometimes shy. She was often forgetful, too. Sally was my dog.

Adolescent dogs (from six months to a year old) are a little bit like human teens. They explore their world and test their own abilities. They love adventures and they often look for attention. One minute they're tired – then suddenly they're lively and energetic. Sometimes it can be hard for others to understand them.

And dogs aren't the only animals with a "teenage" time in their lives. Between the ages of ten and twenty, male African elephants leave their family groups and live in large male gangs. These young elephants don't always behave well. They can be noisy and aggressive. They sometimes terrorize other groups and in some cases they kill other animals for sport.

Male sea otters also have a "teenage" stage. They take risks and ignore their parents' advice. Sometimes they swim near dangerous white sharks and sometimes the sharks eat them. But that doesn't stop other adventurous young otters from playing this dangerous game.

For many animals, the time between childhood and adulthood is difficult. They lose the care and protection which they get from their parents. But they need risk and adventure to learn about the dangers of the world. In other words, impulsive or even crazy behavior is an important part of an animal's education. It is often the key to success as adults. Just like for humans.

2.4 GRAMMAR Simple Past: regular verbs

I can use the Simple Past of regular verbs to talk about the past.

1 🔊 **1.41** Look at the picture. Why is Lee worried? Listen and check.

TAKING CARE OF DAISY

Lee: Amy!
Amy: Lee! What's wrong?
Lee: It's Daisy, Krystal's dog! I can't find her.
Amy: Calm down! What happened?
Lee: We <u>were</u> at the park and I <u>decided</u> to take off the leash to let her run around. But then I answered a call and when I finished talking, Daisy wasn't there. I looked everywhere, but …
Amy: When did this happen?
Lee: About an hour ago.
Amy: Did you go to Krystal's?
Lee: Yes, I did, but Daisy wasn't there. I rushed back here. I didn't know what to do so I called you. Krystal gets back from her vacation today! I promised her I'd take care of her dog, but I didn't. Oh, no!

What's wrong? Calm down!

OUT of class

2 Study the Grammar box and circle the words to complete the rule. Then underline examples of the Simple Past in the dialogue.

Grammar	Simple Past: regular verbs
+	**−**
I called Amy. She walked home. They stopped me.	I didn't call Amy. She didn't walk home. They didn't stop me.
?	
Did you call Amy? When did he arrive?	Yes, I did./No, I didn't.

To make negative sentences and questions in the Simple Past, we use *didn't* and *did* / *do* and *don't*.

GRAMMAR TIME > PAGE 108

3 Look at the verbs below. Write the Simple Past forms in your notebook. Then check in pairs.

> carry end happen help invent
> like listen live open start study
> talk try want watch work

4 🔊 **1.42** Listen and complete the chart with the Simple Past form of the verbs from Activity 3. Then listen again and repeat the verbs.

Speak UP!

1 helped /t/	2 carried /d/	3 ended /ɪd/
liked		

5 Complete the text with the Simple Past form of the verbs in parentheses.

Lee ¹ *asked* (ask) Amy to help him. She ² _____ (not want) to go out, but Lee was desperate so Amy ³ _____ (agree) to help him. At the park, they ⁴ _____ (shout) Daisy's name and ⁵ _____ (walk) around the park, but the dog wasn't there. Finally, Lee ⁶ _____ (suggest) calling the police, but Amy ⁷ _____ (not like) that idea.

6 Write questions from the prompts in your notebook. Go go to page 116 to find the answers.

1 Lee / call / police / ?
 Did Lee call the police?
2 police / help / them / ?
3 what / Amy and Lee / do / ?
4 dog / be / there / ?
5 what / Lee / do / ?

7 In your notebook, write sentences in the Simple Past with the verbs in Activity 3. In pairs, say if your classmate's sentences are true or false.

A: *I talked to a police officer last week.*
B: *False. You didn't talk to a police officer last week.*

And YOU

2.5 LISTENING and VOCABULARY — Pets

I can identify specific information in a conversation and talk about pets.

1 **CLASS VOTE** Read the article and decide which of the pets is good for Liz.

2 **WORD FRIENDS** Look at the Word Friends below. What do they mean? How do you say them in your language?

When you have a pet, you need to …

- [1] feed it
- [ ] take it for a walk
- [ ] train it
- [ ] take it to the vet's
- [ ] wash it
- [ ] empty its litter box
- [ ] brush its fur

3 🔊 1.43 Listen to Liz talking to her friend Jack about getting a pet. Number the Word Friends in Activity 2 in the order you hear them.

4 🔊 1.44 Listen to five dialogues. Circle the correct answers.

1. What kind of pet did Liz decide to get?
   a) a cat   b) a dog   c) a snake
2. How many animals did Jodie offer Liz?
   a) one   b) two   c) four
3. Liz's dad decided to buy something in a pet store. How much was it?
   a) $15   b) $25   c) $50
4. What did Liz's dad want her to do?
   a) train the cat   b) feed it
   c) empty its litter tray
5. Liz and her dad looked for Ginger, Liz's cat. Where was she?

5 Work in pairs. Do you have a pet? If so, who takes care of it? Describe it. Use the Word Friends in Activity 2 and the phrases below to help you.

> It's fun/clean/quiet/boring/dirty/noisy …
> You need to/don't need to …

We have a dog. My mom trained it. I usually take it for a walk. He's fun, but very noisy!

TEENS TODAY

Liz wants a pet, but what kind to get?

Liz loves animals, but she lives in a small apartment downtown. She's very busy and doesn't have much free time. And she hates getting up early. She doesn't have any problems with allergies.

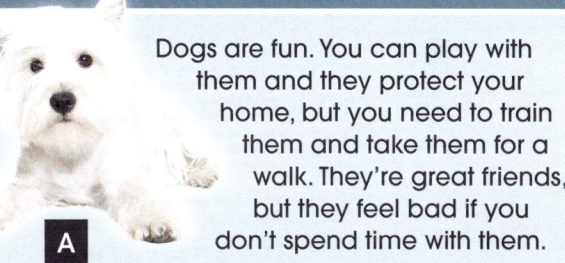

A Dogs are fun. You can play with them and they protect your home, but you need to train them and take them for a walk. They're great friends, but they feel bad if you don't spend time with them.

B Cats are cute and clean, but they scratch the furniture and bring dead animals into the house. They can also give you allergies. They're fun to play with when they're little kittens, but they aren't so friendly when they grow up.

C Fish are quiet and you don't need to take them for a walk. But you can't play with them much and you need to clean their tank. They're beautiful, but they die easily.

2.6 SPEAKING Apologizing

I can make and respond to apologies.

1 **CLASS VOTE** Look at the pictures. How do you think Lee and Krystal are feeling?

2 🔊 **1.45** Listen and read. Then check your answers to Activity 1. Circle the correct option.
1 Krystal (wanted) / didn't want to see Daisy.
2 Krystal thought that Daisy was lost / sick.
3 Daisy was / wasn't at Krystal's house.

I DON'T KNOW HOW IT HAPPENED

Krystal: Hi, Lee.
Lee: Oh, hi, Krystal. Are you home already?
Krystal: Yes, we're just back! The trip was great! So, when can you bring Daisy? I'm missing her so much.
Lee: Um, I'm really sorry, but …
Krystal: Oh, no! Don't tell me she's sick!
Lee: I don't know how it happened. We were at the park and Daisy suddenly disappeared. Amy and I looked for her everywhere and I even contacted the police, but … I feel awful. It's all my fault.
Krystal: She's lost? I don't believe it! How could you be so careless! You promised to take care of her! Oh, she's here! Daisy! Wait! I'm coming! … Lee? Look, I'm sorry I was rude.
Lee: No problem. I totally understand. I'm so glad …
Krystal: Listen, I have to go. Talk to you later. Bye!

I'm so glad. I have to go.	**OUT** of **class**

3 Check (✓) the words and phrases that are used in the dialogue.

Speaking Apologizing

Apologizing
- ✓ I'm (really/so) sorry.
- ☐ I didn't realize.
- ☐ I apologize.
- ☐ It's (all) my fault.
- ☐ I feel awful.
- ☐ It was an accident.

Accepting apologies
- ☐ Never mind.
- ☐ No problem.
- ☐ I totally understand.
- ☐ These things happen.
- ☐ It's not your fault.

Not accepting apologies
- ☐ How can/could you be so careless?
- ☐ You can't be serious!
- ☐ You promised to (take care of her).
- ☐ I'm really angry about this!

4 🔊 **1.46** Use the Speaking box to complete the dialogues. Sometimes more than one answer is possible. Then listen and check. Practice the dialogues in pairs.
1 A: Excuse me. I think you're sitting in my seat.
   B: _I'm so sorry_. I didn't realize!
2 A: _____. I didn't hear you. Could you repeat that?
   B: No problem. It's K-A-R-Y-S.
3 A: I'm sorry I'm late! My bus didn't arrive on time.
   B: _____. The buses are really slow these days!
4 A: I'm afraid there was an accident with your bike.
   B: What!? _____?

5 In pairs, follow the instructions. Use the Speaking box to help you.

And YOU

1 **Student A:** You borrowed Student B's tablet, but you dropped it and it stopped working. Apologize.
   Student B: You don't accept Student A's apology.
2 **Student B:** It was Student A's birthday yesterday. You forgot it. Apologize.
   Student A: It was your birthday yesterday, but birthdays aren't so important to you.

Unit 2

2.7 WRITING — A personal account

I can write a personal account of an event.

1 Read the personal account quickly and answer the questions.

1. Where was Patricia?
   She was in South Africa.

2. Who was she with?

3. What did she look for?

4. How did she describe the experience?

The best experience ever!

by Patricia Gallego

In 2017, I was on vacation in South Africa with my family and something amazing happened. On the weekend, we participated in a safari tour. I was so excited in the morning because it was my dream vacation activity! I really wanted to see an elephant. The safari started in the afternoon. There were lots of wild animals: giraffes, zebras, birds, and many different insects. But there weren't any elephants. At 5:30 p.m. I started to feel sad. Then our guide said "Ssh…listen". We all stopped and listened. There was a loud noise – elephants! I smiled and jumped up. The elephants didn't look happy. "Are they fighting?", I asked. I was a little scared. "No" the guide answered. "They are playing!" I was very surprised, but happy, too. I used my new camera to take some pictures. It was the best experience ever!

2 **I KNOW!** Study the Language box. Circle the prepositions of time in the personal account.

Language — Prepositions of time

IN years: *in 2015*
months and seasons: *in January, in the winter*
parts of the day: *in the morning/evening*

ON days of the week: *on Wednesday/Fridays*
dates: *on April 3*
special days: *on Christmas Day*
other phrases: *on the weekend*

AT holiday periods: *at Christmas*
clock times: *at 12:15*
other phrases: *at night*

! We say *in the evening*, but we say *on Thursday evening*.

3 Study the Writing box. Underline all the examples of the Simple Past in the personal account in Activity 1.

Writing — A personal account

Introduce the situation/event
In 2017, I was …
Last year, my family and I …
It was a sunny day.

Explain how you felt before, during, and after
I was so excited.
After that, I started to feel sad.
I didn't want to leave.

Say what happened
We looked for the island …
I helped the man.
I used my camera to take pictures.

Include direct speech
"What happened?" I asked.
"Be quiet," shouted Dad.

Use adjectives and phrases
It was the best experience ever!
It was awesome/amazing/incredible.
We were careless/silly/impulsive.

4 Write a personal account of an exciting/special/memorable experience.

Writing Time

1. **Find ideas**
   Look at the Writing box. In your notebook, take notes about an exciting/special/memorable experience in your life.

2. **Draft**
   In your notebook, write a draft of a personal account. Look at Patricia's account to help you.

3. **Share**
   Share your text with a student for feedback. Listen to his/her opinion and suggestions. Check the spelling and grammar.

4. **Check and write**
   Make any necessary changes to your text. Do you use a variety of verbs in the Simple Past? Do you use prepositions of time correctly? Do you include direct speech? Write the final version of your text.

WORDLIST   Animals | Personality adjectives | Taking care of pets

adulthood [n]	feather [n]	sharp [adj]
adventurous [adj]	fight [v]	sheep [n]
aggressive [adj]	fish [n]	shy [adj]
ant [n]	flamingo [n]	skin [n]
apologize [v]	fly [n]	snake [n]
aquarium [n]	forgetful [adj]	spider [n]
bear [n]	fur [n]	stripe [n]
bee [n]	giraffe [n]	success [n]
behave [v]	grow up [v]	tail [n]
behavior [n]	impulsive [adj]	tiger [n]
butterfly [n]	kangaroo [n]	tortoise [n]
calm down [v]	kitten [n]	wing [n]
careless [adj]	leash [n]	zebra [n]
cat [n]	lion [n]	zoo [n]
chicken [n]	lively [adj]	
childhood [n]	lovable [adj]	
chimp [n]	monkey [n]	
claw [n]	mouth [n]	
clean [adj]	noisy [adj]	
climb [v]	parrot [n]	
cow [n]	penguin [n]	
criticize [v]	pet [n]	
crocodile [n]	pet store [n]	
cute [adj]	polar bear [n]	
dangerous [adj]	popular [adj]	
decide [v]	promise [v]	
die [v]	quiet [adj]	
dirty [adj]	rabbit [n]	
dolphin [n]	ride [v]	
donkey [n]	rude [adj]	
duck [n]	rush [v]	
elephant [n]	sea otter [n]	
energetic [adj]	shark [n]	

WORD FRIENDS

brush a pet's fur
empty a cat's litter tray
feed a pet
be fun to play with
give you allergies
ignore advice
make a lot of noise
miss somebody/something
protect your home
scratch the furniture
take a dog for a walk
take a pet to the vet's
take care of a pet
take risks
train a pet
wash a pet

VOCABULARY IN ACTION

1 Use the Wordlist to find words for each category. Write them in your notebook.
1. six animals that can fly: *fly, …*
2. six animals that live in or on water:
3. five animal body parts that people don't have:

2 In pairs, say the names of three animals that you think are:
1. quiet *butterfly, …*   3 dangerous
2. noisy   4 cute

3 Complete the Word Friends with the prepositions below. In pairs, say if you agree with the sentences or not.

| for   of   to   ~~with~~ |

1. Tortoises are fun to play __with__.
2. It's difficult to take care _____ a cat.
3. You need to take a dog _____ a walk three times a day.
4. It's a good idea to take your pet _____ the vet every month.

4 Complete the sentences with the correct form of the word in bold.
1. My grandma says her __childhood__ was very hard – she was often hungry. **child**
2. The teacher was very happy with the _____ of her class. **behave**
3. It's _____ to ride a bike at night with no lights. **danger**

5 **PRONUNCIATION** Complete the sentences. Use words below that rhyme with the underlined words. There are two extra words.

| bear   bee   fly   ~~sharks~~   tail   wing   zoo |

1. There aren't any __sharks__ in our local <u>parks</u>.
2. A <u>butterfly</u>'s _____ is a beautiful <u>thing</u>.
3. <u>Why</u> didn't the <u>shy</u> _____ say <u>goodbye</u>?
4. Did <u>you</u> lose a <u>blue</u> <u>shoe</u> at the _____?
5. <u>There</u> was a _____ on the <u>chair</u> over <u>there</u>.

6 🔊 1.47 **PRONUNCIATION** Listen, check, and repeat.

SELF-CHECK

1 Write the names of animals for the definitions.

Animal QUIZ

1. It can fly and it can talk. — *parrot*
2. It's really cute. It's a baby cat. _____
3. It has eight legs and it eats flies. _____
4. It has sharp claws and striped fur. _____
5. It has wings. It can swim, but it can't fly. _____
6. It's a big bird with pink feathers and long legs. _____
7. It jumps very well and keeps its baby in a pouch. _____
8. It's from Africa. It eats leaves from the tops of trees. _____
9. It's a dangerous animal with very sharp teeth. It's green. _____
10. It's a farm animal. It's similar to a horse. _____

2 Complete the adjectives in the sentences. In pairs, ask and answer the questions.

1. Are you a noisy person or are you **q u i e t**?
2. Do you often forget things? Are you f_____?
3. Do you do things suddenly without thinking? Are you i_____?
4. Do you shout at people? Are you a_____?
5. Do you enjoy taking risks and doing extreme sports? Are you a_____?
6. Do a lot of people love you and think you're cute? Are you l_____?
7. Do you often make mistakes and have lots of accidents? Are you c_____?
8. Do you like doing things? Do you have lots of energy? Are you e_____?

A: *Are you a noisy person or are you quiet?*
B: *I'm a very quiet person. I never make a lot of noise.*

3 Complete the Word Friends. Use the words in the correct form. Then, in pairs, say if the sentences are true for you.

1. Animals don't *give* me allergies.
2. We have a cat. I sometimes brush its _____, but I never _____ its litter box.
3. I never _____ my parents' advice.
4. My dad's a good driver. He never _____ risks.
5. Mom says I'm noisy, but I don't think I _____ a lot of noise.
6. We _____ our pet very well – we never give her our food.
7. In the summer vacation I _____ my school friends.

4 Complete the sentences with *was*, *wasn't*, *were*, or *weren't*.

Dolly the sheep

- Why ¹ *was* Dolly famous?
- She ² _____ the first animal clone in the world.
- ³ _____ Dolly from England?
- No, she ⁴ _____. She ⁵ _____ Scottish, from the Roslin Institute near Edinburgh.
- ⁶ _____ there any other clones at that institute?
- Yes, there ⁷ _____, but Dolly ⁸ _____ the first one.

5 Complete the text with the Simple Past form of the verbs below.

| not answer | arrive | ask | call | change |
| need | ~~rush~~ | study | talk | not want |

I ¹ *rushed* home yesterday because I ² _____ to study for the tests. I ³ _____ home at ten to six and then I ⁴ _____ my clothes. From six to eight I ⁵ _____ biology. Then Jamie ⁶ _____ me. I ⁷ _____ to talk to him, but he ⁸ _____ me lots of questions about the test. We ⁹ _____ for an hour, but I ¹⁰ _____ all his questions.

6 In pairs, role-play the situations. Student A: look below. Student B: look at page 117.

Student A

1. You argued with Student B. You shouted and called him/her a bad name. You feel bad. Apologize.
2. Student B posted an embarrassing picture of you online. You are angry. Don't accept the apology.

7 🔊 1.48 Listen, then listen again and write down what you hear.

_____
_____
_____

SELF-ASSESSMENT Think about this unit. What did you learn? What do you need help with?

3

3.1 VOCABULARY Technology

I can talk about technology.

New technology

VOCABULARY
Gadgets and technology | Computer equipment

GRAMMAR
Simple Past: irregular verbs | Relative clauses

Grammar:
Where's my cell phone?
Look at Ruby. How do you think she is feeling? Why?

Speaking:
It all went wrong!
Look at Lee. How do you think he is feeling? Why?

1 Look at the pictures above. Can you name the gadgets in them?

2 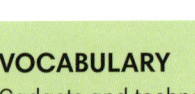 1.49 Look at Vocabulary A box. Listen and repeat the words. Then work in pairs. Ask and answer the questions below.

Vocabulary A	Gadgets and technology		
digital camera	drone	e-reader	games console
smartphone	smart TV	stylus	tablet

Which gadget(s) from Vocabulary A:
- do you have at home?
- would you like to have?

A: *I have a games console and a tablet at home. What about you?*
B: *I have a tablet, but I don't have a games console. I'd like to have a smart TV.*

3 **WORD FRIENDS** Work in pairs. Which gadgets from Vocabulary A box can you use for these activities?

> send instant messages   listen to music   check emails   download files
> take pictures   call a friend   play games   make videos   watch movies
> surf the internet   read a book   stream TV shows and movies

You can send instant messages with a smartphone.

4 Look at pictures A–C. What do you think each gadget can do? Write your guesses in your notebook. Then read the article on page 31 and check them.

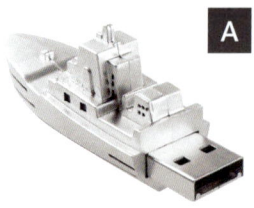
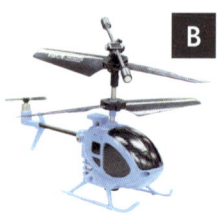

Unit 3

7 Circle the correct option.

1 You can charge your smartphone from your computer's *keyboard* / (*USB port*).
2 Does your smartphone have enough *pictures* / *memory* to download this file?
3 I can play this video game with my keyboard, but it's easier to use a *joystick* / *USB port*.
4 I need to charge the *battery* / *flash drive* on my laptop.
5 I need to buy a new *joystick* / *keyboard* – it's hard to type fast on this old one.

> Do you play **online** games? *adjective*
> Do you play **online**? *adverb*
>
> **Watch OUT!**

COLLECTOR'S CORNER

This week: PRISCILA Jones

I collect USB gadgets – they're small gadgets which you plug into your laptop or tablet. They don't need a battery because they charge from your computer's USB port. I have eighteen different gadgets in my collection, but I'm always looking for new ones!

Some USB gadgets are practical.
For example, my electric USB gloves. You charge them for two minutes in your USB port and they stay warm for hours. They're very useful when I'm at my keyboard in the winter!

Another useful gadget is my special USB flash drive.
It looks like a boat, but it has 128 GB of memory. I keep all my digital pictures on it – I love it.

My favorite gadget is my USB helicopter.
It has a joystick to control it and it really does fly!

5  **1.50** Underline the words in Vocabulary B box in the article. Then listen and repeat the words.

Vocabulary B	Computer equipment
battery joystick keyboard memory flash drive USB port	

6 **I KNOW!** How many words can you add to Vocabulary B box in two minutes? Make a list in your notebook.

8 In pairs, do the quiz. Are you addicted to the internet? Tell your classmate. Use the language in the quiz to help you.

I think I am addicted to the internet because I spend all my free time online.

ARE YOU addicted to the internet?

Five or more "yes" answers means you definitely are!

Do you …
1 enjoy spending time online more than meeting people face-to-face?
2 prefer instant messages to phone calls?
3 often download apps and emojis on your smartphone?
4 often play online games?
5 have more than two social media accounts?
6 prefer using emojis to writing words?
7 sometimes dream about people or situations from your online life?

Unit 3

3.2 GRAMMAR   Simple Past: irregular verbs

I can use the Simple Past of irregular verbs to talk about the past.

1 🔊 **1.51** Describe the picture. Why are Lee and Ruby arguing? Listen and read Part 1 and check your answer.

WHERE'S MY CELL PHONE? (Part 1)

Ruby: Lee! Where's my cell phone?
Lee: I left it in your room ten minutes ago.
Ruby: No, you didn't!
Lee: Yes, I did!
Ruby: Well, it's not there now! Dad! Lee stole my new cell phone!
Lee: Ruby! I didn't steal your phone!
Ruby: You lost it, then! Oh! I only bought it a week ago. It cost a fortune!
Dad: Calm down, Ruby! Lee, did you take your sister's cell phone?
Lee: No, I didn't! Well, yes, I did. The battery died on my phone, so I took Ruby's. I sent *one* message and put the phone back in your room. I only had it for five minutes!
Ruby: Where did you put it?
Lee: I put it in the pocket of your jeans.
Ruby: Which jeans?
Lee: Your black jeans. They were on your chair.
Ruby: What!? Oh, no! I saw those jeans in the washing machine. Mom!

It cost a fortune!
Calm down!
The battery died.

 **OUT of class**

2 Study the Grammar box and circle the correct option. Then underline examples of the Simple Past in the dialogue.

Grammar	Simple Past: irregular verbs
+	**–**
You took my phone.	I didn't take your phone.
?	
Did you take my phone?	Yes, I did. / No, I didn't.
Where did you put it?	

GRAMMAR TIME ▸ PAGE 109

In negative sentences and questions, we use the *base* form / *irregular past* form of the verb.

3 In your notebook, write the Simple Past forms of the verbs. Some of them are in the dialogue.

~~buy~~   cost   do   forget   go   give   have
leave   lose   put   see   send   steal   take

buy – bought

4 Complete the sentences with the Simple Past form of the verbs in parentheses.

1 Ruby's mom ____*put*____ (put) her blue jeans in the washing machine.
2 Ruby _____ (find) the phone in her jeans.
3 Lee _____ (take) the phone out of the jeans.
4 Ruby _____ (give) her mom the phone.

5 🔊 **1.52** Listen to Part 2. In your notebook, rewrite the sentences in Activity 4.

1 *Ruby's mom didn't put her blue jeans in the washing machine. She put her black jeans in the washing machine.*

6 In your notebook, write questions in the Simple Past for these sentences.

1 I went to France on vacation. (Where …?)
   Where did you go on vacation?
2 I didn't do anything last weekend. (What …?)
3 I got two gifts for my last birthday. (How many …?)
4 I bought some new sneakers yesterday. (When …?)
5 I left home at 7:30 this morning. (What time …?)

7 In pairs, ask and answer the questions in Activity 6. Then join another pair. Say if your classmates' answers are true or false.

Unit 3

3.3 READING and VOCABULARY A journal entry and a blog

I can include missing sentences in texts and talk about using technology.

1 🔊 **1.53** Listen and read Tim's journal entry and Tina's blog. Complete blanks 1–4 with sentences a–e. There is one extra sentence.

a Now I can listen to it any time I want!
b That's why I didn't finish it.
c Then I played a game on my phone.
d Phone calls are expensive!
e My friend Cara texted me.

May 11, 1984

Today at school we used a computer with 64 kB of memory! Fantastic!

Later, I told my friend Ian about it. He lives in Texas, but we keep in touch on the phone. Unfortunately, my dad asked me to **hang up** after two minutes. ¹ __d__ And anyway, my mom needed to use the phone.

I heard a Michael Jackson song on the radio. It was great! I wanted to hear it again, so I listened to the radio for hours. I'm glad I didn't **give up** because they played it again and I recorded it on my cassette player. ² _____ Technology is great!

Tim

www.tinasblog.com

April 14, 2017

When I got home from school, I looked at the time on my cell phone. It was early, so I listened to music on my new headphones and downloaded a new app. ³ _____ After that, I **turned on** my tablet, **checked out** Facebook and sent some messages to my friends. I also read some of my favorite blogs and watched videos on YouTube. ⁴ _____ She wanted me to help her with her homework. So I called her on Messenger. We **looked for** some information on Wikipedia together.

You can't live without technology today!

3 Translate the highlighted phrasal verbs in the texts into your language. Then use them to complete the questions. Ask and answer the questions in pairs.

1 What was the last gadget you __turned on__ last night?
2 Where do you usually _____ information?
3 Did you _____ on anyone yesterday? Why?
4 What was the last YouTube video that you _____?
5 When did you last _____ because you couldn't complete a level on a video game?

Reading tip

In order to help you include sentences in a text, make sure you understand the context and the words that come before and after the blanks

2 Read the texts again. Complete the sentences with *Tim* or *Tina*.

1 __Tina__ worked with a friend.
2 _____ talked to a friend on the phone.
3 _____ used a computer with very little memory.
4 _____ used a cell phone to do more than one thing.
5 _____ communicated with friends in different ways.
6 _____ waited a long time to listen to a song.

4 In pairs, say how you keep in touch with friends. Use the ideas below to help you. Say which way you prefer and why.

chat online   meet my friends face-to-face
call   send text messages
send emails   visit friends at home
use social media (e.g., Twitter)

I often use Twitter to keep in touch with my friends.

3.4 GRAMMAR Relative clauses

I can use relative clauses to be specific about people, things, and places.

1 Look at the comic strip. What is the robot thinking in panel 3? Circle the best caption.
a "Why can't humans be more like robots?" b "Housework is so much fun!"
c "I'm super intelligent and I'm cleaning a house. How depressing!"

This is the scientist who invented a super-intelligent robot.
It's a super-intelligent robot that can do a thousand amazing things.

This is a store where they sell the super-intelligent robot.
These are some things which the robot can do.

These are the people that bought the robot.
This is the house where they live.
And these are the things that the robot does.

2 Study the Grammar box. Underline the relative pronouns in the comic strip. Then find one sentence for each rule and write them in your notebook.

Grammar	Relative clauses

We use relative clauses to say which person, thing, or place we are talking about.
1 We use *who* or *that* for people.
   An inventor is a person **who** / **that** invents things.
2 We use *which* or *that* for things.
   This is the machine **which** / **that** Leonard invented.
3 We use *where* for places.
   This is the university **where** Leonard works.

GRAMMAR TIME > PAGE 109

1 *This is the scientist who invented a super-intelligent robot.*

3 In your notebook, combine the sentences with relative pronouns.
1 This is a robot. It cleans floors.
   This is a robot which/that cleans floors.
2 She is a woman. She makes things.
3 I bought a clock. It plays music.
4 That's the store. I bought my gloves there.
5 Is that your friend? She studies IT.

4 Complete the sentences with *who*, *which*, or *where*. Then complete the word for each definition.
1 It's a thing ___which___ you use to charge a cell phone. c _ _ _ _ _ _ _
2 It's a place _____ you plug in USB gadgets. USB p _ _ _ _
3 This is a person _____ collects things. c _ _ _ _ _ _ _ _ _
4 It's a thing _____ takes pictures. c _ _ _ _ _ _
5 This is a person _____ works in a laboratory. s _ _ _ _ _ _ _ _ _

5 Complete the sentences with *who*, *which*, or *where*.
1 The person ___who___ I admire the most is …
2 The place _____ I want to live when I'm older is …
3 The next electronic gadget _____ I want to buy is …
4 One place _____ I feel really happy is …
5 The first person _____ I saw this morning was …
6 I'd love to have a robot _____ can …

6 In your notebook, complete the sentences in Activity 5 to make them true for you. Then compare with a classmate.

3.5 LISTENING and VOCABULARY — Favorite websites

I can identify specific information in a conversation and talk about websites.

1 **CLASS VOTE** What websites do you use the most often?

2 Read the sentences. Work in pairs. Write the name of a website you use for each definition.

1 You can buy and sell things on this website: _eBay_

2 On this website you can **watch** videos. You can also **upload** your own videos to **share** them with other people: _____

3 You can use this to **search** the web for other website content to **download**: _____

4 With this website you can keep in touch with friends and **chat** online: _____

5 On this website you can read articles and **click** on links to find out more information: _____

3 1.54 **WORD FRIENDS** Complete the text with the correct form of the highlighted verbs from Activity 2. Listen and check.

I needed to find a program for making movies, so I ¹ _searched_ the web and found one. I ² _____ on the link and saw it was free, so I ³ _____ the program. After I finished making my movie, I wanted to ⁴ _____ it with other people so I ⁵ _____ my video to YouTube. In the first week, three hundred people ⁶ _____ my video and now some of them want to ⁷ _____ online with me.

4 1.55 Listen to a radio interview about YouTube. Complete the notes with one or two words in each blank.

YouTube
- It started in ¹ _February 2005_.
- The first video was ² _____ long.
- In ³ _____ Google bought it for $1.65 billion.
- Every ⁴ _____ people watch hundreds of millions of hours of videos.
- Every minute people upload ⁵ _____ hours of videos.
- There are YouTube videos in ⁶ _____ languages.

5 1.56 Listen to the second part of the interview. Circle the correct answer.

1 *Upload* is a
   a computer program.   (b) radio show.
   c website.
2 Alex likes YouTube because
   a he likes watching famous people.
   b it's always funny.
   c it shows many different kinds of videos.
3 How many reasons does Alex give for liking YouTube?
   a Two.   b Three.   c Four.
4 Howard Davies-Carr made a very popular
   a family video.   b music video.   c website.
5 How many times did people watch *Charlie bit my finger* in nine months?
   a 9 million.   b 12 million.   c Over 800 million.

6 In pairs, ask and answer the questions about your favorite websites. Use the Word Friends in Activity 3.

1 What kind of website is it?
2 What can you do on it?
3 How popular is it?
4 Do you know how and when it started?
5 How often do you visit it?
6 Why do you like visiting it?

My favorite website is … You can use it to …

Unit 3 35

3.6 SPEAKING — Putting events in order

I can put events in order when talking about the past.

1 🔊 **1.57** What can you see in the picture? What do you think Lee's problem is? Listen and read the dialogue. Then check your ideas.

IT ALL WENT WRONG!

Lee: Hi, Amy.
Amy: Hi, Lee. What's up?
Lee: You know my new song?
Amy: Of course I do. You played it a hundred times last weekend!
Lee: Yeah, anyway, I wanted to make a video of the song and upload it to YouTube, but it all went wrong. My cell phone wasn't working, so I used a digital camera. <u>First</u>, the battery in my camera died after only one minute. Then I couldn't find the charger, so I had to buy a new battery. After that, my microphone didn't work. I didn't know where to plug it in. In the end, it worked and finally, I finished recording the song, so then I went online to upload it to YouTube.
Amy: Yeah?
Lee: And my computer crashed!
Amy: Oh, no!
Lee: Listen, I really need to fix it. Can you come over and give me a hand?
Amy: Yeah, OK.
Lee: Thanks, Amy.
Ruby: Lee, do you know …? Oh! I don't believe it! Mom! Lee's using my cell phone again!
Lee: Ruby! I can explain. You see, the thing is …

OUT of class
What's up? Anyway, …
Give me a hand.

2 **WORD FRIENDS** What problems can you have with gadgets and computers? Check (✓) the ones that Lee had in the dialogue.
- ✓ My computer crashed.
- ☐ My computer got a virus.
- ☐ My internet connection stopped working.
- ☐ I couldn't download a program.
- ☐ I couldn't connect a microphone.
- ☐ The battery in my camera/phone died.

3 Study the Speaking box. Underline the words and phrases in the dialogue. How do you say them in your language?

Speaking	Putting events in order

- At first/First/First of all
- Then/Next/After that/Suddenly
- An hour/A few days/Two weeks later
- Finally/In the end

4 🔊 **1.58** Use the Speaking box to complete the story of Lee's dream. Listen and check.

I dreamed that I uploaded the video of my song to YouTube. At ¹ _first_, it wasn't very successful. But then ² _____ it became popular. Millions of people saw it. A few days ³ _____ a music company asked me to go to New York to make a professional video. That was really successful, too. ⁴ _____ that, they asked me to write a song for a movie! In the ⁵ _____ I won an Oscar for the song!

5 🔊 **1.59** Listen to part of the dialogue again. Pay attention to how Lee says the words you underlined in Activity 3. Then, in pairs, practice reading the extract, changing your intonation to add emphasis.

Speak UP!

6 In pairs, use the Speaking box to tell a story. Choose from the ideas below. Use intonation to add emphasis.
- A time when you had technical problems.
- A day when you invited friends to your house.
- A dream you had.

I had a dream. At first, I was on the subway and …

3.7 WRITING A blog post

I can write a blog post about advantages and disadvantages of using a cell phone.

1 Read Matt's blog post and circle the most appropriate title.

a Do you use your cell phone too much?
b What are the advantages of cell phones?
c Do teenagers like cell phones more than adults?

www.matt'sblog.com

1 Let's talk a little about cell phones. I use my phone from the minute I wake up! I check my messages immediately and reply to my friends who sent me messages late at night. I also look at Twitter – I follow my favorite sports stars there.

2 On the one hand, it's good to be connected to so many different people and feel close to people that I admire. I can watch cool videos and read interesting messages.

3 On the other hand, I waste a lot of time online. I check Instagram every few minutes, but I don't know why! I sometimes check my cell phone for new messages at dinner. My parents don't like that, and I understand why.

4 So, in conclusion, I probably use my cell phone too much. I would like to use it less. What about you?

Tweet 13   Like 2

2 Read the blog post again and complete the chart with the advantages and disadvantages Matt mentions.

Advantages	Disadvantages
good to be connected to so many people	

3 Match paragraphs 1-4 to the information each one provides.

____ disadvantages of cell phones
____ a conclusion
_1_ what I use my cell phone for
____ advantages of cell phones

4 Study the Writing box. Underline the phrases Matt uses in his blog post.

Writing | An opinion blog post

Introduce the topic
Let's talk a little about …   I want to talk about …
Explain advantages
On the one hand, …   I like that …
A good thing is …
Explain disadvantages
On the other hand, …   I don't like that …
A bad thing is …
Write a conclusion
In conclusion, …   To finish, …

5 Write a blog post answering the question in the title of the blog post in Activity 1.

Writing Time

1 **Find ideas**
Look at the Writing box and the chart in Activity 2. Make your own chart in your notebook.

2 **Draft**
Write a draft of your blog post. Look at Matt's text to help you. Pay attention to the structure of paragraphs. Make sure you include advantages and disadvantages of using a cell phone.

3 **Share**
Share your text with a classmate for feedback. Listen to his/her opinion and suggestions. Check the spelling and grammar.

4 **Check and write**
Make any necessary changes to your text. Do you organize the blog post into paragraphs? Do you introduce your paragraphs with different phrases? Write the final version of your text.

WORDLIST — Gadgets and equipment | Computers and technology | Phrasal verbs

addicted to [v]
admire [v]
after that [adj]
app [n]
at first [adv]
battery [n]
blog [n]
calm down [v]
cassette player [n]
cell phone [n]
charger [n]
check out [v]
collector [n]
crash (e.g., a computer) [v]
die (e.g., a battery) [v]
digital camera [n]
drone [n]
e-reader [n]
electric [adj]
electronic [adj]
email (address) [n]
(computer) equipment [n]
finally [adv]
first (of all) [adv]
flash drive [n]
gadget [n]
games console [n]
give up [v]
hang up [v]
in the end [adv]
instant message [n]
internet connection [n]
invent [v]

inventor [n]
joystick [n]
keyboard [n]
laptop [n]
(a few weeks) later [adv]
look for [v]
memory [n]
mouse (computer) [n]
next [adv]
online [adv]
online (games) [adj]
plug in/into [v]
practical [adj]
print [v]
printer [n]
professional [adj]
record [v]
robot [n]
scientist [n]
smartphone [n]
smart TV [n]
software [n]
successful [adj]
suddenly [adv]
switch off/on [v]
tablet [n]
technical (problems) [adj]
technology [n]
then [adv]
turn on/off [v]
unfortunately [adv]
USB port [n]
website [n]

WORD FRIENDS
call a friend
charge a phone/battery
chat online
check emails/updates
click on links
connect a microphone
download files/videos
follow somebody (on Twitter)
get a virus (computer)
go wrong
keep in touch (with people)
listen to music
make phone calls
make videos
meet (people) face-to-face
play games
read a book
search the web
send emails/instant messages
share files/videos
spend time online/offline
stop working
stream TV shows and videos
stylus
surf the internet
take pictures
text friends
upload files/videos
use social media
visit a website
visit friends
waste time (online)
watch movies/videos

VOCABULARY IN ACTION

1 Use the Wordlist to find twelve examples of electronic equipment/gadgets. Write them in your notebook.
drone, …

2 Work in pairs. In your notebook, write which items from Activity 1:
1 often have an internet connection *e-reader, games console, printer, smartphone, tablet*
2 quite often crash/go wrong/stop working
3 can get a virus
4 can help you keep in touch with people
5 you can use to listen to music
6 you are addicted to

3 Complete the sentences with the correct form of the word in bold.
1 Marie Curie was a great ___scientist___. **science**
2 Your videos are great – you did a really _____ job! **profession**
3 Does anybody remember who was the _____ of the tablet? **invent**

4 Complete the Word Friends. In pairs, say if the sentences are true for you.
1 I got a virus after I clicked ___on___ a link.
2 A famous person follows me _____ Twitter!
3 I often _____ the internet for new fashion ideas.
4 I sometimes forget to _____ my cell phone and the battery dies.

5 🔊 1.60 **PRONUNCIATION** Listen to how you pronounce the underlined letters in each word and repeat.

/ə/   **a**ddress   batt**e**ry   cam**era**
computer   digit**a**l   int**e**rnet

6 🔊 1.61 **PRONUNCIATION** In pairs, practice saying these words with an /ə/ sound. Listen and check.

invent**or**   micr**o**phone   print**er**   tabl**e**t   vir**u**s

Unit 3

SELF-CHECK

1 Match words from A to words from B to make phrases. In pairs, choose four phrases and write sentences in your notebook.

A: ~~instant~~   digital   USB   email   flash   games

B: address   console   ~~message~~   drive   camera   port

instant message

2 Complete the words in the text.

> **New short courses for fall 2021**
> 1 **Online Media (6 weeks; $90)**
> During this six-week course, students have a chance to ¹t*ake*_____ pictures and make ²v_____. Students also learn how to ³s_____ their videos and ⁴u_____ files and videos to the internet.
> 2 **Learn to Love Your Smartphone (4 weeks; $60)**
> Do you want to learn how to use your smartphone to keep in ⁵t_____ with friends and family? This four-week course is the answer! Learn how to ⁶s_____ emails and messages, ⁷t_____ friends, and chat ⁸o_____.
> 3 **Vegetable Gardening (8 weeks; $85)**
> Do you spend all day surfing the ⁹i_____? Do you feel you ¹⁰w_____ time online? Are you looking for ways to ¹¹s_____ more time offline? Try a new skill and meet ¹²p_____ face-to-face in the fresh air!

3 Rewrite the sentences in your notebook, replacing the underlined phrases with the phrasal verbs below.

hang up   plug (sth) into   look for   ~~check out~~   give up

Check out
1 Wow! <u>Take a look at</u> these games consoles.
2 Don't <u>stop trying</u>. You need practice to become a good photographer.
3 Can you help me <u>try to find</u> my flash drive?
4 He started shouting so I decided to <u>end the phone call</u>.
5 I'm not surprised your printer isn't working. You forgot to <u>connect</u> it <u>to</u> the USB port.

4 Complete the text with the Simple Past form of the verbs in parentheses. Use the verb list on page 118 to help you.

> Ada Lovelace lived in England in the early 1800s. She ¹ *was* (be) the daughter of Lord Byron, a famous poet. Ada's mother ² _____ (not want) Ada to be a poet like her father, so she ³ _____ (teach) her math and science. In 1833, Ada ⁴ _____ (meet) Charles Babbage, the inventor of a counting machine (a primitive computer). In 1843, Ada ⁵ _____ (write) an algorithm for Babbage's machine: perhaps the world's first computer program. So ⁶ _____ (Ada/have) her father's amazing imagination after all?

5 Complete the information about the story in Activity 4. Circle the correct option.

1 *Ada Lovelace* was the person (who)/ *which* probably became the first computer programmer.
2 _____ was the country *that* / *where* Ada lived.
3 _____ was the poet *who* / *which* was Ada's father.
4 _____ was the early computer *where* / *which* Babbage invented.
5 _____ was the skill *where* / *that* Ada inherited from her father.

6 In pairs, use linking words (*first/then* …) to tell a story. Student A: look below. Student B: look at page 117. Then switch roles.

Student A

Choose a topic:
- A time you nearly gave up, but didn't.
- A time when you didn't finish something because you spent too long online.

7 🔊 **1.62** Listen, then listen again and write down what you hear.

_____
_____
_____
_____
_____

4 My home, my town

VOCABULARY
Things in the house | Prepositions of place | Chores | Adjectives to describe a house | Places in town

GRAMMAR
Adverbs of manner | Modal verbs: *can*, *have to*, and *must*

Grammar:
It's not fair!
Look at the picture. What do you think Amy, Krystal, and Ruby are talking about?

Speaking:
I moved in this morning
Krystal and Amy are talking to a boy. Who do you think he is? How do you know?

4.1 VOCABULARY Things in the house

I can talk about things in the house.

Unusual rooms

A bathroom

This spacious bathroom has really big windows. But there are no curtains, so you can always admire a beautiful view of the Caribbean Sea.

1 **CLASS VOTE** Look at the pictures. Which room would you most like to visit?

2 🔊 1.63 Study Vocabulary A box. Listen and repeat the words. Then underline the things you can see in the pictures.

Vocabulary A	Things in the house

- **kitchen:** cabinet   counter   faucet   refrigerator   sink   stove
- **bedroom:** bed   chair   closet   nightstand
- **bathroom:** bathtub   shower   toilet   washbasin
- **living room:** armchair   coffee table   couch   fireplace
- **different rooms:** ceiling   curtains   desk   floor   lamp   mirror   rug   switch   table   wall

3 **I KNOW!** How many words can you add to Vocabulary A in two minutes? Write them in your notebook.

4 Complete the descriptions of the rooms in the pictures with words from Vocabulary A.

A The Caribbean bathroom has a ¹ _bathtub_ , but no shower. There's a ² _____ . There's a mirror on the ³ _____ and a ⁴ _____ with one faucet. On the floor there is a white ⁵ _____ .

B In the living room in the Ice Hotel, there are two ¹ _____ and a round ² _____ in front of the ³ _____ .

C The aquarium bedroom has a big ¹ _____ . There is a ² _____ and a low ³ _____ near the window. There are some orange ⁴ _____ on the window.

D In the upside down kitchen, there's a ¹ _____ and three ² _____ . There's a ³ _____ for cooking food, a ⁴ _____ to keep food cold, and lots of ⁵ _____ for the plates and glasses.

5 In pairs, think of an item from Vocabulary A. Ask up to ten *Yes/No* questions to find out what your classmate is thinking of.

A: *Is it usually in the living room?*
B: *Yes, it is.*
A: *Do you sit on it?*

B living room

The armchairs are cold, so you need to sit close to the fireplace in the living room of the Ice Hotel near Kiruna, Sweden.

C bedroom

Can't sleep? That's no problem in this underwater hotel bedroom in Dubai. You can get up and watch the fish in the aquarium. It's very relaxing!

D kitchen

No, these people can't fly. They're in the kitchen of the Upside Down House in Moscow, Russia. The furniture is on the ceiling and they are on the floor. Turn the book around to see!

6 🔊 1.64 Study Vocabulary B box. Listen and repeat the words. Then look at the rooms above again and circle the correct option.

Vocabulary B	Prepositions of place

above   behind   between   in   in front of
near   next to   on   opposite   under

1 There are some drinks *near / (on)* the kitchen table.
2 The bathtub is *in / next to* the window.
3 The toilet is *between / opposite* the bathtub and the washbasin.
4 The coffee table is *behind / in front of* the fireplace.

7 Look at the picture and complete the text with one word in each blank.

This is my room. There's a ¹ _closet_ opposite the bed with lots of clothes in it. There's an armchair ² _____ to the closet and ³ _____ the armchair is my guitar. I love music. There's a poster of my favorite group ⁴ _____ the wall above my ⁵ _____ . I like astronomy, too. That's my telescope ⁶ _____ the bed and the armchair. My room isn't very organized. There are lots of shoes ⁷ _____ the bed. That's my laptop computer on the ⁸ _____ in front ⁹ _____ the closet and that's my games console near the ¹⁰ _____ .

8 In pairs, find four things which are in the same places in your homes. Use Vocabulary A and B to help you.

A: *There's a couch under the window in my living room.*
B: *No, in my living room the couch is opposite the window.*

Unit 4 41

4.2 GRAMMAR Adverbs of manner

I can use adverbs of manner to describe how people do things.

1 CLASS VOTE What was your favorite house chore when you were a child?

2 🔊 1.65 WORD FRIENDS Listen and read the text. Then complete the Word Friends.

> ¹ *make* your bed   ² _____ out the trash
> ³ _____ your room   ⁴ _____ /clear the table
> ⁵ _____ the dishwasher/washing machine
> do the grocery shopping/cooking/ironing/
> the vacuuming   wash/dry the dishes
> sweep the floor

Kids and chores – your emails

Toby (4) tries very hard. He sets the table slowly and carefully with a smile on his face. The only problem is that he usually gets it wrong. But he does one thing perfectly. He takes out the trash so well! ❤️

Suzy (13) cleans her room regularly. She does it once a week if she needs to or not! 😊 She makes her bed really quickly, but she does it so badly! She loads the dishwasher every night, but she does it noisily and often wakes up the baby!

Jenny, New York

3 In pairs, say what chores from Activity 2 you do or don't do.

I take out the trash, but I don't do the ironing.

4 Study the Grammar box and circle the correct word to complete the sentence. Then read the text again and underline the adverbs of manner.

Grammar	Adverbs of manner
adjective	*adverb*

He is slow. → He does things slowly.
She is noisy. → She does things noisily.

- We use *very*, *really*, and *so* before adjectives and adverbs.
  He is very/really/so careful.
  → He does things very/really/so carefully.
- We use adverbs of manner to describe *how / when* things are done.
- Some adverbs are the same as the adjectives: hard, fast, right, wrong, early, late.
- The adverb for *good* is *well*.

GRAMMAR TIME ▶ PAGE 110

5 Complete the sentences with adverbs from the adjectives in parentheses. In pairs, say if the sentences are true for you.

1. I make my bed really *badly* . (bad)
2. My mom doesn't cook very _____. (good)
3. I load the dishwasher very _____. (careful)
4. I clean my room so _____. (fast)
5. I never arrive _____. (late)
6. I like getting up _____. (early)
7. My parents do the grocery shopping _____. (slow)
8. My grandfather eats very _____. (noisy)

I don't make my bed badly. I make it very well. How about you?

6 In groups, make adverbs from the adjectives below. Then use them to talk about what you all did yesterday. Are your classmates' sentences true or false?

> good bad quick slow wrong hard
> careful angry happy early late

A: *I sang happily on my way to school.*
B: *I don't believe you. It's false.*

7 🔊 1.66 Complete the text with one word in each blank. Listen and check.

My mom works ¹ *hard* and she's always ² _____ tired when she gets home. So we all help ³ _____ the chores. My brother Tom usually ⁴ _____ the grocery shopping. He can drive, so he does it very ⁵ _____ – in under an hour. My sister Bea is the cook because she cooks really ⁶ _____. I set and ⁷ _____ the table and I ⁸ _____ the vacuuming every Sunday. I take ⁹ _____ the trash, too. But I don't ¹⁰ _____ the dishwasher anymore because Bea says I don't do it very well.

8 Work in pairs. Tell each other who does the chores in your house and how well they do them. Use Activity 7 to help you.

My parents usually do the cooking. My dad cooks really well and …

4.3 READING and VOCABULARY — A mystery story

I can make inferences from a narrative and describe places.

1 **CLASS VOTE** Do you enjoy mystery stories? If so, what's your favorite?

2 Look at the illustration at the bottom of the page. What do you think the story is about?

3 🔊 **1.67** Listen and read an extract of the the story. Were your guesses in Activity 2 correct?

Reading tip

As you read the extract, ask yourself questions, such as:
- What details are included?
- Why did the author tell you that?
- What details have been left out?

4 Read the story again. Mark the sentences ✓ (true), ✗ (false), or ? (doesn't say).
1. [✗] The story takes place in Tom's house.
2. [ ] The house is near a lake.
3. [ ] Tom heard the cat before he saw it.
4. [ ] Tom knew how the kitten got out of the attic.
5. [ ] Tom's grandmother doesn't like cats.
6. [ ] The girl wanted Tom to help her get the kitten.

5 In pairs, find the furniture and rooms in the story. Write them in your notebook.
- Furniture and things in a house: *lamp, ...*
- Rooms and parts of a house:

6 🔊 **1.68** Match the highlighted words in the story to their opposites below. Listen and repeat the words.

Vocabulary — Adjectives to describe a house

bright – 1 *dark*
small – 2 _____
wide – 3 _____
modern – 4 _____
clean – 5 _____
uncomfortable – 6 _____

7 Complete the description of the house in the story to words from the Vocabulary box.

My grandma's house isn't 1 *modern* like ours, it's really 2 _____ . I'm writing this in front of the fire in the living room, it's 3 _____ . The house is very 4 _____ – there are five bedrooms. It's really 5 _____ because the curtains are always closed. The corridors are 6 _____ – you can touch both walls at the same time. Upstairs there is a 7 _____ attic full of old furniture.

It was a hot summer night. I woke up because I heard a cat. I was surprised because my grandmother doesn't have a cat. It was **dark**, so I turned on the lamp. I listened really carefully, but I didn't hear anything. Maybe it was a dream, I thought.

The next night I heard the noise again, but this time there was a black kitten on the windowsill. It jumped into the bedroom and ran quickly outside. I followed it along the **narrow** corridor, through the **large** hall and upstairs into the attic. I turned the light on. The room was very **messy**. There were **old-fashioned** rugs, curtains, a **cozy** armchair, and paintings. I looked everywhere, but I couldn't find the kitten. It was a mystery.

In the morning, I told Grandma about the cat. "Don't be silly, Tom," she said laughing. "There aren't any cats in the house."

That night, I woke up and saw a girl sitting on the windowsill. She was beautiful, with long brown hair and soft green eyes.

"You have to help me," she said. She spoke quietly. It was hard to hear her voice.

She took my hand and I followed her to the yard. She pointed to the roof. I looked up. The kitten was near the chimney, but it was difficult to see it. I got closer to the roof. "He is my cat, Toby," the girl said. "He can't come down from the roof. I need your help."

When I turned back to look at the girl, she wasn't there.

8 How do you think the story ends? In pairs, write the last paragraph of the story in your notebook.

9 Work in groups. Use the Vocabulary box to describe your school or your house.

I think our school is very ...
There is/are ...

And YOU

Unit 4 43

4.4 GRAMMAR — Modal verbs: *can*, *have to*, and *must*

I can talk about permission and obligation.

1 🔊 **1.69** Look at the picture. What is happening? Listen and read, then answer the questions in your notebook.

1. Where are the girls?
2. Why is Ruby not happy?
3. Does Amy agree with Ruby? Why? / Why not?

IT'S NOT FAIR!

Ruby: What time is it?
Amy: Almost eleven.
Ruby: Cool! I <u>have to</u> go to bed at ten normally!
Krystal: Ten! That's early! I don't have to go to bed until eleven … and I can stay up later on weekends. What time do you have to go to bed, Amy?
Amy: Any time I want.
Ruby: You're lucky! My parents are really strict with me. I have to clean my room. I have to come home straight after school. I must not forget to do my homework. I can't wear make-up. I can't stay out late. But Lee can stay out late …
Krystal: What time does Lee have to come home?
Ruby: He doesn't have to come home until ten! It's not fair!
Amy: Yeah, he's older, Ruby. My cousin Meg's thirteen and she must go to bed at nine!
Ruby: Oh!

OUT of class
Cool! You're lucky! It's not fair!

2 Study the Grammar box and complete the sentences with *can*, *have to*, *don't have to*, *must*, or *must not*. Then underline examples of modal verbs in the dialogue.

Grammar	Modal verbs: *can*, *have to*, *must*

Can you stay up late?
I can/can't stay up late on the weekend.

Do I have to go to bed?
You have to/don't have to go to bed now.

You must not leave your clothes on the floor.

- We use _____ to say something is permitted/ not permitted.
- We use _____ / _____ to say something is necessary.
- We use _____ to say something is prohibited.
- We use _____ to say something isn't necessary.

GRAMMAR TIME > PAGE 110

3 🔊 **1.70** Listen to extracts of the dialogue. How is *have to* pronounced?

Speak UP!

4 🔊 **1.71** Circle the correct option. Then listen to Ruby and Krystal and check.

R: Krystal, ¹(can you) / do you have to invite friends to your house any time you want or ²can you / do you have to ask your parents for permission?

K: I ³can / have to invite friends any time I want. I ⁴don't have to / must not ask my parents. But if my parents are watching TV, we ⁵don't have to / must not make a lot of noise.

5 Complete the sentences to make them true for you.

How strict are your parents?

1. I _____ stay up late on weekends.
2. I _____ go to bed at _____ during the week.
3. I _____ get up early on weekends.
4. I _____ eat with my family on weekdays.

6 In groups, ask about the information in Activity 5. Who has strict parents?

Can you stay up late on weekends?
What time do you have to go to bed?

And YOU

4.5 LISTENING and VOCABULARY Describing your town

I can identify specific information in a conversation and talk about my town.

SURVEY RESULTS

Best things about Laconia
1. Friendly people
2. Beautiful lakes
3. Nice old buildings
4. Great cafés and stores
5. Big Pumpkin Festival

Worst things about Laconia
1. Nothing to do in the winter
2. Not enough stores
3. No public transportation in the evenings
4. Too many tourists in summer
5. Everybody knows your business

1 Work in pairs. Look at the pictures. What do they show? What type of place is Laconia?

village   small town   city   capital city

2 🔊 1.72 **I KNOW!** Listen and repeat the words in the Vocabulary box.

Vocabulary	Places in town

art gallery   café   castle   church   city hall
hotel   library   park   movie theater   museum
post office   police department   station
shopping mall   visitor center

3 🔊 1.73 Listen to a recorded message from the tourist information line in Laconia. Fill in the blanks with a word or phrase.

Vacation in Laconia
- For maps and pamphlets go to the ¹ *visitor center* open ² _____
- Top attraction – ³ _____
- Popular sport: ⁴ _____
- Places to stay: ⁵ _____ and cabins

4 In pairs, look at the results of a survey answered by Laconia teenagers and answer the questions in your notebook.
1. What are the three biggest problems for young people in Laconia?
2. What are the three most popular reasons why Laconia is a good place to live?

5 🔊 1.74 Listen to four teenagers answering the survey. In your notebook, write the best (+) and worst (-) things they mention. One answer is mentioned twice.
1. Danny *(+) friendly people; (-) not enough stores*
2. Louise
3. Annie
4. Brett

6 🔊 1.74 Listen again and match statements a–e to speakers 1–4. There is one extra statement.
1. [c] Danny   3. [ ] Annie
2. [ ] Louise   4. [ ] Brett

a. doesn't like the tourists.
b. enjoys riding his/her bike.
c. lived in another town when he/she was younger.
d. is planning to live in a different place.
e. lives outside the town.

7 What are the best and worst things about your town/city? Tell the class. Use the survey answers in Activity 5 and the Vocabulary box to help you.

For me, the best things about our town are the nice old buildings and the music festival. The worst things are …

And YOU?

Unit 4   45

4.6 SPEAKING Advice

I can ask for, give, and receive advice.

1 Krystal and Amy meet a new neighbor. In your notebook, write three questions you think they ask him.

What's your name?

2 🔊 **1.75** Listen to Part 1. Complete the information. Did the girls ask any of your questions in Activity 1?
1 Name: _Billy Smith_
2 Place of birth: _____
3 Age: _____
4 Birthday: _____

3 🔊 **1.76** Listen and read Part 2. Which place is Billy going to visit today?

I MOVED IN THIS MORNING - PART 2

Krystal: Hi, Billy.
Billy: Hi.
Krystal: Where are you going?
Billy: I want to explore my new town. Can you give me some advice about what to do?
Amy: I think you should go for a walk by the canal. It's beautiful.
Krystal: You're kidding, right? That's an awful idea, Amy. You shouldn't go to the canal, Billy. It's not safe there.
Billy: Yeah, I don't think that's a good idea. What do you think I should do, Krystal? Where should I go?
Krystal: Why don't you go to the mall? It's a good place to hang out.
Billy: That's a good idea, thanks.
Krystal: We're going there now. Do you want to come?
Billy: Yeah, why not? OK!

OUT of class
You're kidding, right?
It's a good place to hang out.

4 🔊 **1.77** In pairs, study the Speaking box and complete the dialogues below. Listen and check.

| Speaking | Advice |

Asking for advice
- Where should I ...?
- What do you think I should ...?
- Can you give me some advice about ...?

Giving advice
- You should/shouldn't ...
- Why don't you ...?
- I think/don't think you should ...

Accepting advice
- That's a good idea.
- Thanks for the advice.

Rejecting advice
- That's an awful idea!
- I don't think that's a good idea.

1 Amy: You ¹ _shouldn't_ argue with Peter. He gets angry very easily.
  Billy: Thanks ² _____ the advice, Amy.
2 Billy: Can you give me some ¹ _____ about how to do better in French?
  Teacher: I think you ² _____ do extra homework.
  Billy: That's a good ³ _____ . Thanks.
3 Dad: I don't think you ¹ _____ stay in bed so late. Why ² _____ you help me wash the car?
  Billy: That's an ³ _____ idea! You ⁴ _____ take it to the car wash.

5 In your notebook, write advice for a new student in your town. Use the ideas below.

how to get to school
people to hang out with
clothes to wear/not to wear at school
places to go to/to avoid   things to do/not to do

You should walk to school. It's not far.

6 Work in pairs. Imagine you are new in town. Ask for and respond to the advice you get. Use your ideas from Activity 5 and the Speaking box to help you.

Where should I meet friends after school?

4.7 WRITING — A comment on a post

I can write a comment on a forum post.

1 In pairs, ask and answer the questions.
1. How often do you read and comment on forums?
2. Do you think forums are useful? Why?

2 Read the forum post. Answer the questions in your notebook.
1. Who wrote it?
2. What information does she want?

Forum: moving to a new town

Hey, guys! I need a little help. My dad got a new job in Carmel-by-the-Sea, (but) I don't know the town. Can you tell me anything about it? I want to know more before we move! Thanks. @melania007

Hi there, @melania007! Carmel is on the central coast of California. It's pretty small, but it's a nice town. Do you like surfing? Because the beach is a cool surf spot! I hope that helps.

I'm from Carmel! It's small, almost like a village, but there are a lot of fun things to do. There are museums and there's a famous historic library. I live in a little cottage near downtown. Welcome to Carmel-by-the-Sea!

Hello from another Carmel resident! My apartment is by the beach, in a bright apartment building, and with a great view. There is lots of marine life in Carmel-by-the-Sea and you can even see whales. There are lots of restaurants with delicious seafood, plus several small stores, so you can go shopping on weekends. You'll love it here!

3 Circle the words below in the forum. How do you say them in your language? Use them to complete the sentences.

| and | ~~but~~ | because | so |

1. My town isn't very big, ___but___ there are lots of things to do.
2. We live in Canada, _____ we get a lot of snow in winter.
3. I can walk to school _____ it isn't far.
4. I like the park _____ I like the canal, too.

4 Study the Writing box. Underline the phrases that are used in the comments.

Writing: Posting a comment on a forum about moving to a new town

Greet the person who wrote the post
Hey, ...
Hi, there!
Thanks for your post.

Describe the place
The town is called ...
It's on the central coast of ... / in the south of ... / near ... /
It's very big / pretty small.
It seems nice / isn't very interesting.
There's a famous historic library. / There are museums. / There are lots of restaurants.
The apartment/house isn't very big/modern.
It's on the seventh floor.
It's on a quiet street.

End your comment
I hope that helps.
Let us know how it goes.
You'll love it here!

5 Imagine melania007 is not moving to Carmel, but to your town. Write a comment to help her.

Writing Time

1. **Find ideas**
Look at the Writing box and take notes about your town. Include information about the place, what it is like, what teenagers like to do there, and where you live.

2. **Draft**
In your notebook, write a draft of your comment. Look at the comments in Activity 2 to help you. Connect your sentences using *and*, *but*, *so*, and *because*.

3. **Share**
Share your text with another student for feedback. Listen to his/her opinion and suggestions. Check the spelling and grammar.

4. **Check and write**
Make any necessary changes to your text. Do you use a variety of phrases? Do you connect your sentences correctly? Write the final version of your text.

Unit 4

WORDLIST
Things in the house | Prepositions of place | Chores | Adjectives to describe a house | Places in town

above [prep]	desk [n]	painting [n]	wall [n]
apartment [n]	downtown [n]	park [n]	washbasin [n]
armchair [n]	faucet [n]	police department [n]	wide [adj]
art gallery [n]	fireplace [n]	post office [n]	window [n]
attic [n]	floor [n]	public transportation [n]	windowsill [n]
bathroom [n]	furniture [n]	reasonable [adj]	yard [n]
bed [n]	hall [n]	refrigerator [n]	
bedroom [n]	hotel [n]	relaxing [adj]	**WORD FRIENDS**
behind [prep]	in [prep]	roof [n]	clean your room
between [prep]	in front of [prep]	room [n]	clear/set the table
bright [adj]	kitchen [n]	rug [n]	do the cooking
building [n]	lake [n]	shopping mall [n]	do the housework
cabinet [n]	lamp [n]	shower [n]	do the ironing
café [n]	large [adj]	sink [n]	do the shopping
canal [n]	library [n]	small [adj]	do the vacuuming
capital city [n]	light [adj]	spacious [adj]	dry the dishes
castle [n]	living room [n]	station [n]	hang out with someone
ceiling [n]	mall [n]	stove [n]	listen carefully
chair [n]	messy [adj]	street [n]	live next door
chimney [n]	mirror [n]	strict [adj]	load the dishwasher/the washing machine
church [n]	modern [adj]	switch [n]	make your bed
city [n]	movie theater [n]	table [n]	move to a new apartment/house/town
city hall [n]	museum [n]	toilet [n]	speak quietly
clean [n]	narrow [adj]	tourist [n]	stay out late
closet [n]	near [prep]	town [n]	stay up late
coffee table [n]	neighbor [n]	traffic [n]	sweep the floor
corridor [n]	next to [prep]	trash [n]	take out the trash
cozy [n]	nightstand [n]	uncomfortable [adj]	turn on/off a lamp/the light
couch [n]	old-fashioned [adj]	under [prep]	wash the car
countryside [n]	on [prep]	upstairs [adv]	wash the dishes
curtains [n]	opposite [prep]	view (of/over sth) [n]	
dark [adj]	oven [n]	village [n]	
		visitor center [n]	

VOCABULARY IN ACTION

1 Find in the Wordlist and write in your notebook:
1. six things that you usually find in a bathroom: *mirror, …*
2. six things that you usually find in a kitchen:
3. eight things that you can find in different rooms:
4. ten public places that are in your town/city:

2 Use the letters to write the words connected with the categories below.

Furniture: h a m i c r a r – *armchair*, g r u – _____ , s k e d – _____
Rooms: n i c k e t h – _____ , c i t a t – _____ , d r e b o m o – _____
City places: s u m e m u – _____ , s l e c a t – _____
Adjectives: r a k d – _____ , z c o y – _____

3 Complete the Word Friends. In pairs, say which things you usually do and when.
1. <u>sweep</u> the floor
2. _____ out late
3. _____ quietly
4. _____ your room
5. _____ out with friends in the park
6. _____ the table
7. _____ the light on

I usually sweep the floor on Wednesdays.

4 🔊 1.78 **PRONUNCIATION** In pairs, find one word in each group that is different from the others. Use the underlined letters to help you. Listen, check, and repeat.

1. <u>o</u>ven / <u>u</u>pstairs
   <u>u</u>nder / l<u>a</u>rge (circled)
2. r<u>u</u>g / p<u>a</u>rk
   ab<u>o</u>ve / unc<u>o</u>mfortable
3. sm<u>a</u>ll / fl<u>oo</u>r
   w<u>a</u>ll / c<u>o</u>ffee table

Unit 4

SELF-CHECK

1 Complete the words in the sentences. In pairs, make the sentences true for you.

1 I don't like cities. I prefer the
   c _o_ _u_ _n_ _t_ _r_ _y_ .
2 I always put my clothes in the
   c _ _ _ _ _ _ .
3 I don't look at myself in the
   m _ _ _ _ _ _ very often.
4 We don't have a bathtub in our bathroom. We have a s _ _ _ _ _ _ _ .
5 The c _ _ _ _ _ _ _ c _ _ _ _ _ of my favorite country is Dublin.
6 There's one f _ _ _ _ _ _ for water in our kitchen s _ _ _ _ .
7 I often borrow books from the
   l _ _ _ _ _ _ _ _ .
8 I can't sleep with the l _ _ _ _ _ on. So I turn it off.

I don't like the country. I prefer city life. What about you?

2 Complete the questions with the opposites of the underlined words. In pairs, ask and answer the questions.

1 Is your bedroom <u>messy</u> or _clean_ ?
2 Are the corridors in your school <u>narrow</u> or _____ ?
3 Is your kitchen <u>dark</u> or _____ ?
4 Is your living room <u>cozy</u> or _____ ?
5 Do you live in a _____ or big city?
6 Do you prefer <u>modern</u> or _____ buildings?
7 What's on the wall <u>above</u> your bed? And what do you keep _____ your bed?

3 Complete the text with one word in each blank. Then, in your notebook, write sentences to say what housework from the text you did and didn't do last week.

First, I ¹ _made_ my bed. Then I set the ² _____ for breakfast. After eating, I ³ _____ the table and ⁴ _____ the dishes. I didn't ⁵ _____ the dishes, I left them on the sink. After that, I loaded the ⁶ _____ machine and did the vacuuming. After lunch, I did the grocery ⁷ _____ at the grocery store and then I ⁸ _____ the ironing. I don't enjoy doing ⁹ _____ chores, so my parents were really surprised!

I made my bed every day last week. I didn't …

4 Complete the questions with the correct form of the words in parentheses. In pairs, ask and answer the questions.

1 Do you work very _hard_ (hard) at school?
2 Do you eat _____ (quick) or _____ (slow)?
3 Did you get up _____ (early) last Sunday?
4 Did you sleep _____ (good) or _____ (bad) last night?
5 Do you sometimes get up really _____ (late)?
6 Do you usually get math problems _____ (right) or _____ (wrong)?
7 Do you write text messages _____ (careful)?

5 Circle the correct option.

Dear Mom and Dad,
You ¹(can)/ have to come into my room, but you ² have to / must not knock first.
You ³ don't have to / must not touch my games console when I'm not at home.
You ⁴ can't / have to try to remember my friends' names.
You ⁵ can't / have to stay in my room when my friends are here.
You ⁶ don't have to / must not bring us drinks, but you ⁷ can / can't if you like.
You ⁸ have to / must not ask me to do the chores when I have homework.
Love, Teri
P.S. ⁹ Can you / Do you have to call me "baby" in front of my friends? It's embarrassing!

6 In pairs, role-play the situations. Student A: look below. Student B: look at page 117.

Student A
1 You want to change the decoration in your bedroom. Ask Student B for advice. Then accept or reject the advice.
2 Give Student B advice for the surprise party he/she wants to organize. If he/she rejects your ideas, give him/her different advice.

7 🔊 1.79 Listen, then listen again, and write down what you hear.

SELF-ASSESSMENT   Think about this unit. What did you learn? What do you need help with?

5

Take care

VOCABULARY
Parts of the body | Accidents and injuries | Keeping fit | Snacks | Sleep | Symptoms and illnesses

GRAMMAR
Countable and uncountable nouns | Quantifiers | Past Continuous and Simple Past

Grammar:
What are you having for lunch?
Look at Billy and Amy. What do you think they are talking about?

Speaking:
What's wrong?
Billy has a health problem. What do you think it is? Why does he have it?

5.1 VOCABULARY The body

I can talk about the body, injuries, and keeping fit.

1 lips
2
3
4
5
6
7
8
9

1 **I KNOW!** Work in pairs. How many parts of the body can you name in a minute?

2 **I KNOW!** Use the letters to write the names of the parts of the body.

1 r a m   arm
2 h o t u m   _____
3 t e t e h   _____
4 g e l   _____
5 y e e   _____
6 o s e n   _____
7 f o t o   _____
8 h a d e   _____
9 a r e   _____
10 a r h i   _____
11 c a b k   _____
12 d a h n   _____

50 Unit 5

3 🔊 **2.01** Match the words in the Vocabulary box to the parts of the body 1–9 in the pictures. Listen and check. Then listen again and repeat the words.

Vocabulary	Parts of the body

ankle elbow eyebrow finger knee ~~lips~~
neck shoulder toes

4 🔊 **2.02** Read the information in *Our Amazing Bodies* and follow the instructions.

1 Listen and repeat the highlighted words. How do you say them in your language?
2 Share with your classmates the facts you find interesting.

> **Our Amazing Bodies**
> ⬡ It takes seven seconds for food to get from your mouth to your **stomach** – even when you stand on your head!
> ⬡ A typical man grows about ten meters of **beard** in his lifetime.
> ⬡ In your lifetime, you lose about eighteen kilograms of **skin**.
> ⬡ A ballet dancer can stand on her big toe and carry 150 kilograms at the same time.
> ⬡ Your **heart** beats about three billion times in your lifetime.
> ⬡ Your nose and ears grow all the time!
> ⬡ The **muscles** in your eyes are very hard-working – they move about 100,000 times a day.
> ⬡ Cyclists on Tour de France burn about 12,000 calories per day in the race – that's the energy you get from 100 large bananas! And the race lasts 21 days!
> ⬡ Your **brain** is 80 percent water – that's why it's important to drink a lot of water!
> ⬡ A quarter of your **bones** are in your feet.

5 Complete the sentences with the words from the text and Activities 2 and 3.

1 An adult usually has thirty-two ___teeth___.
2 The _____ is a symbol of love.
3 _____ can be straight, wavy, or curly.
4 Yoga exercises are great for your stomach _____.
5 I have to be careful in sunny weather – my _____ is pale so I get a sunburn easily.
6 I never work at my desk – I always sit with my laptop on my _____.

6 🔊 **2.03** Look at the picture and say what you can see. Then listen and answer the questions in your notebook.

1 What type of exercise do Ellen and Owen do?
2 Why are they in the emergency room?

7 🔊 **2.03** **WORD FRIENDS** Listen again. Circle the correct option.

1 This morning Ellen hurt her (back) / knee.
2 Last week she fell and twisted her knee / ankle.
3 Owen says it's easy to break your arm / leg when you play rugby.
4 Owen cut his knee / finger.

8 🔊 **2.04** **CLASS VOTE** Listen and decide who trains harder – Owen or Ellen.

9 🔊 **2.04** **WORD FRIENDS** Listen again. Complete the sentences with the words below.

do (3x) have go (3x) ~~keep~~ play

1 It's important for me to ___keep___ fit.
2 I _____ rugby (soccer/basketball) every week.
3 I _____ exercises at home every morning.
4 I _____ to the gym regularly.
5 I _____ weight training.
6 I _____ running (cycling).
7 I _____ yoga (T'ai chi).
8 I _____ fitness classes (PE lessons) every day/week.
9 I _____ swimming once a week.

10 In pairs, change the sentences in Activity 9 to make them true for you. **And YOU**

I don't do exercises at home, but I go to the gym once a week.

Unit 5 51

5.2 GRAMMAR Countable and uncountable nouns | Quantifiers

I can talk about quantities and amounts of food.

1 **2.05** **CLASS VOTE** Listen and repeat. Which of these snacks do you usually eat at school?

Vocabulary	Snacks
cake candy bars fruit hamburgers hot dogs nuts potato chips salad sandwiches soup	

I sometimes eat potato chips, but I never eat cake.

2 **2.06** Look at the picture and describe it with a classmate. Listen, read, and answer the questions in your notebook.

1 Are Billy's lunches usually healthy?
2 What is Amy having for lunch today?

WHAT ARE YOU HAVING FOR LUNCH?

Billy: Ah, lunchtime! I'm so hungry!
Amy: What's this? Potato chips and a banana! You never have any healthy food for lunch, like some sandwiches, some salad, or some soup.
Billy: Bananas are healthy! I don't have any time to make sandwiches – I always have too many things to do before school!
Amy: You're kidding! It doesn't take much time to make a nice lunch! Today I have some chicken sandwiches and some delicious Thai soup.
Billy: Amy, how many sandwiches do you have today? I don't have much food.
Amy: Three! And I want them all! But I have a lot of soup. Do you want some?
Billy: Yes! Thanks!
Amy: Help yourself. Careful, it's hot … Billy! Are you OK?

OUT of class
You're kidding!
Help yourself.

3 **I KNOW!** In pairs, say if the underlined words in the dialogue are countable or uncountable.

4 Study the Grammar box and complete the sentence. Then circle examples of quantifiers with nouns in the dialogue.

Grammar	Quantifiers
Countable nouns	**Uncountable nouns**
some sandwiches	some salad
a lot of vegetables	a lot of fresh fruit
too many fries	too much chocolate
not many things	not much time
not any apples	not any bread
How many burgers?	How much salad?

- We use quantifiers to talk about quantities and amounts. In affirmative sentences, _____ and _____ are quantifiers we can use with countable and uncountable nouns.

GRAMMAR TIME ▶ PAGE 111

5 Look at what Amy and Billy ate for lunch in one week. Complete the sentences with quantifiers. There is often more than one possible answer.

Amy – week 1
2 apples, 3 kiwi fruit,
4 bananas, 1 orange,
0 candy bars,
10 salami sandwiches

Billy – week 1
1 banana,
7 chocolate bars,
5 bags of potato chips,
0 sandwiches

- Amy eats ¹ _a lot of_ fruit. She doesn't eat ² _____ candy bars. She doesn't eat ³ _____ oranges. She eats ⁴ _____ sandwiches.
- Billy eats ⁵ _____ chocolate. He doesn't eat ⁶ _____ fruit. He doesn't eat ⁷ _____ sandwiches. He eats ⁸ _____ potato chips.

6 In pairs, say how much of these things you eat and drink. **And YOU**

| iced tea   coffee   water   fruit juice   soda |
| meat   fruit   vegetables   snacks   candy |

I don't drink much coffee. What about you?

Unit 5

5.3 READING and VOCABULARY   An advice column

I can find specific information in an online advice column and talk about sleeping habits.

1 **CLASS VOTE** Do you agree with statements a–c?

a It's hard for me to get up in the morning.
b I sleep more than my parents.
c I never go to bed before 11:00 p.m.

2 🔊 **2.07** Listen and read the advice column, then answer the questions in your notebook. What's Polly's advice

a for weekdays?   b for the weekend?

Ask Polly

Dear Polly,
Last night at 10:00 p.m. I was online when my dad told me to get ready for bed. Two hours later, I was in bed with my eyes open. I didn't feel sleepy, so I got up. My parents were on the couch. They always fall asleep in front of the TV. They don't go to bed when they are sleepy, so why do I have to go to bed? Then last Saturday my mom woke me up at 11:00 a.m. She says I'm lazy, but that's not fair. I always feel tired in the morning, but I get up early and work hard all week so why can't I stay in bed on weekends?
Josh, 15

Hi Josh,
Your parents don't want you to stay up late because they think you need to sleep. And they're right! Teenagers need a lot of sleep. How much? Usually about nine hours a night – that's more than adults!

But it's difficult for teens to wake up early and go to sleep early. Often they feel lively at night when adults feel sleepy. That's because teenagers' brains produce melatonin* later in the day. When you see bright lights, your brain stops making melatonin. That means you can't sleep well. So during the school week, you shouldn't use your cell phone or watch too much TV before bedtime. It's better to read or listen to music.

Sleep is important for our health. If you don't get much sleep, your memory and concentration suffer. So try to go to bed early during the week, but tell your parents you need to stay in bed late on weekends.
Polly

*a hormone which makes you sleepy

Reading tip

When answering multiple-choice questions, look for key words in the items and find similar words in the text. Read the question and the text carefully again.

3 Read the advice column again. Circle the correct answer.

1 Josh says that last night he fell asleep
   a before his parents.   **(b)** after his parents.
2 Josh's mother woke him up last Saturday because
   a he wanted to get up early.
   b she thinks it's wrong to stay in bed late.
3 Polly says
   a teenagers need a lot of sleep.
   b adults think teenagers are lazy.
4 Teens like staying up late and getting up late because
   a they make hormones differently from adults.
   b they watch too much TV.

4 **WORD FRIENDS** Look at the highlighted phrases in the advice column and complete the Word Friends.

| feel tired / ¹ _sleepy_ |
| fall ² _____ |
| get ³ _____ for bed |
| go to ⁴ _____ / sleep |
| get / wake up ⁵ _____ / late |
| sleep ⁶ _____ / badly |
| stay up / stay in bed / sleep ⁷ _____ |

5 🔊 **2.08** Listen to the Word Friends. Which part is stressed – the verb or the complement? Answer in your notebook.

Speak UP!

6 Read the Sleep Quiz and circle the correct words to complete the questions.

SLEEP QUIZ

1 What time did you *(go)* / *sleep* to bed last night?
2 What time did you *get* / *stay* up last Saturday morning?
3 What do you do when you can't *fall* / *wake* asleep?
4 What do you do to help you *go* / *wake* up early?
5 How many hours do you usually *fall* / *sleep* at night?
6 Do you ever *feel* / *go* sleepy in class?

7 In groups, do the Sleep Quiz in Activity 6.

And YOU

A: *What time did you go to bed last night?*
B: *I went to bed early because …*

Unit 5   53

5.4 GRAMMAR Past Continuous and Simple Past

I can talk about an event in the past and what was happening around it.

1 Look at the picture. What's happening? Why do you think it's happening?

2 🔊 **2.09** Listen and read the text to check your ideas. Then work in pairs and say what happened to Wayne and Stephanie.

Wayne fell off a ladder. He cut …

ACCIDENTS!

We asked some people to describe accidents they had. What were you doing when the accident happened?

WAYNE
Yesterday afternoon I <u>was painting</u> the ceiling. My little brother was holding the ladder, but he wasn't paying attention. While I was coming down, the ladder moved and I fell. I cut my hand, hurt my back, and broke my arm. It was really painful.

STEPHANIE
My basketball team was playing a game. We weren't playing well and the other team was really good. They were winning 34–21 when I got the ball. Unfortunately, when I was trying to score a basket, I twisted my ankle and fell. I hit my head and broke my nose. I was lucky I didn't break my neck!

3 Study the Grammar box and check (✓) the correct options. Underline examples of the Past Continuous in the text.

Grammar	Past Continuous and Simple Past
+	**−**
I was playing. They were playing.	I wasn't running. They weren't running.
?	
Were you playing? Yes, I was. / No, I wasn't.	
Were they playing? Yes, they were. / No, they weren't.	
What was she doing yesterday at 5 p.m.?	

Past Continuous and Simple Past
While/When I was coming down the ladder, I fell.
I was coming down the ladder when I fell.

- ✓ We often use the Past Continuous with the Simple Past.
- ☐ We use the Simple Past for a short/complete action.
- ☐ We use the Past Continuous for a longer activity in progress.
- ☐ The actions don't happen at the same time.
- ☐ Before the Past Continuous we use *while* or *when*.

GRAMMAR TIME ▶ PAGE 111

4 Circle the correct option.
1 My cousin (had) / was having an accident when he rode / was riding a motorcycle.
2 My mom hit / was hitting her head when she got / was getting into the car.
3 While my dad played / was playing tennis, he hurt / was hurting his back.
4 I twisted / was twisting my ankle while I ran / was running to school.

5 Complete the conversation with the correct form of the verbs in parentheses.

A: What ¹ <u>were you doing</u> (you/do) when the accident ² _____ (happen)?
B: I ³ _____ (drive) my kids to school when they ⁴ _____ (begin) to shout, so I ⁵ _____ (tell) them to be quiet. I ⁶ _____ (not look) at the road so I ⁷ _____ (not see) the dog. It ⁸ _____ (cross) the road. I ⁹ _____ (drive) into a tree. Fortunately, nobody was hurt.

6 Work in groups. Describe a time when you got hurt. Use the questions below to help you.

1 How old were you?
2 What were you doing when you got hurt?
3 What happened after that?

I was ten years old. I was walking to school when …

5.5 LISTENING and VOCABULARY Symptoms and illnesses

I can identify specific information in a conversation and talk about illnesses.

1 Look at the picture. Why is tomorrow a big day for Bridgeton United?

_____

_____

"We're Bridgeton United five-a-side soccer team. We're playing in the championship final tomorrow. Come and support us!"

2 🔊 **2.10** Listen and repeat the phrases. How do you say them in your language?

Vocabulary | Symptoms and illnesses

Symptoms
- feel sick/ill
- have a headache/a stomachache/ a sore throat/a fever/a cough
- cough/sneeze

Illnesses
- I have hay fever/the flu/a cold/a food allergy.

3 🔊 **2.11** What symptoms do the players in Bridgeton United have? Complete the sentences. Then listen to Jerry and check.

1 Nathan is _____sneezing_____.
2 James has a _____.
3 Ben has a _____ and a _____.
4 Chris has a _____.

4 In pairs, say what the symptoms are for these illnesses.

   a cold   food allergy   the flu

When you have a cold, you sneeze a lot and …

5 Use the Vocabulary box to complete the sentences.

1 If you ___sneeze___ when you're near flowers, maybe you have _____.
2 You have a very high _____ – it's 40° Celsius! I think you have the _____.
3 I ate too much and now I have a _____.
4 I was shouting and now I have a _____.

6 🔊 **2.12** Listen to the coach of Bridgeton United talking to the players. Answer the questions.

1 Why couldn't Ben play?
   He had the flu.
2 Why was Nathan sneezing?
   _____
3 Why did James have a stomachache?
   _____
4 Why couldn't Chris play?
   _____
5 What did Tom get at the end?
   _____

7 🔊 **2.13** Listen to Jerry talking to a friend about the five-a-side soccer game. Circle the correct answer.

1 They played the game on
   a Wednesday. **b** Saturday. **c** Sunday.
2 While Jerry was visiting friends, he got
   a a cold. **b** the flu. **c** allergies.
3 On the day of the game, Jerry felt
   a great. **b** sick. **c** very well.
4 Ben didn't finish the game because he
   a twisted his ankle. **b** broke his leg.
   c hurt his back.
5 Jerry's team won the game
   a 2-1. **b** 3-1. **c** 3-2.

8 In pairs, ask and answer the questions.

- How often do you have a cold or the flu?
- Are you allergic to anything?
- What kind of things can give you a headache?

I have a cold once or twice a year.

Unit 5   55

5.6 SPEAKING — Health and illnesses

I can talk about feeling sick and give advice.

1 In pairs, look at the picture. What do you think is happening?

2 🔊 **2.14** Listen and read Part 1. Why did Billy go to see the school nurse?

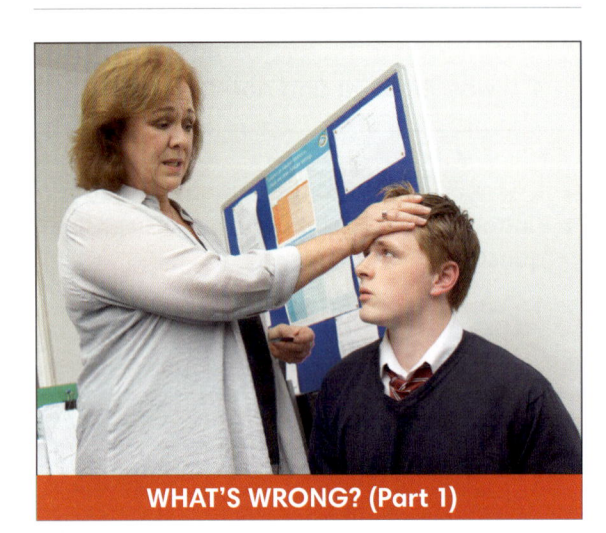

_____
_____

WHAT'S WRONG? (Part 1)

Nurse: William Taylor! What's the matter?
Billy: I feel awful.
Nurse: Hmm, well you don't have a fever. Are you feeling sick?
Billy: No, I'm not. I have a really bad stomachache.
Nurse: Well, when did you start feeling sick?
Billy: Just after lunch.
Nurse: I see. What did you have for lunch?
Billy: Just the usual – some potato chips and a banana. Oh, hold on, and some of Amy's Thai soup …
Nurse: Ah! You're probably allergic to something in the soup. Here, have some water. You should drink a lot of water. And maybe you should make an appointment with your doctor immediately … after school. OK! I think you can go back to class now.
Billy: Oh!

> **OUT of class**
> *I see. Just the usual.*

3 🔊 **2.15** Listen to Part 2. What was Billy's problem?

_____
_____

4 Study the Speaking box. Then underline the words and phrases from the dialogue.

Speaking — Health and illness

Asking what the problem is
- What's wrong / <u>What's the matter?</u>
- How are you feeling?

Talking about symptoms
- I feel sick/ill/awful.
- I have a stomachache/headache/toothache/ a fever/a sore throat/a cold/the flu.
- My leg/back/ankle/tooth hurts.

Advice
- Sit down.
- Have some water/herbal tea.
- You should lie down/stay in bed/make an appointment with the doctor/go to hospital.

5 🔊 **2.16** Complete the dialogues with one word in each blank. Listen and check.

1   A: What's ____*wrong*____?
    B: I have a fever.
    A: I think you should _____ down.
2   A: _____'s wrong?
    B: My ankle hurts. Maybe I twisted it.
    A: I think you _____ go to the hospital.
3   A: _____ are you feeling?
    B: I have a really sore throat.
    A: You should make an _____ with the doctor.

6 Work in pairs. Suggest what the people should do. Use the Speaking box to help you.

1   Billy has the flu. *Billy should stay in bed.*
2   Lee has hay fever.
3   Amy's tooth hurts.
4   Krystal's stomach hurts.

7 In pairs, follow the instructions. Use the Speaking box and Activity 5 to help you.   **And YOU**

1   **Student A**: ask how Student B is feeling. Listen and give advice.
2   **Student B**: you feel sick. Tell Student A your symptoms.
3   Switch roles.

5.7 WRITING   An instant message conversation

I can write an instant message conversation about a health problem.

1 Read the instant messages and answer the questions. Then use the phrasal verbs underlined to complete the definitions.

a Why can't Keegan go to soccer practice?

b Why is Liv surprised?

Conversation 1

- Hey, Pete. Can't come to soccer practice tonight. Can you tell the coach?
- What's up, Keegan?
- I keep <u>throwing up</u>.
- Oh, poor you! Did you go to the doctor's to <u>check out</u> what's wrong?
- Not yet. Think I'm <u>coming down</u> with a stomach bug.
- Go to the doctor's, bro! You need 2 <u>find out</u> what's wrong.
- OK, OK!

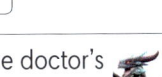

Conversation 2

- Want to come with me to that new vegan restaurant, Liv?
- Vegan restaurant, Jen?
- LOL I'm <u>giving up</u> meat! Want to <u>look after</u> my health better and red meat isn't good for you.
- But u love BBQ, Jen!
- True. OK. I'm <u>cutting down on</u> red meat then. I can still have BBQ sometimes.
- And r you <u>taking up</u> a sport?
- Calm down, sis! One thing at a time!

1 stop doing something: _give up_
2 discover, learn: _____
3 start a hobby or activity: _____
4 verify: _____
5 take care: _____
6 vomit: _____
7 do something less often: _____
8 become sick: _____

2 Study the Writing box. Underline the phrases and abbreviations that are used in the instant messages in Activity 1.

> **Writing** | Instant messages about a health problem
>
> **Omit personal and object pronouns**
> Like my new laptop?
> Can't call you, sorry.
> Speak later.
> **Use abbreviations**
> LOL (laugh out loud) / u (you) / r (are) / 2 (to)
> **Use informal language, such as phrasal verbs**
> What's up?
> I think I'm coming down with something.
> My dog keeps throwing up.
> **Use friendly language**
> Poor you!
> Go to the doctor's, bro!
> Calm down, sis!

3 Write an instant message conversation.   *Writing Time*

1 **Find ideas**
Imagine you are sick and can't go to an event. Take notes for a conversation between you and a friend about this topic.

2 **Draft**
In your notebook, write a draft of your conversation. Look at the messages in Activity 2 and the Writing box for help.

3 **Share**
Share your text with another student for feedback. Listen to his/her opinion and suggestions. Check the spelling and grammar.

4 **Check and write**
Make any necessary changes to your instant message conversation. Is the language informal? Write the final version of your text.

Unit 5 57

WORDLIST
Parts of the body | Accidents/injuries | Keeping fit | Snacks | Health/illness

accident [n]
ankle [n]
appointment [n]
arm [n]
back [n]
beard [n]
body [n]
bone [n]
brain [n]
break [n]
burn [v]
cake [n]
calorie [n]
candy [n]
candy bar [n]
check out [phr v]
ceiling [n]
coach [n]
coffee [n]
cold (illness) [n]
come down with [phr v]
cough [v]
cut [v]
cut down on [phr v]
delicious [adj]
doctor [n]
ear [n]
elbow [n]
exercise [n]
eye [n]
eyebrow [n]
fever [n]
find out [phr v]
finger [n]
five-a-side soccer

food allergy [n]
foot (feet) [n]
fruit [n]
fruit juice [n]
game [n]
give up [phr v]
goalkeeper [n]
go off [phr v]
gym [n]
hair [n]
hamburger [n]
hand [n]
hay fever [n]
head [n]
headache [n]
health [n]
healthy [adj]
heart [n]
hit [v]
hot dog [n]
hurt [v]
illness [n]
knee [n]
ladder [n]
leg [n]
lips [n]
look after [phr v]
meat [n]
menu [n]
mouth [n]
muscle [n]
neck [n]
nose [n]
nuts [n]
paint [v]

potato chips [n]
pick up (illness) [phr v]
rugby [n]
salad [n]
salt [n]
sandwich [n]
score [v]
shoulder [n]
sick [adj]
sickness [n]
skin [n]
sleepy [adj]
snack [n]
sneeze [v]
soccer practice [n]
soda [n]
soup [n]
stomach [n]
stomachache [n]
sugar [n]
symptom [n]
take up [v]
tea [n]
the flu [n]
throw up [phr v]
toe [n]
tooth (teeth) [n]
toothache [n]
train [v]
vegetable [n]
vegetarian [adj]
water [n]

WORD FRIENDS
cut your knee/finger
do exercises/yoga/T'ai chi
fall asleep
feel ill/sick/sleepy/terrible/tired
get ready for bed
get up early/late
go running/cycling/swimming
go to bed/sleep
go to the gym
good/bad for you
have hay fever/a cold/a cough/the flu/a headache/fever/a sore throat/a stomachache/toothache
have a dream
have fitness classes/P.E. classes
hit your head
hurt your hand/back
make an appointment (with the doctor)
pay attention to sth
play soccer/basketball/tennis/
ride a motorcycle/bike
score a basket
sleep easily/well/badly
stay up (late)
stay in bed late
twist your ankle/leg
wake up early/late

VOCABULARY IN ACTION

1 Use the Wordlist to find and write in your notebook:
1. five things you can drink. *soda, …*
2. eight items of food or drink that are bad for you.
3. ten parts of the body that you always have two of.
4. three health problems ending with *-ache*.

2 Complete the sentences.
1. I can't stop ___sneezing___ ! Achoo!
2. You need to _____ some tea for your headache.
3. My baby brother has a fever - his temperature is high.
4. Oh, I _____ really sick.

3 Complete the sentences with the words below. In pairs, say which sentences are true for you.

~~fever~~   have   hay fever   ride   sleep   up

1. I sometimes ___fall___ asleep in class.
2. I _____ my bike to school every morning.
3. I usually _____ badly on the night before a test.
4. I usually _____ a cold all winter!
5. I love staying _____ late on Friday night.
6. My family and I always get _____ at the beginning of spring.

4 🔊 **2.17** **PRONUNCIATION** Listen to the words below and decide if you hear the underlined letter(s). Then listen again and repeat.

cho**c**olate   jui**c**e   **k**nee   mus**c**le
san**d**wich   temp**e**rature   ti**r**ed   veg**e**table

58   Unit 5

SELF-CHECK

1 Write the correct word for each definition.

1. You have this when you are sick
   s _i c k n e s s_
2. You do this when you have a cold.
   s _ _ _ _ _ _
3. This can be high when you have the flu.
   f _ _ _ _ _
4. It can stop you from eating some foods.
   a _ _ _ _ _ _ _ _
5. This is the healthiest thing you can drink.
   w _ _ _ _
6. He/She looks after you when you are sick.
   d _ _ _ _ _
7. This can hurt when you eat too quickly.
   s _ _ _ _ _ _
8. Feeling well, not sick. **h** _ _ _ _ _ _

2 Complete the Word Friends in the text with the verbs below.

> cut   had (x2)   hit   hurt   ~~twisted~~

> Our vacation in the mountains was a disaster. First of all, my mom [1] _twisted_ her ankle when we were climbing a mountain – she couldn't walk for days. Grandpa [2] _____ his back from carrying a heavy backpack. My sister [3] _____ a very bad stomachache after she ate a sheep's cheese pizza. My dad [4] _____ his head every time he stood up in the tent. I [5] _____ my finger when I was opening a can of soup. And finally, my grandma [6] _____ a sore throat from shouting at all of us!

3 Circle the correct option.

A: I'm so hungry! Is there anything to eat?
B: Well, we have [1]any / (some) cheese and [2]any / some eggs.
A: OK! How [3]many / much eggs?
B: Four.
A: That's [4]not much / not many!
B: But we have [5]a lot of / any potatoes.
A: Great! So we can have fried eggs and French fries!
B: No, we can't. You need [6]a lot of / much time to cook French fries and we don't have [7]much / many time. And you eat [8]too many / too much French fries! But we have [9]a lot of / too many vegetables so you can make us a nice vegetable omelet!

4 Complete the text with the Simple Past or the Past Continuous form of the verbs in parentheses.

> Yesterday I [1] _was studying_ (study) in my room when suddenly I [2] _____ (hear) a noise from the living room. I [3] _____ (run) into the room and saw that my dad [4] _____ (lie) on the floor.
> "What happened?" I [5] _____ (ask) Dad.
> "I [6] _____ (look) for a book! I [7] _____ (stand) on a chair, but I [8] _____ (not pay) attention and the chair moved and I fell. My shoulder hurts, too! Maybe it's broken – look!"
> His shoulder looked fine. Dad is a hypochondriac.
> "What book [9] _____ (you/look) for?" I asked.
> "*The Book Of Family Health.* It's here somewhere."

5 In pairs, talk about feeling sick. Student A: look below. Student B: look at page 117.

Student A
1. Say hello to Student B. Ask him/her how he/she is feeling. Listen to Student B's news.
2. Give some advice: Have some tea. / Make an appointment with the dentist.

6 🔊 2.18 Listen, then listen again and write down what you hear.

6

Shopping around

6.1 VOCABULARY Types of stores | Containers

I can talk about stores and what they sell.

VOCABULARY
Types of stores | Containers
Shopping malls | Money

GRAMMAR
Comparatives and superlatives of adjectives | *going to* and the Present Continuous

Grammar:
Are you coming with us?
Look at the picture. Who do you think Lee is talking to? Why?

Speaking:
New shoes
Look at Amy. Why does she seem to be annoyed?

1 In pairs, ask and answer the questions.
1. When was the last time you went shopping?
2. What did you buy?
3. Where do you usually go shopping? Why?
4. Who do you go shopping with?

2 🔊 2.19 **I KNOW!** Listen and repeat the words. How do you say them in your language? In your notebook, add more words to the list.

Vocabulary	Types of stores

bakery   bookstore   clothing store   drugstore   flower shop
greengrocer   meat market   newsstand   shoe store

A clothing store   B   C   D

Unit 6

3 In pairs, use the clues below and in the picture to label stores A–I with the words from the Vocabulary box.

- The shoe store is closed at the moment.
- There's a store that sells fruit and vegetables between the bookstore and the newsstand.
- There are a lot of special offers at the clothing store.
- The store between the shoe store and the flower shop sells meat.
- The bakery is next to the drugstore and it's always very busy.

4 Which stores from the Vocabulary box are there in your neighborhood? Which stores aren't there? Discuss in groups.

There's a bakery, but there isn't a bookstore.

5 **WORD FRIENDS** How do you say the words in bold in your language?

a **bag** of apples   a **bar** of chocolate
a **bunch** of flowers   a **bottle** of shampoo
a **box** of cereal   a **can** of soda   a **jar** of honey
a **loaf** of bread   a **package** of cookies

6 🔊 2.20 Listen and complete Julia's shopping list. What did she forget to buy?

shopping list
- greengrocer – apples
- bakery – 1 __bread__ , cookies
- 2 _____ – shampoo
- newsstand – magazine, 3 _____,
  4 _____
- flower shop – 5 _____

7 Circle the correct option.
1 a *bag / can* of sugar
2 a *jar / bottle* of water
3 a *bar / package* of potato chips
4 a *bunch / box* of matches

8 🔊 2.21 Match questions 1–5 to answers a–e. Listen and check.

1 [c] What's its name?
2 [ ] Where is it?
3 [ ] What does it sell?
4 [ ] How often do you go there?
5 [ ] Why do you like it?

a It sells video games.
b I go there about once a month.
c My favorite store is called Go2 Games.
d They have a good choice of games and the people who work there are very helpful.
e It's in the mall downtown.

9 In pairs, ask and answer questions about your favorite store. Use Activity 8 to help you.

And YOU

A: *What's your favorite store?*
B: *My favorite store is called …*

Unit 6   61

6.2 GRAMMAR — Comparatives and superlatives of adjectives

I can compare things.

1 **CLASS VOTE** Look at the text in Activity 2. What type of text is it? How often do you read it? Why? Answer in your notebook.

2 🔊 **2.22** Look at the adjectives below, then listen and read the text. Do people generally have a good opinion of the headphones?

| enjoyable   heavy   low   trendy   (un)comfortable |

HENNSIZER M13 HEADPHONES
Just $25.99 – lowest ever price

OWEN ★★★★★
This is my second pair of Hennsizer headphones – I'm their biggest fan! They're heavier and bigger than my old ones, but the most important thing is that they sound awesome!

ROSIE ★★★★★
They really are the trendiest headphones! They're comfortable – going to school is definitely more enjoyable these days.

LEAH ★★★★☆
You can buy cheaper headphones, but they aren't as good as these. They're definitely better than the headphones I had.

3 Study the Grammar box and circle the correct options. Then underline examples of comparatives and superlatives in the text in Activity 2.

Grammar	Comparatives and superlatives of adjectives	
old	older	the oldest
nice	nicer	the nicest
thin	thinner	the thinnest
pretty	prettier	the prettiest
important	more important	the most important
good	better	the best
bad	worse	the worst

They are not as good as my old headphones.
We use comparative adjectives to compare *two things / more than two things* and superlative adjectives to compare *two things / more than two things*.

GRAMMAR TIME ▶ PAGE 112

4 In pairs, compare cell phones A–C on page 116 using the comparative forms of the adjectives below or your own ideas. In your notebook, write as many sentences as you can in three minutes.

| thin   modern   old   big   small   ugly |

Cell phone A is older than cell phone B.

5 In pairs, make sentences with superlatives about cell phones A–C on page 116. Write them in your notebook.

Cell phone A is the oldest.

6 Complete the review with the comparatives or superlatives of the adjectives in parentheses.

CALLY ★☆☆☆☆
My Hennsizer FL40 headphones stopped working. The M13 headphones are ¹ *more expensive* (expensive), but I bought them. That was my ² _____ (big) mistake! They're ³ _____ (uncomfortable) than my old headphones. I think the quality isn't as good as the FL40 and the sound is ⁴ _____ (bad), too. The ⁵ _____ (annoying) thing is that the cable is too long! I was ⁶ _____ (happy) with my ⁷ _____ (cheap) headphones!

7 In your notebook, rewrite the sentences with *not as ... as* and the adjectives in parentheses.

1 This laptop is lighter than my old one. (heavy) *This laptop isn't as heavy as my old one.*
2 The prices in the bookstore are higher than on the internet. (low)
3 The tablet is cheaper than the cell phone. (expensive)

8 In pairs, ask and answer the questions.
- What was the most expensive thing you bought last year?
- What did you buy that was the biggest waste of money? Why?

And YOU?

6.3 READING and VOCABULARY — A magazine article

I can find specific information in a magazine article and talk about shopping malls.

1 In pairs, guess the answer to the questions about shopping malls. Check your answers on page 116.

Why …
1. do they play music all the time?
2. is it hard to find the exit?
3. is it a long way from the up escalators to the down escalators?

2 🔊 **2.23** Listen and read the magazine article and answer the questions in your notebook.
1. What was Victor Gruen's profession?
2. When and where did he build Southdale?
3. Was Southdale a success?

Reading tip

Before a reading activity, read the questions and underline the information that you need to look for in the text.

3 Read the article again. Mark the sentences ✓ (right), ✗ (wrong), or ? (doesn't say).
1. ✓ Victor Gruen wanted shopping malls to be more than just a place to buy things.
2. ☐ Southdale wasn't as nice as other shopping malls.
3. ☐ Southdale was the busiest shopping mall in the USA.
4. ☐ Victor got a nice surprise when he went back to Vienna.
5. ☐ His invention didn't do what he wanted.

4 🔊 **2.24** Underline the words and phrases below in the article. Listen and repeat.

Vocabulary — Shopping malls

department store   escalators   food court
multiplex   parking lot   public restrooms
shoppers   shopping carts

5 Use the Vocabulary box to complete the definitions below.
1. You put your shopping in it: *shopping cart*
2. A large store that sells lots of different things: _____
3. A way to move from one level to another: _____
4. A place to see movies: _____

Who invented the shopping mall?

In 1938, an Austrian architect called Victor Gruen arrived in New York with eight dollars and no English. He started designing stores and quickly became one of the most successful architects in the city.

Victor thought American cities were uglier than European cities like Vienna. He wanted to make them more beautiful. His dream was to make shopping malls like traditional European downtown areas: beautiful places with parks, schools, and homes around them. So, in 1956, he built Southdale, a shopping mall near Minneapolis. It had the usual stores, department stores, public restrooms, and a big parking lot. But Southdale was more pleasant than other shopping areas. All the stores were under the same roof. It was on two levels with escalators to take shoppers and their shopping carts up and down. And in the middle there was a garden with a café.

Southdale was very popular. Afterwards, most new shopping malls followed the Southdale model. Unfortunately, they didn't become the center of beautiful new towns. Instead, they were ugly out-of-town buildings with seas of cars around them.

In 1978, Victor went back to Austria, but what did he find in Vienna? A large ugly shopping mall with a multiplex and a food court! It was more popular than the traditional stores and many of them had to close.

Victor Gruen invented the modern shopping mall to make the USA more like Vienna, but in the end his invention made Vienna more like the USA.

6 In groups, ask and answer the questions.
- Do you like shopping malls? Why? / Why not?
- How often do you go to shopping malls? Who do you go with?

And YOU?

Unit 6

6.4 GRAMMAR *Going to* and the Present Continuous

I can talk about intentions and arrangements.

1 🔊 **2.25** Listen to Part 1. Check (✓) the things Lee and Ruby plan to do on Saturday.

☐ take the subway ☐ go for a pizza
☐ watch a movie ☐ go shopping

ARE YOU COMING WITH US? (Parts 1 & 2)

(Part 1)

Lee: Hi, Amy. Listen – it's my mom's fortieth birthday next Tuesday and Ruby and I want to buy her something special. So we're going to take the subway to the mall on Saturday, get mom a gift, and then we're going to see a movie at the multiplex. Oh, and I'm going to buy some new sneakers. Can you come with us? Hope so! Oh, we're not going to tell anybody – it's a surprise.

(Part 2)

Amy: Hi, Lee.
Lee: Hey, Amy! Are you coming with us tomorrow?
Amy: Yes, but what time are we taking the subway? I can't remember.
Lee: We're not taking the subway anymore. The bus is cheaper. So we're taking the X4 bus from the bus stop on Mandela Avenue at 10:15. Oh, and I checked the movie times. They're showing *Fast Cars* at the multiplex at 2:30. Billy's meeting us there.
Amy: Great! See you tomorrow at 10:15!

> **OUT of class**
> *Hope so!*
> *It's a surprise.*

2 🔊 **2.26** Listen and read Part 2. Answer the questions in your notebook.
1 Is Amy going with Lee and Ruby on Saturday?
2 How are they going to the mall?
3 What time are they meeting?

3 🔊 **2.27** Now listen to Part 3. Where's Amy?

4 Study the Grammar box. Complete the chart with *intentions and plans* or *arrangements*. Underline examples of *going to* and the Present Continuous in the voicemail message and in the dialogue.

Grammar — Talking about the future

I'm going to buy some sneakers.
We're not going to tell anybody.
Are you going to study?
_____

They're showing *Fast Cars* at 2:30.
We're not taking the subway tomorrow.
Are you coming with us?

GRAMMAR TIME ▶ PAGE 113

5 🔊 **2.28** Complete the sentences with *going to* and the verbs in parentheses. Then listen to Ruby and Lee, and check.

1 I **'m going to buy** (buy) something to drink.
2 He _____ (come) with me to the shoe store.
3 _____ (you/come) with us?
4 I _____ (go) to the bookstore first.
5 I _____ (not spend) all my money.

6 🔊 **2.29** Listen to two people say the sentence below. What do you notice about the pronunciation of *going to*?
I'm going to do my homework.

Speak UP!

7 🔊 **2.30** Listen and underline *to* if the speaker uses a weak sound (/ə/), and circle *going to* if it is pronounced *gonna*.
1 We're going to eat ice cream.
2 Is she going to come, too?
3 They aren't going to see the movie.
4 I'm going to stay in bed.

8 In your notebook, write three intentions for the near future with *going to* and three arrangements for next week with the Present Continuous. In groups, compare your sentences.

I'm going to start running.

And YOU

Unit 6

6.5 LISTENING and VOCABULARY A radio call-in show about how to save money

I can identify specific information in conversations and talk about money.

1 **CLASS VOTE** Does money make people happy? Vote *yes* or *no* and then say why.

2 🔊 2.31 Read the quiz. Then listen and circle Greg's answers. What does he ask Gemma for at the end?

_____

How important is MONEY to you?

1. One day you **get** $10 as <u>allowance</u> and **earn** $20 babysitting. Do you put the money …
   a in a piggy bank?
   b in your wallet/pocket?

2. You get $50 for your birthday. Do you …
   a **save** some and **spend** the rest?
   b spend it all immediately?

3. You get too much change in a store. Do you …
   a keep the money?
   b tell the salesclerk?

4. You need a new pair of jeans. Do you …
   a wait for the sale?
   b buy the pair you like without looking at the price?

5. Some friends want to **borrow** $30. Do you …
   a tell them you never **lend** money?
   b give them the money and say they can **pay** you **back** any time?

Watch OUT!
borrow – take something from someone else and give it back later
lend – give something to someone for some time

---

3 🔊 2.32 Listen and repeat the words and phrases in the Vocabulary box, then underline them in the quiz. Use the words to complete the sentences.

Vocabulary	Money

allowance   change   piggy bank
price   sale   wallet

1 My dad has a ___wallet___ , but I keep my money in my pocket.
2 The price of a book is $6.69 and you pay $10. How much _____ do you get?
3 How much _____ do you get a week?
4 Prices are always lower in the summer _____.
5 I have a _____ on a shelf in my room.

4 **WORD FRIENDS** Complete the sentences with the highlighted verbs in the quiz.
1 I think I should ___get___ more **allowance.**
2 It's better to _____ **money** than to **spend it.**
3 I sometimes _____ **money** to my friends.
4 When I _____ **money**, I always **pay it back**.
5 Teenagers should work to _____ their **money.**

5 In pairs, do the quiz. Check your score on page 116.

6 🔊 2.33 Listen to a radio call-in show about money. Mark the sentences true (T) or false (F).
1 [T] Emily has to work to get an allowance.
2 [ ] She has a lot of money in her piggy bank.
3 [ ] She never buys any clothes in the stores.
4 [ ] She doesn't lend money to her friends.
5 [ ] She thinks it's good to save money before you buy things.
6 [ ] She's saving her money for something special.

7 🔊 2.34 Listen to an interview with an expert on saving money. Circle the correct answer.
1 Molly thinks Emily
   a is intelligent.
   (b) should spend more money.
   c isn't telling the truth.
2 Molly thinks it's good to
   a earn more money.
   b make a list.
   c spend nothing.
3 Molly says it's a good idea to
   a stop using your cell phone.
   b go shopping often.
   c find the lowest prices.

8 In pairs, discuss the sentences from Activity 4.
A: *Do you think you should get more allowance?*
B: *I think …*

And YOU?

Unit 6   65

6.6 SPEAKING — Shopping for clothes

I can go shopping for clothes and other things.

1 🔊 **2.35** In pairs, describe the picture. Is Lee going to buy the red sneakers? Listen and check.

NEW SHOES

Salesclerk (SC): Can I help you?
Lee: Yes, I'm looking for a pair of sneakers.
SC: These ones are on sale.
Lee: How much are they?
SC: $30.99.
Amy: That's a good price, Lee. You should get them.
Lee: Can I try them on, please?
SC: Of course. What size are you?
Lee: Forty-one.

Two minutes later

Lee: Oh! They're too small … Excuse me, Do you have them in a bigger size?
SC: I think so … Just a second … Here you are.

Two minutes later

Lee: These ones are the right size.
Amy: Great, because I'm bored! This is the fifth store we …
Lee: … but I don't like the color. Excuse me! Do you have these in blue?
Amy: Lee! Are you going to buy them or not?
Lee: Yes! I'll take them. Here you are … Amy! Wait for me!
SC: Don't forget your change!

2 In pairs, underline ten phrases that are in the dialogue.

Speaking	Shopping for clothes
You need to understand	**You need to say**
• Can I help you?	• I'm looking for …
• These ones are on sale.	• How much is it/are they?
• What size are you?	• Can I try it/them on, please?
• The changing rooms are over there.	• It's/They're too big/small.
• Don't forget your change.	• Do you have it/them in a smaller/bigger size/another color?
	• I'll take it/the blue one.
	• I'll take them/these ones.

3 🔊 **2.36** Complete the dialogue with the phrases from the Speaking box. Listen and check.

Salesclerk: Hello, can I help you?
Customer: ¹ _I'm looking for a T-shirt._
SC: This one's on sale.
C: ² _____?
SC: $9.99.
C: ³ _____, please?
SC: Yes, of course. The changing rooms are over there.
C: Oh! It's too big. ⁴ _____?
SC: Yes, here you are. Oh, yes, that's better.
C: ⁵ _____.
SC: Great. Don't forget your change. Goodbye.

4 Complete the sentences with *one* or *ones*.

1 Do you want the black shoes or the brown _ones_?
2 This belt is too small. Do you have a bigger _____?
3 I'll take the pink shirt, but I don't want the green _____.
4 My headphones aren't as good as these _____.
5 I like these sneakers, but they aren't as comfortable as those _____.
6 This black jacket is on sale, but not that blue _____.

5 In pairs, buy and sell the things below. Student A: you are the customer. Student B: you are the salesclerk. Use the Speaking box to help you. Switch roles.

a hat   a pair of jeans   a coat/jacket

A: *Good morning! Can I help you?*
B: *Yes, I'm looking for …*

And YOU

6.7 WRITING Notes and messages (making arrangements)

I can write notes and messages to make arrangements.

1 Work in pairs. Choose the best format a–d for your messages in situations 1–4.

1. [a] You're working on a school project and your bedroom is messy. You leave a message asking your mom not to organize your papers.
2. [ ] You're meeting a friend, but your bus is late. You want to let him/her know.
3. [ ] It's your birthday next week and you decide to invite all your friends to a party.
4. [ ] You need to tell your sensei that you're sick and can't go to judo classes next week.

a a note on a piece of paper
b a post on social media
c a text sent from your phone
d an email

2 Read Lee's messages. Which one:
1. includes an invitation and makes an arrangement? [ ]
2. only gives information? [ ]

A
Hi Amy,
1. I'm going downtown to buy some guitar strings.
2. Would you like to come?
3. I should be outside the mall at 2:30.
4. Let me know!
Lee

B
Hi Mom,
1. I'm going to the music store to buy some new guitar strings. I should be back about 5:00.
4. See you soon!
Lee

3 Study the Writing box. Underline the phrases which are in Lee's messages.

4 Read messages C and D from Amy. Which message is a reply to Lee's invitation? What surprise is Amy planning?

C
Hi,
Sorry, but I'm really busy right now. Maybe we could meet tonight? See you soon. Amy

D
Hi,
It's Lee's birthday today and I want to organize a surprise party for him at my house. Would you like to come? The party's starting at 7 p.m.
Amy

Writing Notes (making arrangements)

1. **The information you want the other person to know**
   - I'm having a party.
   - I'm going downtown.
   - Help! I don't understand my homework.
   - I'm really sick – I can't come.
   - The bus is really late. ☹

2. **A request, offer, or invitation (optional)**
   - Would you like to come?
   - Can you help?
   - Maybe we could meet tomorrow?
   - Please wait for me.

3. **Arrangements**
   - I should be outside the mall at 2:30.
   - Let's meet in front of the movie theater at 8:00.
   - The party's starting at 10:00.
   - I'm planning to be online at 9:00.

4. **Ending**
   - See you there! / See you soon!
   - Let me know!
   - I hope you can come/help.

Watch OUT! We often use imperatives (e.g. *Don't call at ... / Please come/wait ...*) in notes.

5 Write a note to a friend and a note to your mom/dad. *Writing Time*

1. **Find ideas**
   Think about what information you want to include in your note. Write it in your notebook.

2. **Draft**
   Write a draft of your note. Look at the Writing box and at Lee's and Amy's messages to help you.

3. **Share**
   Share your draft with another student for feedback. Listen to his/her opinion and suggestions. Check the spelling and grammar.

4. **Check and write**
   Make changes to your note. Do you use a variety of phrases, different expressions, and imperatives? Write the final version of your text.

Unit 6

WORDLIST
Types of stores | Containers | Shopping malls | Money | Shopping

allowance [n]	low [adj]	shopping cart [n]	borrow money from sb
bakery [n]	message [n]	shopping list [n]	earn money
bookstore [n]	mistake [n]	shopping mall [n]	forget your change
busy [adj]	model [n]	size [n]	get change
buy [v]	modern [adj]	sound [v]	get an allowance
change [n]	money [n]	special offer [n]	get/give sb a gift
changing rooms [n]	multiplex [n]	supermarket [n]	give information
cheap [adj]	music store [n]	surprise [n]	go for a pizza
closed [adj]	neighborhood [n]	traditional [adj]	go shopping
clothing store [n]	newsstand [n]	trendy [adj]	invite friends to your house
comfortable [adj]	nice [adj]	try (something) on [v]	keep money in your pocket/ wallet
cost [v]	note [n]	uncomfortable [adj]	leave a message
department store [n]	opinion [n]	update [n]	lend money to sb/lend sb money
drugstore [n]	out-of-town [adj]	voicemail message [n]	make a list
enjoyable [adj]	parking lot	wallet [n]	make an arrangement
escalator [n]	pay [v]		meet friends
exit [n]	piggy bank [n]	**WORD FRIENDS**	organize a (surprise) party
expensive [adj]	pocket [n]	a bag of apples/sugar	pay (sb) back
flower shop [n]	popular [adj]	a bar of chocolate	plan a surprise party
food court [n]	price [n]	a bottle of shampoo/water	save money
generous [adj]	problem [n]	a box of cereal/matches	show a movie
greengrocer [n]	public restrooms [n]	a bunch of flowers	spend money
headphones [n]	quality [n]	a can of soda/lemonade	spend time (doing sth)
heavy [adj]	reply [n]	a good choice	take the subway
interview [n]	sale [n]	a good/high/low price	the right size
invention [n]	sales clerk [n]	a jar of jam/honey	(a) waste of money
invitation [n]	sell [v]	a loaf of bread	
level [n]	shoe store [n]	a package of cookies	
light [adj]	shopper [n]	a piece of paper	
look for [v]	shopping [n]	be on sale	

VOCABULARY IN ACTION

1 Use the Wordlist to find and write in your notebook:
1. three places where you can keep your money: *pocket*, …
2. six containers:
3. ten types of stores:

2 In pairs, complete the words in the text.

I didn't make a ¹**s**_hopping_ list before I went to the mall. That was a big ²**m**_____ . If you don't know what you're going to buy, you buy things you don't need – especially when they are on ³**s**_____ . In my favorite clothing stores the ⁴**p**_____ were very low. I tried on lots of things in the ⁵**c**_____ **r**_____ . I bought a ⁶**t**_____ bag and I also bought a birthday ⁷**g**_____ for my brother.

3 Complete the Word Friends. In pairs, say if the sentences are true for you.
1. I want to ___earn___ a lot of money one day.
2. I often _____ parties for my friends.
3. I _____ the train to school.
4. We _____ shopping for food every weekend.
5. I'm going to do some _____ after school.

4 🔊 2.37 **PRONUNCIATION** Listen and underline the word(s) in each phrase with a weak sound (/ə/). Listen again and check.
1. make a list (x1)
2. take the train (x1)
3. the right size (x1)
4. a jar of jam (x2)
5. a loaf of bread (x2)
6. a waste of money

SELF-CHECK

1 Complete the sentences.
1 It costs $6.49. You pay $10. How much ___change___ do you get?
2 It's not the right _____. It's too big!
3 I bought a _____ of flowers at the flower shop.
4 There's a _____ of chocolate in my bag.
5 Can you get a _____ of cookies from the bakery?
6 I got some nice sausages at the _____.

2 Complete the text with the words and phrases below. There is one extra item.

> department store   ~~escalator~~   exit
> food court   multiplex   parking lot
> public restroom   shopping carts

It wasn't a good shopping trip. First, the ¹ ___escalator___ wasn't working so we had to use the stairs. We went to all the stores and a big ² _____, but I didn't find anything to buy. There weren't any free tables in the ³ _____, so we didn't eat anything. There wasn't anything good on at the ⁴ _____, so we didn't see a movie. And at the supermarket there weren't any ⁵ _____, so we had to carry a heavy basket. Finally, we spent ten minutes looking for our car in the ⁶ _____ and then we couldn't find the ⁷ _____!

3 Circle the correct option. Then, in pairs, read the dialogue.
A: Let's go ¹(*for*) / *to* a pizza.
B: Good idea, but can you ² *borrow* / *lend* me ten dollars?
A: What? But you ³ *borrowed* / *lent* ten dollars from me yesterday!
B: I know, but I promise to pay you ⁴ *back* / *for* tomorrow.
A: Why do you always ⁵ *earn* / *spend* all your money? You should try to ⁶ *save* / *spend* some.
B: I don't have a job, so I don't ⁷ *earn* / *pay* any money and I don't get an allowance. But I ⁸ *bought* / *made* you a gift with the money you lent me. Here you are.

4 Compare the stores with the words in parentheses and *than* or *as … as*. Write sentences in your notebook.

	Ali's	Lido	C2
How big is the store?	60m²	500m²	3500m²
How much do people usually spend there?	$37.85	$29.49	$33.10
How popular is the store?	★★★★☆	★★★★☆	★★★☆☆

1 Lido / Ali's (big) *Lido is bigger than Ali's.*
2 Lido / C2 (small)
3 Ali's / C2 (expensive)
4 Lido / C2 (cheap)
5 Ali's / Lido (popular)

5 In your notebook, write superlative sentences about the stores in Activity 4, using the adjectives in parentheses.

C2 is the biggest store.

6 Circle the correct option.
1 I'm *winning* /(*going to win*) the Nobel Prize.
2 I'm *lying* / *going to lie* down when I get home. I'm really tired.
3 I'm *meeting* / *going to meet* some friends at my house tonight. Do you want to come?
4 They're *showing* / *going to show* the Lego movie on CBC at 6 p.m.

7 In pairs, role-play the situations. Student A: look below. Student B: look at page 117.

Student A
1 You go to a sports store to buy a new sweatsuit. You can't decide between a white one and a blue one.
2 You are a salesclerk in a shoe store. Help Student B buy a new pair of shoes.

8 🔊 2.38 Listen, then listen again, and write down what you hear.

_____
_____
_____

SELF-ASSESSMENT   Think about this unit. What did you learn? What do you need help with?

7 Learning to work

VOCABULARY
Work and jobs
School and education

GRAMMAR
Will for future predictions
First Conditional | Adjectives with prepositions

Grammar:
If you don't study …
Look at the picture. What do you think Lee and his mom are talking about?

Speaking:
I'll definitely pass.
Look at the picture. Where do you think Amy, Billy, and Lee are? What are they talking about?

7.1 VOCABULARY Jobs

I can talk about people and their jobs.

WHAT JOBS ARE GOOD FOR YOU?
Do the flow chart to find out.

START HERE

- I want to work indoors.
  - I want to work in an office.
    - I prefer to work in one place.
      - accountant
      - receptionist
      - writer
    - I don't want to stay in an office all the time.
      - architect
      - engineer
      - lawyer
  - I think office work is boring.
    - I want to work with my hands.
      - I want to help people.
        - doctor/nurse
        - salesclerk
        - teacher
      - I want a creative job.
        - artist
        - chef
        - hairdresser
      - I want to fix things.
        - electrician
        - IT specialist
        - mechanic
- I prefer an outdoor job.
  - I don't want a dangerous job.
    - I want to travel in my job.
      - I prefer to work alone.
        - bike courier
        - driver
        - mail carrier
      - I want to work with other people.
        - journalist
        - pilot
        - tour guide
  - I don't mind danger. I want a challenging job.
    - firefighter
    - police officer
    - soldier
    - I prefer to work in one place.
      - builder
      - farmer
      - gardener

1 🔊 2.39 Listen and repeat the words in the Vocabulary box. Circle the jobs in the pictures.

Vocabulary	Jobs

accountant   architect   artist   bike courier   builder   (chef)   doctor   driver
electrician   engineer   farmer   firefighter   gardener   hairdresser   IT specialist
journalist   lawyer   mail carrier   mechanic   nurse   pilot   police officer
receptionist   salesclerk   teacher   soldier   tour guide   writer

2 **I KNOW!** Work in groups. How many more jobs can you think of in two minutes? Make a list in your notebook.

Unit 7

3 Follow the job chart on page 70 to find a good job for you. In pairs, compare your jobs.

A: *What jobs does the flow chart give you?*
B: *Artist, chef, or hairdresser.*
A: *What do you think of them?*
B: *I'd like to be a chef because …*

4 In pairs, discuss the questions.

1 In your opinion, which job from the Vocabulary box is …
- the most dangerous?
- the easiest?
- the best paid?
- the most stressful?

2 Which job would you most like to have?

5 Find jobs from the Vocabulary box for the people in the sentences below.

He/She …
1 works in a hospital.   *doctor/nurse*
2 helps people on vacation. _____
3 draws pictures of buildings. _____
4 makes parks look beautiful. _____
5 answers the phone in an office or a hotel.
   _____

6 **WORD FRIENDS** In pairs, check if you understand the phrases below. Then find jobs from the Vocabulary box for Jane, Brett, and Charlotte. There is more than one job for each person. Write your answers in your notebook.

> work from nine to five   be happy at work
> work indoors/outdoors   work on a team
> get to work on time   work weekends
> earn (good) money   wear a uniform   work alone

Jane – lawyer, accountant, ….

7 🔊 **2.40** Complete the text with the Word Friends from Activity 6. Guess the speaker's job. Listen and check.

> I don't ¹ *earn* much money, but I don't mind because I'm ² _____ at work. I really like working on a ³ _____. My co-workers are great. I don't work from nine to ⁴ _____. Sometimes I work during the day and sometimes at night. I have to wear a ⁵ _____, but that's all right. I look good in it! In my job it's really important to get to work on ⁶ _____ because people can die if you're late.

The speaker is a/an _____.

8 In pairs, choose a job from the Vocabulary box. Find out your classmate's job asking ten questions. He/She can only answer *yes* or *no*.

A: *Do you work indoors?*
B: *Yes, I do.*
A: *Do you wear a uniform?*
B: *No, I don't.*

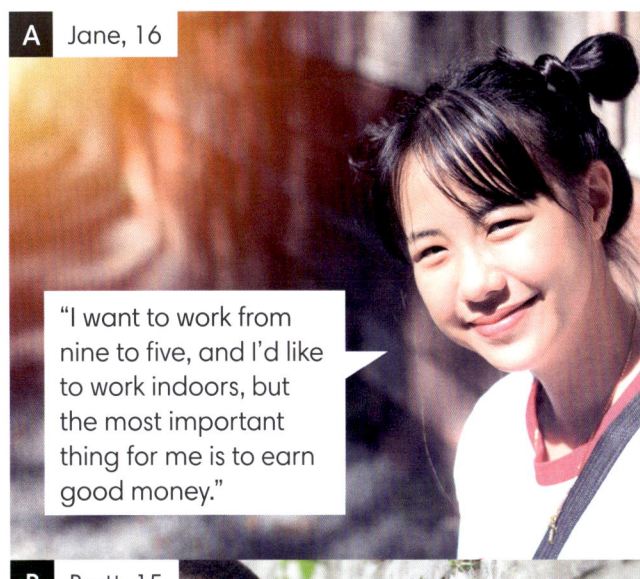

A Jane, 16

"I want to work from nine to five, and I'd like to work indoors, but the most important thing for me is to earn good money."

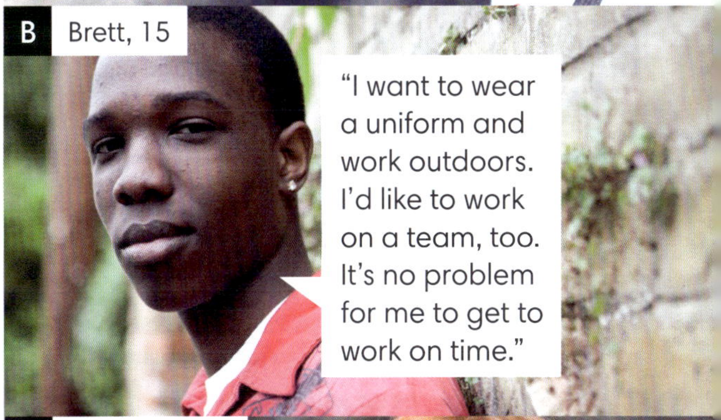

B Brett, 15

"I want to wear a uniform and work outdoors. I'd like to work on a team, too. It's no problem for me to get to work on time."

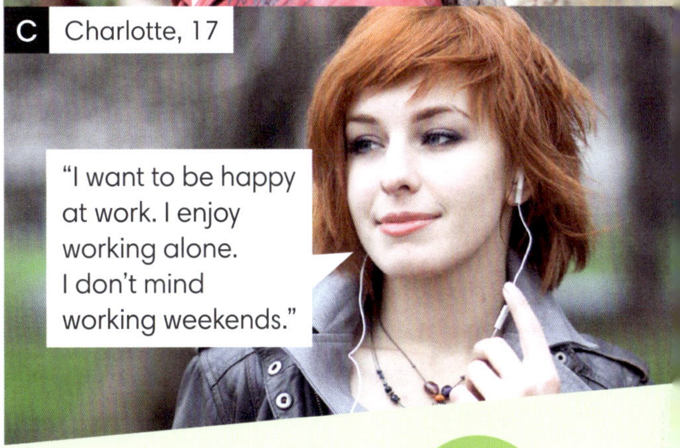

C Charlotte, 17

"I want to be happy at work. I enjoy working alone. I don't mind working weekends."

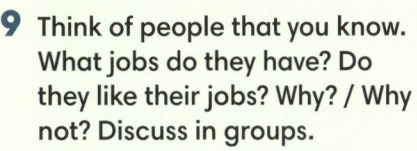

9 Think of people that you know. What jobs do they have? Do they like their jobs? Why? / Why not? Discuss in groups.

My uncle works in an office. He's a receptionist. He loves his job because …

And Y?U

7.2 GRAMMAR *Will for future predictions*

I can use *will* to talk about future predictions.

1 **CLASS VOTE** What is your favorite part of the school day? Why?

2 🔊 **2.41** Listen and read the article and check (✓) the things the writer mentions. Would you like to have all your classes at home?

- ✓ test
- ☐ classroom
- ☐ homework
- ☐ schedule
- ☐ school uniform
- ☐ textbook

A school day in 2035?

**Higson Corporation Global Schools –
Monday May 5, 2035 8:57 a.m.**

> Good morning, Emily!
> Your math test **will start** in three minutes. There's an online meeting with your Chinese teacher at 10 a.m. Have a nice day!

Education will be very important in 2035, but children won't go to school. So how will they learn? They will study in their bedrooms at home. Computers will organize the schedule for each day. Students will do all their homework and tests online, because we won't have paper textbooks. They'll only have contact with their teachers through the internet. But will they enjoy all their classes? No, they won't – some things will never change!

3 Study the Grammar box and circle the correct word to complete the sentence. Then underline examples of *will/won't* in the article in Activity 2.

Grammar	*Will* for future predictions
+	–
I will work hard. They will play.	I won't work hard. They won't play.
?	
Will you study a lot? Will children play games? How will they learn?	Yes, I will. / No, I won't. Yes, they will. / No, they won't.
I don't think this will happen. NOT I think this won't happen.	

Time expressions:
in 2035/twenty years/the next five years/the future
by (= before) 2035/Christmas/my twentieth birthday

We use *will* and *won't* + verb to talk about future actions we *are / aren't* 100% sure about.

GRAMMAR TIME > PAGE 113

4 Complete the text with *will* or *won't* and the verbs in parentheses.

English ¹ **won't be** (not be) so popular in 2035. But Chinese and Portuguese ² _____ (become) very important. Students ³ _____ (not learn) in class: instead, students ⁴ _____ (chat) to students their age in other countries to practice languages. In the future, students ⁵ _____ (not have) the chance to gossip with friends between classes because everyone ⁶ _____ (learn) at home. So ⁷ _____ students in 2035 _____ (feel) lonely?

5 🔊 **2.42** The short form of *will* is *'ll*. In pairs, say the sentences below. Then listen, check, and repeat.

Speak UP!

I'll be home tonight.
She'll call you at 6.
We'll be busy then.
You'll see him tomorrow.
They'll visit the job fair.

6 In pairs, say if and when you think these predictions will come true. Use time expressions with *in* or *by*.

1 All schools will give laptops to their students.
   I think this will happen by 2025.
2 Students won't learn languages – everyone will use cell phones to translate.
3 Students will use the internet in tests.
4 Robots will do all the manual jobs.

7 Check (✓) the things you think you will do before your twentieth birthday.

- ☐ learn to drive
- ☐ go to college
- ☐ live with a roommate
- ☐ buy a house or apartment
- ☐ work or study abroad

8 In pairs, ask and answer the questions in Activity 6. Add extra information.

And YOU?

A: *Will you learn to drive before your twentieth birthday?*
B: *No, I won't. Actually, I don't want to have a car.*

7.3 READING and VOCABULARY   A blog post

I can infer the author's purpose in a blog post and talk about jobs.

1 Work in pairs. Read the blog post quickly and find the names of seven famous people. What do you know about them?

2 🔊 2.43 Listen and read the blog post. What jobs did the people in Activity 1 have before fame?

Johnny Depp sold pens.

Tammy's blog

BEYONCÉ WASHED MY AUNT'S HAIR!

When I tell people that many years ago, Beyoncé washed my aunt's hair, most people don't believe me. But it's true! Some celebrities, like Beyoncé, know what it's like to look for a job and to work from nine to five. For example, did you know that Johnny Depp sold pens before he became an actor?

And the American actor is not the only famous person who had a normal job before fame. Megan Fox worked as a server. Jennifer Lopez had a temporary job in a lawyer's office. And Tom Cruise had a part-time job delivering newspapers.

Some celebrities had jobs that don't seem surprising. Writer J.K. Rowling was an English teacher. She had a full-time job in a school in Portugal before she wrote the Harry Potter book series.

But other famous people had more surprising jobs. Brad Pitt, for example, once had a very strange job. He had to dress up as a giant chicken to attract customers to a restaurant! It was better than being unemployed, but I don't think he wasn't upset when he lost that job.

My point here is to show that people with ordinary jobs can become extraordinary. Maybe the salesclerk in the games store will win a Nobel Prize one day. And maybe that young server with a summer job in your local café will become a movie star. Who knows?

Beyoncé, hairdresser's assistant

Reading tip

Paying attention to how the author ends the text can help you infer his/her purpose for writing it. Does he/she conclude by:
- giving his/her opinion?
- summarizing the facts?
- giving readers the opportunity to form their own opinions?

3 Read the text again. Mark the sentences ✓ (right), ✗ (wrong), or ? (doesn't say).

1. [✗] In the writer's opinion famous people don't know about normal people's lives.
2. [ ] Famous people only have unusual jobs.
3. [ ] The author thinks that celebrities need to focus on their talents.
4. [ ] J.K. Rowling started writing Harry Potter during her lunch breaks at work.
5. [ ] The writer isn't sure the server in her local café will become a movie star.

4 Read again the last part of the blog post. What point does Tammy make? Check (✓) the correct answer.

1. [ ] People with normal jobs can't become famous.
2. [ ] People with normal jobs can change careers and become famous.
3. [ ] People with unusual jobs will become famous.

5 🔊 2.44 Underline the phrases below in the text. Then listen and repeat. How do you say them in your language?

Vocabulary   Work and jobs

Types of jobs
full-time job   part-time job   summer job   temporary job

Work
work in an office   work for a company   look for a job
work as a (server)   be unemployed   get/have/lose a job

6 🔊 2.45 Use the Vocabulary box to complete the text. Listen and check.

I don't have a full-time job. I have two ¹ *part-time* jobs. In the morning, I work ² _____ the city hall. I'm a gardener. And in the evening, I work ³ _____ a server in a café. It's tiring, but I don't want to be ⁴ _____. Last year I had a ⁵ _____ job in a restaurant at the beach. The money was great! Unfortunately, I ⁶ _____ my job when fall came.

7 In pairs, choose three summer jobs you would both like to do in the future. Explain why.

And YOU?

babysitter   bike courier   guide in a local museum
lifeguard at a swimming pool
activity instructor at a summer camp

Unit 7   73

7.4 GRAMMAR   First Conditional

I can use the First Conditional to talk about possible consequences in the future.

1 🔊 **2.46** What's happening in the picture? Why is Lee's mom angry with him? Listen to Part 1 and check.

IF YOU DON'T STUDY … (Part 1)

Mom: Where do you think you're going?
Lee: I'm just going to see Billy and Krystal.
Mom: Oh no, you're not, Lee Marshall! You're taking important tests next week. You can go back to your room and start studying for your tests! <u>If you don't study, you won't pass your tests</u> – it's as simple as that!
Lee: Billy's mom lets him go out in the evenings! It's not fair!
Mom: Billy always gets good grades. You'll have to attend summer school if you don't get better grades. And if you have to attend summer school, you won't be with your friends for three months.
Lee: OK! OK! I'll go and study now.

OUT of class
It's as simple as that!
It's not fair!

2 🔊 **2.46** **WORD FRIENDS** How do you say these Word Friends in your language? Listen again and check (✓) the phrases Lee's mom uses.

- ☐ study for a test
- ☐ have/take a test
- ☐ cheat in a test
- ☐ get the results (of a test)
- ☐ pass/fail a test
- ☐ get a good/bad grade

3 In pairs, talk about your last big test. What happened? Use Word Friends from Activity 2.

4 Study the Grammar box and check (✓) the correct order. Then underline examples of the First Conditional in the dialogue.

Grammar   First Conditional

If I *get* a bad grade in the test, my parents *will be* angry.
You*'ll have* to attend summer school *if you don't get* a better grade.
To form the First Conditional, we use:
- ☐ *if* + *will* + verb, Simple Present
- ☐ *if* + Simple Present, *will* + verb

GRAMMAR TIME ▶ PAGE 114

5 🔊 **2.47** Circle the correct option. Then listen to Part 2 and check.

Amy: Hi Lee! How's your studying going?
Lee: Awful! And I'm really tired now.
Amy: So go to bed! If you ¹(get up)/ *'ll get up* early tomorrow, you ²*feel* / *'ll feel* fresher and you'll remember more.
Lee: Yes, maybe. But I had a great idea. I wrote all the dates for the history test on the back of my ruler! If I ³*forget* / *'ll forget* something in the test, I ⁴*check* / *'ll check* it on my ruler.
Amy: You can't do that! That's cheating! And I'm sure they ⁵*catch* / *'ll catch* you if you ⁶*cheat* / *'ll cheat*. And if they ⁷*catch* / *'ll catch* you, you ⁸*get* / *'ll get* a suspension. Don't be stupid, Lee!

6 Complete the sentences with the correct form of the verbs in parentheses.

1. If I ____*pass*____ (pass) all my tests, I'll be so happy!
2. If I get good grades, my grandma _____ (take) me out for ice cream!
3. If Kelly _____ (get) the results of her math test, she'll call me.
4. My mom won't be happy if I _____ (not get) a good grade.
5. We'll have to call the doctor if she _____ (not feel) better soon.
6. If you break it, I _____ (not lend) you anything again!

7 In your notebook, finish the sentences to make them true for you. Then compare with a classmate. **And YOU?**

1. If there's no internet connection at home this weekend, *I'll read a book.*
2. If I get some money for my birthday, I …
3. If I don't understand my homework tonight, I …
4. If my cell phone stops working, I …

Unit 7

7.5 LISTENING and VOCABULARY — An unusual school

I can identify specific information in a conversation and talk about education.

1 In pairs, look at the picture on the right. What do you think is unique about the school?

2 🔊 **2.48** In pairs, check if you understand the words below. Then listen and check your ideas from Activity 1.

gym   library   science lab   high school   sports field

The Green School – classroom

3 🔊 **2.48** Listen again and circle the correct answer.
1 Green School …
 a only has students from Bali.
 b started in the United States.
 (c) has students from all over the world.
2 Students at Green School …
 a have classes every day.
 b help solve problems.
 c don't study in classrooms.
3 All of the students …
 a eat chicken for lunch.
 b try to help the environment.
 c travel in special cars.
4 Green school …
 a doesn't use technology.
 b has classes with themes.
 c doesn't have tests.

4 Work in pairs. Would you like to be a student at Green School? Why? / Why not?

5 🔊 **2.49** Add the words from Activity 2 to the correct category. Listen, check, and repeat.

Vocabulary — School and education

Places of learning
college   elementary school   ¹ *high school*
People in schools
classmates   homeroom teacher   principal
math/English teacher   student
Places/rooms at school
classroom   locker room   ² _____   ³ _____
⁴ _____   ⁵ _____   school yard
teacher's lounge

6 Complete the sentences with words from the Vocabulary box.
1 Luke was late for school, so he had to see the _*principal*_ .
2 The _____ is busy after school because students get ready for sports practices and games.
3 I changed schools last month. My new _____ are a lot nicer.
4 We play soccer on the school _____ , but when it's wet we play in the _____ .
5 The teachers relax in the _____ between classes.

7 🔊 **2.50** **WORD FRIENDS** In pairs, circle the correct option. Listen and check.
1 The best way to study for a test is to *get* / (*take*) notes.
2 We *do* / *make* a lot of grammar activities in English classes!
3 I'm really shy, so I feel nervous before I *give* / *show* presentations.
4 I always *do* / *make* my homework after I get home from school.
5 It's hard to *draw* / *write* essays in class.

8 In pairs, ask and answer the questions.
1 How often do you
 • talk to your principal/ homeroom teacher?
 • use the school library/sports field?
2 What are your favorite subjects at school?

And YOU?

Unit 7   75

7.6 SPEAKING Probability

I can talk about probability.

1 **CLASS VOTE** How do you feel before an important test? Check (✓) the correct answer.

☐ relaxed ☐ nervous ☐ frightened

2 Look at the picture. Who do you think looks most relaxed: Amy, Lee, or Billy? What do you think they're talking about?

3 ▶ 2.51 Listen to Part 1. Then study the Speaking box and underline examples of the phrases in red used in sentences in the dialogue. Who is most confident about passing the test?

_____

Speaking	Probability

- I **will definitely/probably** pass.
- I **may/might** pass.
- I **definitely/probably won't** pass.

I'LL DEFINITELY PASS (Part 1)

Amy: That was a really difficult test.
Billy: Yes! That last question? What a nightmare! I couldn't remember any of the dates. I probably won't get any points for it!
Amy: I definitely won't! I didn't even answer that question – I didn't have time!
Billy: Oh, don't worry, Amy. You'll probably pass!
Amy: I don't know. I might pass. Fingers crossed! How about you, Lee?
Lee: I thought it was easy! I'll definitely pass! In fact, I think I may get an A+.
Amy: But history's your worst subject. You didn't cheat, did you? Because they'll definitely see from your answers if you cheated!
Lee: No, I didn't cheat!
Billy: So, how did you do it?

What a nightmare!
Fingers crossed!

OUT of class

4 **CLASS VOTE** Why did Lee find the history test so easy?
1 He followed his mom's advice and studied hard for the test.
2 He copied important dates on his ruler and on his hand.
3 His uncle is a history teacher and helped him study for the test.

5 ▶ 2.52 Listen to Part 2 and check your ideas in Activity 4.

6 ▶ 2.53 Listen to Part 3. Where would Lee, Billy, and Amy like to go camping this summer?

_____

7 ▶ 2.53 Order the words in parentheses to complete the sentences. Listen to Part 3 again and check.
1 Camping in Florida *will probably be* expensive. (be/will/probably)
2 Billy's uncle _____ them camp on his farm. (let/will/definitely)
3 There _____ space in Ruby's tent for Krystal. (be/will/definitely)
4 Krystal _____ to stay in a tent. (want/won't/probably)
5 Krystal _____ to stay in a five-star hotel. (want/might)
6 Lee's parents _____ with Lee, Billy, and Amy's camping plans. (probably/agree/will)

8 In pairs, use the Speaking box to say if you think these things will happen to you and your country in the future.

And YOU

Will you …
- learn a new language?
- be famous?
- buy a car/motorcycle?
- still live in your hometown?

In our country, will …
- people stop using banknotes and coins?
- food be cheaper?
- everyone use public transportation?

I will definitely learn a new language.

7.7 WRITING A personal statement

I can write a personal statement.

1 Read the personal statement and the summer job ads. Which ad is Ana replying to?

ANA DELGADO
12 RIVERVIEW AVENUE
WESTERVILLE, OH
ana.delgado2@email.co

My name is Ana Delgado and I am in the 8th grade at Westerville Middle School. I am very friendly and confident. I study hard at school, but on Thursday afternoons I read to children at the hospital. I am interested in helping people and I think I am good at making people laugh!

I am crazy about sports, especially volleyball and swimming. I am not afraid of learning new things, so I would like to try new sports. Last summer, I went on an adventure sports camp. It was a great experience – I learned new skills and made new friends.

I am not very good at IT, but I work hard to get better at things I find difficult. So I am taking extra IT classes on Saturdays.

In the future, I'd like to be a lawyer or a nurse.

---

1 APP TESTER
Are you aged 13 to 17? Are you always using your cell phone? We need a part-time app tester to help us during summer vacation.

2 ACTIVITY CAMP INSTRUCTOR
Are you great at working with children? Do you like being outdoors? Join us this summer and be one of our instructors!

2 Read the personal statement again and complete the chart about Ana.

Personal qualities	Hobbies and interests	Experiences
1 *friendly*	3	5
2	4	

3 Study the Writing box. Are any of the sentences true for you? Underline them.

Writing | A personal statement

Describe your personal qualities
I am pretty confident.
I am a very happy person.
I am good at following instructions.

Give examples of your personal qualities
It is easy for me to make new friends.
I look at the positive aspects of a situation.
I am good at building complicated LEGO models.

Talk about your hobbies and interests
I am interested in learning languages.
I like spending time in nature.
I am crazy about horses!

Talk about your experiences
Last year, I went to Italy and I learned some expressions in Italian.
I came in second place in a math competition.

4 Write a personal statement for a part-time or summer job.

Writing Time

1 Find ideas
Think about the job you would like to have. Then, in your notebook, take notes about your personal qualities, hobbies, interests, and experiences. Which of them would be useful for the job?

2 Draft
Write a draft of your personal statement. Look at the text in Activity 1 and the Writing box to help you. Try to use adjectives + prepositions and avoid using contractions. Pay attention to correct verb tenses.

3 Share
Share your personal statement with another student for feedback. Listen to his/her opinion and suggestions. Check the spelling and grammar.

4 Check and write
Make any necessary changes to your text. Do you use adjectives + prepositions correctly? Do you avoid contractions? Write the final version of your personal statement.

WORDLIST

accountant [n]
activity instructor [n]
architect [n]
artist [n]
babysitter [n]
bike courier [n]
builder [n]
break [n]
celebrity [n]
challenging (job) [adj]
cheat (in a test) [v]
chef [n]
city hall [n]
classmate [n]
classroom [n]
co-worker [n]
college [n]
count [v]
creative (job) [adj]
danger [n]
doctor [n]
dress up (as) [v]
driver [n]
education [n]
electrician [n]
elementary school [n]
engineer [n]
farm [n]
farmer [n]
firefighter [n]
full-time (job) [adj]
gardener [n]
gym (at school) [n]
hairdresser [n]
high school [n]
homework [n]
homeroom teacher [n]
IT specialist [n]
journalist [n]
lawyer [n]
(school) library [n]
lifeguard [n]
locker room [n]
look for (a job) [v]
(math/English) teacher [n]
mail carrier [n]
mechanic [n]
nightmare [n]
normal [adj]
nurse [n]
office work [n]
ordinary [adj]
part-time (job) [adj]
personal statement [n]
pilot [n]
police officer [n]
principal [n]
receptionist [n]
schedule [n]
science lab [n]
server [n]
soldier [n]
sports field [n]
stressful [adj]
study [v]
student [n]
subject [n]
summer job [n]
summer school [n]
teacher's lounge [n]
temporary (job) [adj]
test (at school) [n]
textbook [n]
tour guide [n]
translate [v]
unemployed [adj]
(school) uniform [n]
unpleasant [adj]
well/best paid [adj]
writer [n]

WORD FRIENDS

answer the phone
attend summer school
attract customers
be bad at
be afraid of
be crazy about
be good at
be happy at work
be interested in
be late for school/work
be unemployed
become famous
cheat in a test
deliver newspapers
do (grammar) activities
do homework
earn (good) money
get a good/bad grade
get a suspension
get points (in a test)
get the results of a test
get to work on time
get/have/lose a job
give presentations
gossip with friends
go to college
have/take a test
help people
learn languages
learn to drive
live with a roommate
pass/fail a test
study for a test
take notes
wear a uniform
work as a (+ job)
work on the weekend/from nine to five
work for a company
work on a team/alone
work in an office/in one place
work indoors/outdoors
work with your hands
work/study abroad

VOCABULARY IN ACTION

1 Use the Wordlist to find and write in your notebook:
  1 eight jobs in which you spend a lot of time working outdoors. *builder, ...*
  2 four jobs in which you have to be good at counting.
  3 five jobs for which you have to wear a uniform.
  4 six places where people work.

2 In pairs, say how you feel about the ideas below. Use an adjective and a preposition.

  doing grammar activities   reading about celebrities
  cheating in tests   giving presentations
  learning languages   wearing a school uniform

  - I'm (not) interested in …
  - I'm (really) bad …
  - I'm great/good …
  - I'm (not) afraid …

3 Complete the Word Friends.

I spend a long time studying ¹ *for* tests, but something always goes wrong on the day I ² _____ them. The worst thing is when I have to ³ _____ an essay. After that there's the long wait to ⁴ _____ the results and …

4 🔊 2.54 **PRONUNCIATION** Copy the chart into your notebook. Then listen to the underlined letter(s) in each word and decide which sound you hear.

  cheat   chef   college   electrician   danger
  gymnasium   journalist   language   receptionist
  soldier   teacher

1 /dʒ/	2 /ʃ/	3 /tʃ/
		cheat

5 🔊 2.55 **PRONUNCIATION** Listen and check.

SELF-CHECK

1 Complete the words in the sentences.
1. My big brother was **u** n e m p l o y e d for six months, but now he has a **p**_ _ _ _ - _ _ _ _ _ _ _ job.
2. An expensive **a** _ _ _ _ _ _ _ _ _ _ _ is designing that famous singer's new house.
3. I love cooking – I want to work as a **c** _ _ _ when I'm older.
4. I started **h** _ _ _ school last week. My homeroom **t** _ _ _ _ _ _ _ is really nice.

2 Complete the Word Friends. Use the words in the correct form.

First, I wanted to be a lawyer, but you need to study a lot and I'm not crazy about studying for ¹ _tests_. After that I wanted to be a journalist, but I realized that I wasn't interested in ² _____ articles. Next I thought about becoming a driver, but I couldn't ³ _____ my driving test. I started working as a receptionist, but I really hated answering the ⁴ _____ ! It wasn't a surprise when I ⁵ _____ my job. After that I was a salesclerk for a month, but I couldn't get to work ⁶ _____ time. Then I worked ⁷ _____ a bike courier, but found out I don't like ⁸ _____ alone. Finally, I have the perfect job – I walk dogs for a living. I love it!

3 In pairs, talk about adults you know and the jobs they have. Why do you think they chose these jobs?

My grandpa is a mechanic – he's good at working with his hands.

4 Complete the second sentence so that it means the same as the first one.
1. Helen fears to go out alone at night.
   Helen is afraid _of going out alone at night_.
2. Melissa loves learning languages.
   Melissa is crazy _____.
3. Jack works very badly in a team.
   Jack is really bad _____.
4. Mary doesn't enjoy working indoors.
   Mary isn't interested _____.

5 Complete the text with *will* or *won't* and the words in parentheses. Then, in your notebook, write predictions about today's school day.

Our first class today is English. I'm sure we ¹ _'ll talk_ (talk) a lot in English and we ² _____ (play) some cool games. Then it's history. ³ _____ (we/watch) a movie? I hope so! This afternoon isn't so good. Our first class after lunch is math. We ⁴ _____ (probably/do) a lot of activities and I'm sure I ⁵ _____ (not understand) them. After that it's P.E. I'm sure that somebody ⁶ _____ (forget) their shorts and Mr. Hodd ⁷ _____ (shout) at us.

6 Complete the dialogue with the correct form of the First Conditional.

Ann: How are you getting to your job interview?
Bea: By bike. The farm isn't far from town.
Ann: But what ¹ _will you do_ (you/do) if the weather ² _____ (be) bad?
Bea: It's OK. If it ³ _____ (rain), I ⁴ _____ (take) the ten o'clock bus.
Ann: But if the bus ⁵ _____ (arrive) late, how ⁶ _____ (you/get) there then?
Bea: I ⁷ _____ (call) for a taxi if something ⁸ _____ (go) wrong.
Ann: But if there ⁹ _____ (not be) an internet signal, you ¹⁰ _____ (not able to use) the app to get a taxi.
Bea: You worry too much!

7 In pairs, talk about careers. Student A: look below. Student B: look at page 117.

Student A
1. You are a school counselor. Ask Student B what he/she likes doing.
2. Ask Student B about his/her career plans.
3. Give advice: *You definitely/probably won't enjoy being a … / You might be good at …*

8 🔊 2.56 Listen, then listen again and write down what you hear.

_____
_____
_____

8 Close to nature

VOCABULARY
Landscapes, natural features, and countries | Phrasal verbs | Outdoor activities | Sports equipment

GRAMMAR
Present Perfect – all forms | Present Perfect with *already*, *just*, and *yet*

Grammar:
Have you bought a new sleeping bag?
Look at the picture. Lee and Amy are talking about plans. What are they?

Speaking:
Can I ask for a favor?
Look at the picture. Who do you think the man on the right is?

8.1 VOCABULARY Landscapes, natural features, and countries

I can talk about landscapes, natural features, and countries.

A The Aran Islands in the Atlantic Ocean, near the coast of Ireland. Most of the population work in farming.

1 Work in pairs. Look at the pictures. Are there places like these in your country?

2 🔊 2.57 **CLASS VOTE** Listen and read about the places in pictures A–D. Which place would you most like to visit?
I'd like to visit the Sahara.

3 **I KNOW!** Unscramble the letters to write words connected with landscape and natural features. Add them to Vocabulary A box.
1 c h e a b _beach_
2 d e e r s t _____
3 k a l e _____
4 i n o m u t a n _____
5 r e v i r _____
6 a s e _____

Vocabulary A	Landscapes and natural features		
¹ _beach_ cliff coast ² _____		field forest island	
jungle ³ _____ ⁴ _____		ocean rainforest	
⁵ _____ rocks ⁶ _____		volcano waterfall	

4 🔊 2.58 Listen and check your answers in Activity 3. Then listen again and repeat the words.

5 Work in pairs. Match features 1–4 to pictures A–D.
1 [B] mountains, a lake
2 [ ] rainforest, a river, waterfalls
3 [ ] fields, cliffs, a beach
4 [ ] desert, rocks

80 Unit 8

Karymsky Volcano, in east Siberia in Russia, is about 6,000 kilometers from Moscow, the capital city.

The Great Eastern Sand Sea, in the Sahara Desert in Algeria – one of the hottest places on Earth.

Victoria Falls is on the Zambezi River, between Zimbabwe and Zambia. They are more than 100 meters high. Around 500,000 tourists visit them every year.

6 🔊 **2.59** Can you match places 1-9 to a feature from Vocabulary A? Listen and check.

1 The Sahara _desert_
2 Loch Ness _____
3 Mount Everest _____
4 The Mississippi _____
5 Great Britain _____
6 The Pacific _____
7 The Baltic _____
8 Iguazu Falls _____
9 Etna _____

7 **WORD FRIENDS** Study the Word Friends. Then complete the text with the correct prepositions.

in	a forest/a field/a lake/the mountains/the sea/ocean
on	a beach/an island/the coast
by	a lake/a river/the sea/ocean

We had an awesome vacation. We stayed ¹ _on_ the north coast of Spain. We camped ² _____ a field ³ _____ a small river. In the mornings, we swam ⁴ _____ the sea and Mom and Dad sunbathed ⁵ _____ the beach. On hot days we spent our time ⁶ _____ the mountains.

8 🔊 **2.60** Study Vocabulary B box, then listen and repeat the words. How do you say them in your language?

Vocabulary B — Talking about countries

border   capital city   country   flag   official language   population

9 🔊 **2.61** Listen and answer the questions about Ander's country. Can you guess where he comes from?

1 What is the country's population?
   (About) five million people.
2 What colors are the national flag?
   _____
3 What is the country famous for?
   _____
4 Which countries does it share a border with?
   _____
5 What is its capital city?
   _____
6 What is the official language?
   _____

Ander is from _____.

10 In groups, answer the questions in Activity 8 for your country.

My country's population is about one hundred million.

Unit 8

8.2 GRAMMAR Present Perfect – all forms

I can use the Present Perfect to talk about past experiences.

1 CLASS VOTE Do you think it's better to go on vacation abroad or to stay in your own country?

2 Read the interview. How many countries does Todd Morden still have to visit? Which was his favorite country?

Todd Morden is hoping to become the youngest person to visit every country in the world. The twenty-four-year-old Canadian has visited 127 of them and he hasn't finished (there are 195 countries in total)! Planet Discovery talked to Todd.

PD: Tell us about your most exciting experience.
Todd: Where to start? I've swum with dolphins off the coast of Ireland, I've played with bears in Romania, and I've climbed Mount Kilimanjaro.
PD: Have you ever had any bad experiences?
Todd: No, I haven't. Well, I've had some problems with visas. But I've never had any really bad experiences.
PD: Which country have you enjoyed most?
Todd: I think I've enjoyed Thailand most – it's so interesting. But in every country people have been nice to me. I've met a lot of very kind people, especially in the African countries I've visited.
PD: Have you learned a lot from traveling?
Todd: Yes, I have. I've learned that people everywhere are good and basically the same!

3 Study the Grammar box and circle the correct option to complete the sentence. Then underline examples of the Present Perfect in the text.

Grammar	Present Perfect – all forms
+	**−**
I've (have) swum with dolphins. He's (has) visited 127 countries. They've (have) played a lot.	I haven't visited Africa. She hasn't finished. They haven't had problems.

?
Have you traveled a lot?   Yes, I have. / No, I haven't.
Has he enjoyed Libya?   Yes, he has. / No, he hasn't.
Have they finished?   Yes, they have. / No, they haven't.
Which country have you enjoyed most?

We use *has/have* + the *past / past participle* form of the verb to make the Present Perfect.

GRAMMAR TIME ▶ PAGE 114

4 What are the past and past participle forms of the verbs below? Make a list in your notebook.

~~buy~~ ~~come~~ drink eat forget have look meet see sleep travel visit watch write

buy – bought, bought
come – came, come

5 Complete the sentences with the correct Present Perfect form of the verbs in parentheses.

1 I ___'ve met___ (meet) people from all over the world.
2 My friend Glenn _____ (write) a blog about his trips.
3 My parents _____ (not visit) Fiji, but they _____ (be) to Australia.
4 I _____ (spend) a lot of time in Paris, but I _____ (not see) the *Mona Lisa*.

6 🔊 2.62 Listen to some of the sentences in Activity 5. What do you notice about the pronunciation of the contracted form *'ve*?

Speak UP!

7 Complete the questions with the past participle of the verbs in parentheses. Then ask and answer in pairs.

1 Have you ever ___been___ (be) to New York?
2 How many countries have you _____ (visit)?
3 How many times have you _____ (flow) in a plane?
4 Have you ever _____ (eat) something really unusual?
5 Have you ever _____ (swim) in the ocean?

A: *Have you ever been to New York?*
B: *Yes, I have. / No, I haven't.*

8 Tell the class about a surprising thing you have done in your life. Whose fact was most surprising?

I've met/seen/won/lived in/been to/played …

And YOU

Unit 8

8.3 READING and VOCABULARY — A personal story

I can use the context to understand a personal story and talk about personal experiences.

1 In pairs, look at the title of the personal narrative. Answer the questions in your notebook.

1. What do you think the story is about?
2. Do you think the story has a happy ending?

2 🔊 **2.63** Listen and read the personal story. Check your predictions in Activity 1.

INCREDIBLE STORIES

Week 10: **Juliane Koepcke**

Alone in the jungle

It was Christmas Eve. Juliane Koepcke, a seventeen-year-old German girl, was traveling with her mother from Lima, Peru, to Iquitos, in the same country. They were flying over the rainforest when suddenly there was a storm and the pilot lost control of the plane. Many of the passengers started crying, but Juliane calmly held her mother's hand. After that, the plane blew up. Juliane found herself outside the plane, but still in her seat, high above the ground. She fell for more than three kilometers. She remembered seeing the rainforest below her, but after that she fainted.

The next day Juliane woke up. She had a broken shoulder bone and cuts on her leg. She was completely alone. Although she felt afraid, she knew she couldn't give up. Juliane came to a river and started walking down along it – she hoped it would take her to civilization. She walked for nine days. Nights in the jungle were very cold and Juliane was wearing only a dress. She had no food, except for one bag of candy.

On the tenth day, Juliane was very weak and had to stop walking. But she came across an empty boat and knew there must be people nearby. She slept near the boat and the next day she heard men's voices. When the men saw the thin, hungry girl they were surprised, but Juliane talked to them in Spanish about the accident. The men took her to a doctor. She later found out that all the other ninety-one passengers on the plane were dead.

This incredible survival story happened in 1971. There have been two movies about Juliane's adventure and many newspapers and magazines have written about her. Juliane has also written a book, "When I Fell From The Sky". She now works as a zoologist, but has often gone back to the rainforest in Peru. She has had a normal life, although she has often asked herself, "Why was I the only person to survive?"

3 Read the personal story again and answer the questions.

1. Where was Juliane going on Christmas Eve?
   She was going to Iquitos, in Peru.
2. When did the plane hit bad weather?
3. What was wrong with Juliane when she woke up?
4. What happened on the tenth day?
5. Has Juliane returned to Peru?

Reading tip

You don't need to know the meaning of all the words to understand a story. Look around the difficult word – can you understand the context? If so, continue reading. If not, use in a dictionary.

4 🔊 **2.64** Listen and repeat the phrasal verbs in the Vocabulary box. Then underline the phrasal verbs in the story. Can you guess their meaning from the context?

Vocabulary | **Phrasal verbs**

blow up   come across   find out   give up   go back

5 Use the phrasal verbs in the Vocabulary box to complete the sentences.

1. I can't answer your question. I _give up_ !
2. It's hard to _____ to school after the summer.
3. I _____ an old diary when I was organizing grandpa's desk.
4. Luckily, the car engine didn't _____ after the accident.
5. I have to _____ the train times.

6 Tell the class about a time when you got lost. Use the questions below to help you.

1. What happened?
2. How did you feel?
3. Did you ask for help?

Unit 8

8.4 GRAMMAR Present Perfect with *already*, *just*, and *yet*

I can use the Present Perfect to talk about recent events.

1 Look at the picture. What do you think Amy and Lee are planning?

_____

2 🔊 **2.65** Listen to Part 1. Check your answer to Activity 1 and check (✓) the things Lee has done.

Camping vacation
- ✓ buy new sleeping bag
- ☐ buy a map
- ☐ clean the tents
- ☐ buy food
- ☐ pack backpacks

HAVE YOU BOUGHT A NEW SLEEPING BAG? (Part 1)

Lee: Hi, Amy! What's up?

Amy: I'm worried about our camping trip next week. <u>Have you bought</u> a new sleeping bag <u>yet</u>?

Lee: Well, I know exactly what sleeping bag I want to buy – I've already checked its price. But I haven't actually bought it yet … I've bought a map of the local area! … And Dad and I have just cleaned all the tents.

Amy: So you haven't started packing yet?

Lee: Give me a break, Amy! I've already told you – we haven't bought all the food yet, so it's too early to start packing. Anyway, have you heard from Billy yet?

Amy: Yes, I have – he's just called to say his uncle will meet us downtown for lunch and then we'll all drive to the farm in your parents' car.

Lee: Great! This will be an awesome vacation!

Give me a break!   **OUT of class**

3 Study the Grammar box, then complete the sentences with *already*, *just*, and *yet*. Underline examples of these words being used with the Present Perfect in the dialogue.

Grammar	Present Perfect with *already*, *just*, and *yet*
+	**−**
I've *already* checked the price. He's *just* called.	We haven't bought all the food *yet*.
?	
Have you bought a new sleeping bag *yet*?	

1 We use _____ for actions/events that happened faster than expected.
2 We use _____ for actions/events that are expected to happen.
3 We use _____ for actions that happened a short time ago.

> GRAMMAR TIME > PAGE 115

4 Complete the sentences with *already*, *just*, or *yet*.

1 **A:** *Drek 5* is on TV now. Why don't we watch it?
   B: Sorry, but I've <u>already</u> seen it twice!
2 Have you finished on the computer _____? I want to write my essay for the history class.
3 **A:** You look cold and tired!
   B: Yes, we've _____ been back from a long walk.
4 Don't take my plate. I haven't finished _____!
5 You're slow – Jo has _____ finished the exercise!

5 🔊 **2.66** Circle the correct option. Listen to Part 2 and check.

Amy: Hi, Mom! Yes, we've ¹(*just*)/ *yet* arrived. No, we haven't seen Billy's uncle ²*already* / *yet*. We've ³*yet* / *just* gotten off Lee's parents' car. Yeah, everyone's fine. Yes, we've ⁴*already* / *yet* thanked Lee's parents for bringing us along with them. The weather's OK – it hasn't rained ⁵*already* / *yet*! I have to go, Mom. Bye! Billy, has your uncle arrived ⁶*just* / *yet*?

Billy: No, he hasn't. Oh, wait. I've ⁷*just* / *yet* seen him!

6 In your notebook, write five sentences about your news and recent activities. Use *already*, *yet*, and *just*. Then compare with a classmate.   **And YOU**

Unit 8

8.5 LISTENING and VOCABULARY   Outdoor activities

I can identify specific information in personal accounts and talk about outdoor activities.

1 In pairs, discuss which activities in the pictures you would like to do. Explain why.

I would like to go mountain biking. I think it is the most exciting activity.

Kayaking **A**    Snowboarding **B**    Mountain biking **C**    Surfing **D**

2 🔊 **2.67** Listen and repeat the words in Vocabulary A box. Then add each activity to the correct category in the chart – water or land.

Vocabulary A	Outdoor activities

cycling   fishing   hiking   kayaking
mountain biking   pony trekking   rock climbing
scuba diving   skiing   snowboarding   surfing
swimming   wind-surfing

water	land
kayaking, surfing, …	*mountain biking, snowboarding, …*

3 In groups, say which activities in Vocabulary A box you have/haven't tried and which are popular/unpopular in your country.

4 🔊 **2.68** Listen to four people talking about their sports experiences. Match statements a–e to Speakers 1–4. There is one extra statement.

1 ☐   2 ☐   3 ☐   4 ☐

a He/She says the activity can be dangerous.
b He/She is very good at the activity.
c He/She talks about the last time he/she did the activity.
d He/She talks about when he/she did the activity for the first time.
e He/She describes the good and bad sides of the activity.

5 🔊 **2.69** Listen and repeat the words in Vocabulary B box. How do you say the words below in your language?

Vocabulary B	Sports equipment

bike   boots   compass   gloves   goggles   helmet
kayak   life vest   map   paddle   snowboard
surfboard   wet suit

6 🔊 **2.70** Complete the sentences with the correct items of equipment from Vocabulary B. Listen and check.

- **Pony trekking** – you need a ¹ *helmet* for your head, a map, and a ² _____ , so you don't get lost.
- **Wind-surfing** – you need a ³ _____ to float in the water and a ⁴ _____ to keep you warm.
- **Skiing** – you need skis, ski poles, ski boots, ⁵ _____ to protect your eyes, and ⁶ _____ for your hands.

7 In pairs, ask and answer the questions about the different activities in Vocabulary A.

1 Have you ever tried …?
2 When was the last time?
3 Did you enjoy it?
4 Which of the activities would you like to try?

A: *Have you ever tried surfing?*
B: *Yes, I have.*
A: *When was the last time you went surfing?*
B: *Last summer. I was at the beach with some friends and …*

Unit 8   85

8.6 SPEAKING — Asking for, giving, and refusing permission

I can ask for, give, and refuse permission.

1 🔊 2.71 In pairs, look at the picture. Do you think the people are having a good time? Listen and check.

CAN I ASK FOR A FAVOR?

Billy: Is it OK to put our tents up here, Uncle Jack?
Jack: I'm afraid that's not possible, Billy. There's a big bull in this field. He won't like it.
Billy: What about that place, by the lake? Can we camp in there?
Jack: I'm afraid that's not a good idea, either. There's a lot of water over there at the moment. You'll wake up swimming in your tents!
Lee: So is it all right to camp next to the farmhouse?
Jack: Yes, of course. Good idea.
Krystal: Can I ask for a favor? Can we dry our clothes in the house? All my things are soaking wet!
Jack: No problem. Let's meet Lee's parents and Ruby inside and have a cup of hot chocolate. You all look so unhappy!

> *Can I ask for a favor?* — **OUT of class**

2 Underline examples of the phrases from the Speaking box in the dialogue.

Speaking — Asking for, giving, and refusing permission

Asking for permission
- Can I/we …?
- Is it OK (for me/us) to …?
- Is it all right to …?

Giving permission
- Yes, of course.
- No problem.
- Sure – go ahead. (informal)

Refusing permission
- I'm sorry, but you can't.
- I'm afraid that's not possible.
- I'm afraid that's not a good idea.

3 🔊 2.72 Complete the dialogues with one word in each blank. Listen and check.

1. Lee: Is it OK ¹ *for* me to use your bathroom?
   Jack: Sure – go ². _____ .
2. Amy: Can I make myself a cup of coffee and a snack?
   Jack: ³_____ problem! The kitchen's on the left.
3. Krystal: Is it ⁴_____ for me to have a hot shower?
   Jack: Yes, ⁵_____ course!
   Krystal: Oh, and ⁶_____ I borrow a hairdryer?
   Jack: I'm afraid that's not ⁷_____ . We don't have one!

4 Work in pairs. Replace the highlighted phrases in Activity 3 with another phrase from the Speaking box. Then practice reading your dialogue.

5 🔊 2.73 Listen to the end of the story. How many people spent the night in the tents? Answer in your notebook.

6 In pairs, ask for permission. Use the ideas below or your own ideas.

> borrow a pen?
> leave my bag here?
> use your cell phone?
> look at your book?
> ask for a favor?
> visit you this weekend?

A: *Is it OK for me to borrow a pen?*
B: *Sure – go ahead.*

7 In pairs, follow the instructions. Use the Speaking box to help you. **And YOU?**

- **Student A** – Look at page 116. Choose a situation and ask your partner for permission.
- **Student B** – give or refuse permission
- Change roles. Student B, look at page 116.

Unit 8

8.7 WRITING — An email about a trip

I can write an email about a trip.

1 Read the email. What is it about? Circle the correct answer.
   a A trip Sarah took in the past
   b A trip Andrew is planning on taking
   c A trip Sarah is taking

From: sarah_2005@woohoo.com
To: andrewtaylor@ymail.com

Dear Andrew,

As you know, my family and I are huge fans of adventure, so last week we took a plane to Asheville, North Carolina, to try some different outdoor activities. My dad has always been the one who chooses our journeys, but this time I got a say in it: Asheville is definitely the most adventurous city I have ever been to.

So far, we have hiked the Biltmore trails, which I think has been the easiest and the best way to start with – and we were so good at it that our compass wasn't even used. We didn't need any specific equipment for that, just a pair of hiking boots. It only took us thirty minutes to go through all the way around a big castle.

We have just found bikes to rent, so we can go cycling past the forests, waterfalls, and all the natural beauty we have been eager to see!

However, we haven't had the chance to go kayaking yet because we can't decide on a lake to do it. There are so many options and I can't wait to tell you which one we picked.

What about you? What have you done during your vacation? I want to know everything about it!

Love,
Sarah

2 Study the Writing box. Identify the way the author deals with each topic in the email.

Writing — ANn email about a trip

Say where you are and why you chose the place
Last week we took a plane to Asheville, North Carolina. As you know, my family and I are huge fans of adventure. Asheville is definitely the most adventurous city I have ever been to.

Say what you have already done and give an opinion/details
We have hiked the Biltmore trails.
We were so good at it that our compass wasn't even used.
It only took us thirty minutes to …

Talk about what you haven't done yet, but want to do
We haven't had the chance to go kayaking yet because we can't decide on a lake to do it.

Ask the recipient about his/her trip/vacation/time off
What about you?
What have you done during your vacation?

Say goodbye
Love,
Cheers,

3 Write an email telling about a trip.

Writing Time

1. **Find ideas**
   Choose one of the suggestions below and, in your notebook, take notes about the places, activities and people you are traveling with.
   - Things you have already done
   - Things you would like to do
   - Things you are planning on doing

2. **Draft**
   Write a draft of your email. Look at the text in Activity 1 and the Writing box to help you. Pay attention to correct verb tense.

3. **Share**
   Share your email with another student for feedback. Listen to his/her opinion and suggestions. Check the spelling and grammar.

4. **Check and write**
   Make changes to your email. Did you use verb tenses correctly? Does the email make sense? Write the final version of your text.

WORDLIST

Landscapes, natural features, and countries | Phrasal verbs | Outdoor activities | Sports equipment

adventure [n]
alone [adv]
amazing [adj]
beach [n]
backpack [n]
blow up [phr v]
boat [n]
(ski) boots [n]
border [n]
camp [v]
capital city [n]
civilization [n]
cliff [n]
coast [n]
come across [phr v]
compass [n]
country (state) [n]
cut [n]
cycling [n]
dead [adj]
desert [n]
dry [adj]
Earth [n]
(sports) equipment [n]
faint [v]
farmhouse [n]
field [n]
find out [phr v]
fishing [n]
flag [n]
float [v]
forest [n]
give up [phr v]
gloves [v]

go back [phr v]
goggles [n]
GPS [n]
ground [n]
hairdryer [n]
helmet [n]
hiking [n]
hometown [n]
island [n]
jungle [n]
kayak [n]
kayaking [n]
lake [n]
land [n]
landscape [n]
life jacket [n]
map [n]
mountain [n]
mountain bike [n]
mountain biking [n]
natural feature [n]
ocean [n]
official language [n]
outdoor activity [n]
paddle [n]
passenger [n]
pilot [n]
place [n]
plane [n]
pony trekking [n]
population [n]
rain [v]
rainforest [n]
ride [v]

river [n]
rock climbing [n]
rocks [n]
rub [n]
sand [n]
scuba diving [n]
sea [n]
skis [n]
ski poles [n]
skiing [n]
sky [n]
sleeping bag [n]
snowboard [n]
snowboarding [n]
soaking [adj]
storm [n]
sunbathe [v]
surfboard [n]
surfing [n]
survive [v]
swimming [n]
take place [v]
tent [n]
(train) ticket [n]
tourist resort [n]
travel [v]
vacation [n]
visa [n]
volcano [n]
warm [adj]
water [n]
waterfall [n]
weather [n]
wet [adj]

wet suit [n]
wind-surfing [n]
windy [adj]

WORD FRIENDS

a happy ending
a personal story
by a lake/a river/the sea
buy a sleeping bag
climb a mountain
fly in a plane
get lost
get off a bus/train
go on vacation
go the wrong way
have a good/bad experience/vacation
have a good/great time
have a problem (with)
in a forest/a field/a lake/the mountains/the ocean
lose control of (a vehicle)
on a beach/an island/ the coast
pack a backpack
protect your head/eyes
put up a tent
spend the night in a tent
swim in the sea/ocean
try an activity
visit a country/museum

VOCABULARY IN ACTION

1 Use the Wordlist to find and write in your notebook:
  1 eight things you could buy in a sports store. *boots, …*
  2 ten sports activities.
  3 twelve places you could see in a nature documentary.

2 In pairs, say:
  1 three things you have bought in a sports store: *helmet, …*
  2 three sports activities that you enjoy and three that you don't like:

3 Complete the words in the sentences.
  1 When I was kayaking, I dropped my **p a d d l e** and fell in the water. Fortunately, I was wearing a **l_____ v_____**.
  2 We got lost in the mountains because of a bad **s_____**. Fortunately, I had a map and a **c_____** with me.
  3 There were a lot of people waiting to cross the **b_____** into India. Fortunately, my **v_____** was OK and they let us through.

4 Complete the Word Friends.
  1 _put up_ a tent
  2 _____ a backpack
  3 _____ a mountain
  4 _____ in the sea/ocean
  5 _____ on vacation

5 🔊 2.74 **PRONUNCIATION** Listen and write the words below in the correct column.

~~adventure~~ amazing dangerous
equipment museum rainforest
snowboarding vacation volcano waterfall

1 oOo	2 Ooo
adventure	dangerous

6 🔊 2.75 **PRONUNCIATION** Listen, check, and repeat.

SELF-CHECK

1 Circle the correct option. Then write a similar text about your hometown.

> Columbus is a college town ¹*by /(in)/ on* the state of Mississippi. It has a ²*border / flag / population* of about 24,000 people. The town is a popular tourist ³*hometown / landscape / resort* because of its famous museums and its fishing ⁴*lakes / cliffs / fields*. A few miles north of the town there is a bridge over the Mississippi ⁵*ocean / river / water*. Columbus is pretty far from Washington D.C., the ⁶*capital / country / official* city of the United States, in fact, it's around 800 miles away!

2 Match the activities below to the groups of words.

| hiking   kayaking   mountain biking   skiing snowboarding   ~~surfing~~   wind-surfing |

1 _surfing_ – sea, board, wet suit
2 _____ – goggles, mountains, board
3 _____ – helmet, cycling, countryside
4 _____ – lake/sea, board, windy weather
5 _____ – life jacket, river, paddle
6 _____ – map, forest, boots
7 _____ – mountains, poles, gloves

3 Complete the Word Friends and phrasal verbs in the story. Use the words in the correct form.

> I went ¹ _on_ vacation last week. It started very badly. I ² _____ off the bus at the wrong stop! Then I went the ³ _____ way! So I arrived late at the station and missed my train. I had to take a slower train, so it was very late when I got to the hotel. Then I ⁴ _____ a BIG problem. The receptionist said there was no reservation in my name! He said, "I can ⁵ _____ up a tent in the garden for you." I said, "There's no way I'm going to ⁶ _____ the night in a tent!" I almost gave ⁷ _____ and went home. But my story had a ⁸ _____ ending. The receptionist was joking and actually we became friends. We had a great ⁹ _____ together.

4 Complete the text with the Present Perfect form of the verbs in parentheses.

> I ¹ _haven't been_ (not be) on a fitness vacation before. I hope I enjoy it.
> **6 a.m.** – We ² _____ (just/eat) breakfast! Julie says she ³ _____ (never/get) up so early!
> **10 a.m.** – We ⁴ _____ (already/run) ten kilometers and we ⁵ _____ (not/yet/finish)! I ⁶ _____ (never/feel) so tired!
> **1 p.m.** – They ⁷ _____ (just/bring) us lunch – salad and an apple! Andy ⁸ _____ (already/finish). He's still hungry. He ⁹ _____ (never/have) lunch without dessert before!

5 In your notebook, write questions in the Present Perfect. Then, in pairs, ask your questions and answer with *already*, *just*, or *yet*.

1 you / ever / be / to / England / ?
2 you / visit / capital city / your country / ?
3 your brother (or sister) / leave / school / ?
4 you / climb / highest mountain / your country / ?
5 you / send / text / friend / today / ?
6 you / answer / a question / class / today / ?

A: *Have you ever been to England?*
B: *No, I haven't been to England yet.*

6 In pairs, role-play the situations. Student A: look below. Student B: look at page 117.

Student A
1 You want to go mountain biking. Student B has a better bike than yours. Ask for permission to use it. You don't have a helmet. Try to borrow one from Student B.
2 Student B asks for permission to go on a camping trip with you. Give permission. Ask if Student B has a tent. Student B wants to share your tent. Refuse permission – it's a small tent.

7 🔊 2.76 Listen, then listen again, and write down what you hear.

_____
_____
_____
_____

SELF-ASSESSMENT Think about this unit. What did you learn? What do you need help with?

Why do we dance?

Dancing in the UK

Many of us love dancing or watching dancing. But why do you think we do it? It's strange when you think about it. When we dance, we don't go anywhere and we don't make anything, so what's the reason for it?

Today in the UK dance is very popular. About five million people go to dance classes every week. There are many styles, but the most popular are street dancing, ceroc, ballet, and salsa.

Street dancing has many styles, including breaking, hip-hop, and popping. It's popular with young people and you have to be very flexible. Some people say we do this kind of dance to show our friends how strong and skilful we are.

Ceroc is a simple version of swing, salsa, and jive. You can dance ceroc to fast or slow music. It is very popular with middle-aged people because dancing is a good way to keep fit.

Ballet is popular all over the world. There are many spins and jumps in ballet. It's very difficult and you have to do a lot of training to be good at it. Ballet usually tells stories and people think it's very beautiful.

Salsa is from Cuba. The word "salsa" is Spanish for hot and spicy sauce. Salsa dancers have a lot of passion and energy. People usually dance salsa to fast and fun music. One reason people do this dance is to increase their self-confidence.

So there are many reasons why we dance. Whatever the reason, everyone agrees that dancing is great fun.

GLOSSARY
flexible (adj) bends and moves easily
skillful (adj) good at doing something
spicy (adj) a strong, pleasant taste
spin (n) the movement of something turning around very quickly

EXPLORE

1. In pairs, discuss the questions.
   1. Do you like dancing? Are you a good dancer?
   2. How popular is dancing in your country?
   3. Do you know anyone who is a very good (or bad) dancer?
   4. Why do you think we dance?

2. Read the text. Mark the sentences true (T) or false (F).
   1. [F] Street dancing is popular with middle-aged people.
   2. [ ] Ceroc is always danced to fast music.
   3. [ ] Ballet is from Cuba.
   4. [ ] Salsa also means a hot and spicy sauce in Spanish.

3. Work in pairs. Read the text again and find four reasons for why people dance. Are they the same as your ideas in Activity 1?

BBC Young DANCER 2015 – The Young Dancer Award

This competition happens every year. Judges choose the best dancers from four sections – ballet, contemporary, hip-hop, and South Asian.

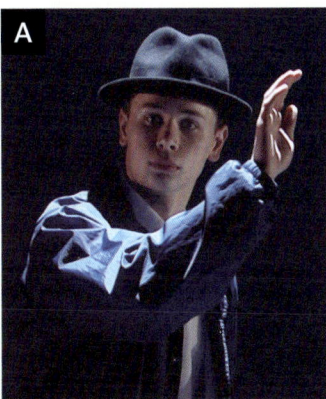

EXPLORE MORE

4. You are going to watch part of a video from the BBC about a dance competition. Read the ad for the TV show on the bottom left. Do you have competitions like this in your country?

5. ▶ 01 Watch Part 1 of the video and match pictures A–E to the names of the contestants 1–5.
   1. [A] Harry Barnes
   2. [ ] Jonadette Carpio
   3. [ ] Jodelle Douglas
   4. [ ] Sharifa Tonkmor
   5. [ ] Kieran Lai

6. In pairs, discuss who your favorite dancer is and why.

7. ▶ 01 Watch Part 1 again. Mark the sentences true (T) or false (F). Correct the false statements.
   1. [F] Harry always feels happy.
   2. [ ] Jonadette was born in a different country.
   3. [ ] Jodelle usually works alone.
   4. [ ] Sharifa doesn't plan her dances.
   5. [ ] Kieran uses machines when he dances.

8. ▶ 02 Watch Part 2 of the video and answer the questions in your notebook.
   1. Who is the winner?
   2. Why do the judges like him/her?
   3. How does the winner react/feel?
   4. What happens next for the winner?

9. Work in pairs. Do you think the winner is the best dancer? Why? / Why not?
   Yes, I agree with the result.
   No, I don't think so. I think …

YOU EXPLORE

10. **CULTURE PROJECT** In groups, use the language and ideas covered in the lesson to create a digital presentation promoting dance and its benefits.
    1. Use the internet to research traditional or popular dances in your country.
    2. Write a short script and include some pictures or video.
    3. Share your presentation with the class.

Why do parrots talk?

Pets around the world

For a long time, people used animals for food and for work. Today, many of us keep animals in our homes as pets and people all over the world love dogs and cats. In the USA, there are more than 80 million pet dogs! Here are some other popular pets that you might find surprising.

Guatemala
A popular pet in Guatemala is the Macaw parrot. It has colorful feathers and can copy words and sounds. These birds live in the rainforest, but there aren't many left now. Because of this, people can only buy them from special places.

China
Chinese people like many different animals, but one very popular pet is the goldfish. For the Chinese the color gold means money and they believe goldfish are lucky. People say that the goldfish has a bad memory – they're very forgetful and can only remember things for five seconds!

Japan
In Japan, they like keeping rabbits. Many Japanese people are vegetarian – they don't eat meat – and rabbits are vegetarian, too! They're gentle animals with soft fur, but when they're angry or frightened, they get aggressive and tap their feet on the ground loudly! They're also very small, which is important for people who live in a small apartment.

The USA
Snakes are very popular in the USA. They can live up to forty years and people don't need to feed them a lot. They don't usually move very much and some snakes sleep for several months every year. Most pet snakes are born in special centers. They're not dangerous or poisonous – unlike the snakes in the wild!

GLOSSARY
gentle (adj) not strong or violent
in the wild (phr) living free in nature
rainforest (n) a forest with tall trees growing in an area where it is hot and it rains a lot
tap (v) to hit lightly

EXPLORE

1 In pairs, discuss the questions.
  1. What's your favorite animal? Why?
  2. What are the most popular pets in your country?
  3. Do you have a pet? Would you like to have one? Why? / Why not?
  4. Do any of your friends have an unusual pet? Can you describe it?
  5. Do you know why parrots talk?

2 Which pets do you think are popular in these countries? Match countries 1–4 to pictures A–D.
  1. ☐ Guatemala
  2. ☐ China
  3. ☐ Japan
  4. ☐ The USA

3 Read the article and check your ideas in Activity 2.

4 Read the article again and answer the questions in your notebook.

Which animals:
  1. can repeat what you tell them?
     parrots
  2. bring you good luck?
  3. are quite rare?
  4. don't eat meat?
  5. are good for small spaces?
  6. are gentle?

EXPLORE MORE

5 In pairs, discuss if you would like to have one of these pets. Why? / Why not?

6 You are going to watch part of a BBC documentary called *Wild at Heart*. Read an ad for the TV show. Do you like watching documentaries about animals?

> **Wild at heart**
>
> This is part of a series of documentaries about animal behavior. Why do our pets sometimes do strange things? Are they playing games or is there another reason?

7 ▶ 03 In pairs, look at the pictures in Activity 5. What activities do these animals often do? Watch the video and check your ideas.

8 Answer the questions in your notebook.
  1. How old are the puppies?
  2. How far do hamsters run every day?
  3. How many words can the parrot speak?

9 ▶ 03 Watch the video again. Answer the questions in your notebook.
  1. Why do puppies play?
  2. Why do hamsters run?
  3. Why do hamsters put a lot of food in their mouths?
  4. Why do parrots talk?

10 Work in pairs. Do you think it's a good idea to keep a pet? Why? / Why not?

  Yes, because pets are like friends.
  No, animals should live in the wild.

YOU EXPLORE

11 **CULTURE PROJECT** In small groups, create a short video about pets.
  1. Use the internet to research popular pets in your country.
  2. Find some pictures or video.
  3. Write a short script and record it with your cell phone.
  4. Share it with the class.

Is there wi-fi in the Sahara?

Unusual places around the world to find wi-fi

Nowadays, people can go online nearly everywhere. We don't have to be at home, work, or school. There are hotspots at cafés, hotels (even in the Sahara!), stores, and hospitals. Although we still can't browse websites or check our emails on all planes, in deserts, or in some rural areas, there are unusual places which do have wi-fi hotspots.

The Moon
Are you surprised? It's true. Scientists placed a satellite and a receiver near the Moon. No one is using this hotspot at the moment. But people might live there and use it in the future? Who knows?

Mount Everest
The highest mountain in the world got wi-fi in 2010. There are hotspots all along the difficult routes up to the top. So, if you want to climb to the very top, the summit, you can take a selfie and share it with your friends!

The North Pole
A Russian team made the difficult journey into the Arctic in 2005. They set up a hotspot at an ice camp eighty kilometers from the Pole. It was the first wi-fi connection in the Arctic.

London black cabs
It usually costs a lot to go online while you're traveling. But now you can do this for free in many London black cabs (taxis). You have to watch a fifteen second ad first, but then you get fifteen minutes of free wi-fi to use on your cell phone, tablet, or laptop. Useful for the "cabbies", too!

Engineers are still working to bring wi-fi to a lot of remote areas all over the world. Small African villages might soon have wi-fi, just like the big hotels!

GLOSSARY
browse (v) to look for information
cabbie (n) a taxi driver
receiver (n) a piece of equipment which receives signals
remote (adj) far away
summit (n) the top of a mountain

EXPLORE

1. In pairs, discuss the questions.
   1. What is a wi-fi hotspot?
   2. Are there a lot of hotspots in your town/neighborhood?
   3. How often do you use them?
   4. Is there wi-fi everywhere in your country?
   5. Which parts of the world do you think *don't* have wi-fi?

2. Read the article and check (✓) the things 1–7 that we learn about.
   1. ✓ hotspots
   2. ☐ how hotspots work
   3. ☐ possible future hotspots
   4. ☐ advertising for hotspots
   5. ☐ hotspots on transportation
   6. ☐ places where there are no hotspots
   7. ☐ the cost of hotspots

3. In pairs, discuss what you learned about the items you checked in Activity 2.

4. Now answer the question in your notebook: Is there wi-fi in the Sahara?

EXPLORE MORE

5. You are going to watch part of a BBC program about the internet. Read an extract from an ad about the TV show. Do you enjoy watching TV shows about technology?

The digital revolution

The internet changed our lives in many ways, but 60 percent of the world is still not connected.

EXPLORE MORE

6. ▶ 04 Watch Part 1 of the video and answer the questions in your notebook.
   1. Why is today an important day for this small town in Africa?
   2. Why is Tim Berners-Lee important?
   3. What was his idea?
   4. What is he showing people?
   5. What questions does the speaker ask?

7. Is the internet good or bad for us? In pairs, write a list of good and bad points in your notebooks.

8. ▶ 05 Watch Part 2 of the video and check your ideas in Activity 7. Are your ideas the same as in the video?

9. Mark the sentences true (T) or false (F).
   1. T Kudjo is a farmer who grows crops.
   2. ☐ Kudjo also teaches his friends about the internet.
   3. ☐ He uses the internet to learn the costs of his competitors' crops.
   4. ☐ Sir Tim Berners-Lee sold his invention for a lot of money.

10. Work in pairs. Do you think Tim Berners-Lee made the right decision?

    Yes, because I believe that everyone should use the internet.
    No, it's better if you earn money from your own inventions.

YOU EXPLORE

11. **CULTURE PROJECT** In small groups, create a digital presentation about an online company.
    1. Use the internet to research a new and exciting company that does everything online.
    2. Write a short script and include some pictures or video.
    3. Share your presentation with the class.

Why are there houses on stilts?

HOUSES AROUND THE WORLD

In the United States and Australia, people's houses are often made of wood from trees. In the UK, people often live in brick houses with two floors and a yard. In some countries, the houses are very different. Is there a reason for this?

Underground houses
People in North Africa and southern Europe started to live in underground houses a long time ago, in the seventh century. Underground houses kept them safe from enemies – people who wanted to hurt them – and the hot sun. Today in Adelaide, South Australia, some people still live in underground houses that miners (people who work underground) made a hundred years ago. Adelaide can get very hot and these houses are nice and cool.

Snow houses
In some very cold parts of the world like the Arctic, Alaska, and Greenland, people build their houses from blocks of snow. It's strange, but inside the snow walls the temperature can be fifteen degrees when outside it's minus forty!

Stilt houses
In some parts of Asia, South America, and West Africa, people live in stilt houses. The stilts lift the houses above the ground or the water. This protects the houses when the sea level rises in bad weather. Sometimes the sea gets very high. On land, the stilts stop animals, like rats and mice, from getting into the house. And over or near the water, the stilts stop dangerous animals, like crocodiles.

People everywhere build houses to protect them from different dangers, like the weather, enemies, and animals. It seems that the shape and the size of our houses depend on what we need.

GLOSSARY
brick (n) a hard block of material for building walls, houses
enemy (n) someone who wants to harm you
protect (v) to keep something safe
stilt (n) a long stick made of wood

EXPLORE

1 In pairs, discuss the questions.
1. What sort of house do you live in?
2. Are there some unusual houses in your country?
3. Why do you think houses aren't the same in every country?

2 Read the article and match the houses from the text 1-3 to pictures A-C.

A

B

C

1. [B] underground house
2. [ ] snow house
3. [ ] stilt house

3 Read the article again and answer the questions in your notebook.

Which house:
1. is good when the weather is cold?
2. is good when the weather is hot?
3. is safe from animals?
4. is good for rainy and stormy weather?

4 How do houses in your country protect people from the cold and the heat?

EXPLORE MORE

5 You are going to watch part of a BBC program about room makeovers. Read an ad for the TV show. Do you have TV shows like this in your country? Do you watch them?

I want my own room!

Every week the team at *I want my own room!* helps kids to design the room of their dreams.

EXPLORE MORE

6 ▶ 06 Watch Part 1 of the video. In pairs, answer the questions in your notebook.
1. What is Freya's hobby?
2. What is Hattie's hobby?
3. What is their mom's hobby?
4. Why do the girls want to change their bedroom?
5. What is Michelle's job?

7 What would you like to change about *your* bedroom?

8 ▶ 07 Watch Part 2 of the video. Mark the sentences true (T) or false (F).
1. [F] The girls paint pictures for the walls.
2. [ ] Their mom throws away everything in the front room.
3. [ ] The girls put pictures on the wallpaper.

9 ▶ 08 Watch Part 3 of the video. Check (✓) things 1-9 which are NOT in the room. Where are the other things?
1. [✓] a blue cabinet
2. [ ] a red butterfly
3. [ ] an orange closet
4. [ ] a pink blind
5. [ ] a pink and red doorstop
6. [ ] a purple rug
7. [ ] a yellow pull-out bed
8. [ ] some black and white cushions
9. [ ] a blue chair

10 In pairs, discuss the questions.
1. What's your favorite thing in the room?
2. What do you not like? Why?

YOU EXPLORE

11 **CULTURE PROJECT** In small groups, prepare a presentation about unusual buildings.
1. Use the internet to research two unusual buildings in your country.
2. Find out why people built them like this.
3. Write a short script and include some pictures and videos.
4. Share your presentation with the class.

BBC CULTURE

Is chess a sport?

Strange sports

Soccer, tennis, hockey, and cricket are all popular sports around the world. But when is a sport not a sport? Most people think that in a sport we must be strong, use our mind, and want to win. So what about these activities?

1 Chess boxing
People play chess all over the world. Chess players need to be fit – in body and mind. Sometimes they need to sit and think hard for seven hours a day. In some competitions, they play for eleven days! There's also a hybrid sport called "chess boxing." Boxers fight and then play chess! It's popular in Germany, the UK, India, and Russia.

2 Makepung
Every summer in West Bali there are special buffalo races. A team of one man and a pair of buffaloes race against another team. They race over muddy ground for a long time – sometimes five hours. The men often fall off and get dirty. The crowd likes that!

3 Haggis hurling
In Scotland, some people like to do haggis hurling. They have to throw a haggis – this is a hard ball of special meat which is a traditional Scottish food. They have to throw the haggis a long way and also very carefully. The haggis shouldn't break when it hits the ground. So, you have to be strong, but also smart.

What do you think? Are these games or sports? Would you like to see them in the Olympics?!

GLOSSARY
competition (n) an event in which people or teams compete against each other
mind (n) your thoughts
muddy (adj) wet and dirty
race (n) a competition in which people or animals compete to be the fastest and finish first
traditional (adj) existing for a long time

EXPLORE

1 In pairs, discuss the questions.
   1 How many sports or games can you name in two minutes?
   2 Do you do any sports? Do you do them for fun or for competition?
   3 Do you know anyone who is very good at a sport or game?
   4 What's the difference between a sport and a game?

2 Read the article and match sports 1-3 to pictures A-C.

   1 [B] Chess boxing
   2 [ ] Makepung
   3 [ ] Haggis hurling

3 Read the article again. Write the name of the game or sport.
   1 This only happens at a certain time of year. _Makepung_
   2 People do this with something small that we can eat. _____
   3 People sometimes laugh when they watch this. _____
   4 People don't move for a long time in this activity. _____
   5 This is a mixture of two games/sports. _____

4 In pairs, discuss the final questions in the article.

EXPLORE MORE

5 You are going to watch part of a video from a BBC series about unusual sports and games. Read an ad for the TV show. Do you know anyone who does an unusual sport?

Unusual sports

People do some very unusual sports and this series shows us just a couple of them.

EXPLORE MORE

6 ▶ 09 Watch Part 1 of the video. Mark the sentences true (T) or false (F).
   1 [T] At the World Alternative Games, there are thirty sports.
   2 [ ] Backwards running started in the United States.
   3 [ ] Backwards running is good for the brain.
   4 [ ] Backwards running is a difficult sport.

7 What advice does the speaker give at the end of the video? Why?

8 ▶ 10 Watch Part 2 of the video and answer the questions in your notebook.
   1 How and why did wrong pong start?
   2 How is wrong pong different from normal table tennis?
   3 How many different tables did you see in the video?

9 ▶ 11 Watch Part 3 of the video and complete the sentences.
   1 This race is called _the wife carrying race_.
   2 It started in _____.
   3 Usually the man _____.
   4 In the race today, for the first time _____.

10 Work in pairs. Would you like to try any of the unusual sports in this lesson? Why? / Why not?
   I would like to try wrong pong because I think it's fun.

YOU EXPLORE

11 **CULTURE PROJECT** In small groups, create a presentation about an unusual sport.
   1 Use the internet to research sports that people do in your country.
   2 Invent a new hybrid sport from two of these sports.
   3 Write a short description of the new sport.
   4 Share your presentation with the class.
   5 Vote on the most popular new sport!

Where can you buy a town?

Amazing things sold on eBay

Most people love shopping. It's a popular hobby, but our shopping habits don't always stay the same. They change. Today we can buy things in many places and more and more people are buying things online. There are lots of websites where you can buy normal things, but if you want something really unusual, go to an online auction site, like eBay. eBay started in the United States more than twenty years ago, but now operates in thirty different countries. Here are some of the amazing things people sold on the site.

Bridgeville
In 2008, the small town of Bridgeville in California was for sale and someone paid 1.25 million dollars for it! It's a very small place – in 2008 it had only thirty people, eight houses, a post office, a café, and a cemetery. The town needed a lot of money and work and the new owner sold it again a few years later.

A life
Ian Usher was very sad after his wife left him. He decided to put his whole life for sale on eBay! He sold everything that he had – his house, his car, introductions to his friends, and his job. Someone paid 300,000 dollars and Ian started a new life with the money.

A forehead
Kari Smith sold her forehead for advertising space! A company paid her 10,000 dollars to tattoo the name of their company on her forehead!

A yacht
One of the most expensive things for sale on eBay was a big yacht. Roman Abramovich (who owned Chelsea soccer club) bought it for 168 million dollars. It had a gym, a movie theater, a spa, and an elevator.

Do you have something unusual you would like to sell on eBay?

GLOSSARY
auction (n) a public sale where things are sold to the person who offers the most money for them
cemetery (n) a piece of land in which dead people are buried
forehead (n) the part of your face above your eyes and below your hair
introductions (n) telling two people each other's names when they first meet and explain who they are
operate (v) to work

EXPLORE

1. In pairs, discuss the questions below.
   1. Do you prefer to buy things online or in stores? Why?
   2. Do you have a favorite shopping website or online store?
   3. What's the most interesting thing you bought last month?
   4. Do you know someone who recently bought something unusual? What did they buy?

2. Read the article. In pairs, answer the questions.
   1. How old is eBay?
   2. Why was the town for sale again after a few years?
   3. Why was the life for sale?
   4. How much did the life sell for?
   5. Why did a woman sell her forehead?
   6. Who bought the yacht?

3. In pairs, discuss the final question in the article.

EXPLORE MORE

4. You are going to watch part of a video from the BBC about shopping in different cities. Read an ad for the program and answer the question.

   ### City shopping
   Some big cities have famous places to go shopping. Do you know any? This show is about some of them.

EXPLORE MORE

5. ▶ 12 Watch Part 1 of the video. Mark the sentences true (T) or false (F).
   1. **F** On Oxford Street, everything costs a lot of money.
   2. ☐ People go to a special event on Oxford Street in November.
   3. ☐ The air on Oxford Street is very clean.
   4. ☐ On Portobello Road, there is a big market every day.
   5. ☐ You can buy old clothes at Portobello market.

6. Work in pairs. In your opinion, which is better – a day on Oxford Street or a day on Portobello Road? Why?

7. ▶ 13 Watch Part 2 of the video and complete the sentences.
   1. The Apple Store on Fifth Avenue is interesting because *it is a wonderful glass cube*.
   2. You might get tired at Macy's because _____.
   3. Shibuya Crossing is famous because _____.
   4. Trendy young people go to Shibuya because _____.

8. Work in pairs. Imagine you have $5,000 to spend. Will you go to London, New York, or Tokyo? Why? What are you going to spend your money on?

YOU EXPLORE

9. **CULTURE PROJECT** In small groups, create a presentation about a shopping area.
   1. Use the internet to research a popular city shopping mall or area in your country.
   2. Write a short script and include some pictures or video.
   3. Share your presentation with the class.

CULTURE

Will robots do our jobs?

Robots in the future

1 _____

Robots and machines can do a lot of jobs today that people did in the past. Should we be worried because we might lose our jobs? Or should we be happy because they can do jobs we don't enjoy?

2 _____

Technology is progressing very quickly now. Robots and computers can do more and more jobs. Over 800,000 machines are doing jobs today that people did fifteen years ago and experts say that fifteen million people will lose their jobs in the future.

3 _____

This change started a long time ago. Robots started to build cars in 1961 in the United States and trains without drivers began thirty years ago. At that time, scientists were building robots and machines to do the boring and routine work in manufacturing. Then they started to replace other jobs to make life easier and quicker for people. Today there aren't many secretaries, travel agents, librarians, airport check-in assistants, or farm workers. Robots can also do the jobs of receptionists, pharmacists, and soldiers.

4 _____

Robots might replace a lot of us in the future, but some jobs will always need people. If you have a job which is about looking after people, or talking to people, or finding answers to problems and being creative, you'll be safe. They say that there will always be teachers, restaurant staff, hairdressers, care workers, and top businesspeople who make important decisions. Of course, there will be new jobs, too, because we'll need lots of computer specialists and people to teach everyone to code and design new machines.

But who really knows? There's already a robot bartender in Germany who can mix cocktails and talk to customers! And you can check in to a very unusual hotel in Japan.

GLOSSARY
bartender (n) someone who makes and serves drinks in a bar or restaurant
care worker (n) someone who looks after people who are sick or old
expert (n) someone who knows a lot about something
progress (v) to become better
replace (v) to take the place of someone

EXPLORE

1. In pairs, discuss the questions below.
   1. Write down as many jobs as you can in two minutes.
   2. Which of these jobs do you think robots can do now?
   3. Which jobs do you think robots will do in the future?
   4. Which jobs do you think that robots will not be able to do in the future? Why?

2. Read the article and check your ideas in Activity 1.

3. Read the article again and match headings A–D to paragraphs 1–4 in the text.
   - A ☐ Which jobs are in danger?
   - B ☐ 1 Some questions we need to ask.
   - C ☐ Which jobs are safe?
   - D ☐ How big is the problem?

4. Which of the pictures below does the text not mention? What do you learn about the others?

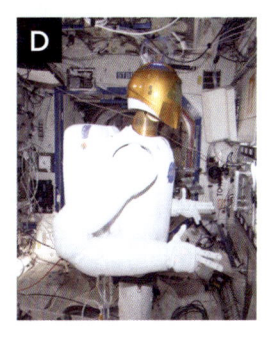

5. In pairs, discuss the questions.
   1. Who do you think will lose their jobs in the future – people who earn good money or people who don't earn much money? Why?
   2. Do you think robots will be good or bad for society in the future? Why?

EXPLORE MORE

6. You are going to watch part of a BBC program about an unusual hotel in Japan. Read an ad for the TV show. Do you ever stay in hotels when you're on vacation?

   Click — The BBC's technology series tells us about a new hotel in Japan and why it's very special.

7. ▶ 14 Watch Part 1 of the video and answer the questions in your notebook.
   1. Why is the Henn Na Hotel unusual?
   2. Why is the visitor surprised by the second receptionist?
   3. Do the receptionists speak English?
   4. Why does the visitor laugh when he's at reception?
   5. Why does a machine take his picture?

8. Work in pairs. What do you think the visitor's hotel room will be like?

9. ▶ 15 Watch Part 2 of the video and check your ideas in Activity 8.

10. ▶ 15 Watch Part 2 of the video again and complete the sentences in your notebook.
    1. It takes a long time to get to his room because …
    2. There aren't any light switches in the room because …
    3. The visitor needs to use a book because …
    4. The visitor has a problem because …

11. Work in pairs. Would you like to stay at this hotel? Why? / Why not?

YOU EXPLORE

12. **CULTURE PROJECT** In small groups, create a presentation about a robot.
    1. Use the internet to research a new and clever robot that works in your country.
    2. Write a short script and includes some pictures or video.
    3. Share your presentation with the class.
    4. Vote for the smartest robot.

How many fish ... ?

Ocean life numbers

Fish is a popular meal for many people. It's healthy, tasty, and often cheap because there are lots of fish in the ocean. But are there? Maybe you've noticed that sometimes we can't buy our favorite fish. The reason is that in the last thirty years we've taken too many fish out of the sea. Fishermen must stop catching some fish for a while and catch others instead. Man has caused lots of problems for other sea animals, too.

There aren't many sea turtles left in the world. People kill them for food and many also die when they get caught in fishermen's nets. Another problem for turtles is that they lay their eggs on beaches. We have built more and more houses and hotels on the coast. When the baby turtles come out of their eggs, they need to get to the sea. But many of them don't survive because they get lost or sea birds kill them. Today in many places, like Cancun in Mexico, people help them to get to the sea.

Seabirds are also becoming rarer. Beautiful birds, like the albatross, spend nearly all their lives in the air and eat fish to live. Some types of fishing are very dangerous for these birds. Like the turtles, they get caught in fishing nets and drown. Some areas, like the South Georgia Islands in the Atlantic have created big protected areas to help these birds. Also conservation groups are encouraging fishermen to use new fishing techniques.

All sea birds need to catch fish to live. So for them and for us we need to control fishing.

GLOSSARY
conservation group (n) people who work to protect animals, plants, etc.
drown (v) to die from being under water for too long
get caught (v) to be in a situation that you cannot easily get out of
lay their eggs (v) to produce eggs
net (n) something used for catching fish, insects, or animals

EXPLORE

1. In pairs, discuss the questions below.
   1. Do you like eating fish?
   2. Do people in your country eat a lot of fish?
   3. Has the type of fish that people eat changed in recent years? How?

2. Read the article. Write *T* (for turtles), *S* (for seabirds), or *B* (for both).
   1. [T] People eat them.
   2. [ ] Fishermen catch them accidentally.
   3. [ ] Today, there are buildings in the places where they always left their eggs in the past.
   4. [ ] Their young often die soon after birth.

3. In pairs, discuss the questions below.
   1. Is it important to know how many fish there are in the sea? Why?
   2. Is it possible to count them?

EXPLORE MORE

4. You are going to watch part of a BBC program about fishing. Read an ad for the TV show. Is fishing an important industry in your country?

   Coast
   The series *Coast* is about different ways that humans relate to the sea. This episode asks the question, "How many fish are in the ocean?"

5. Work in pairs. What do you think "overfishing" means?

6. ▶ 16 Watch Part 1 of the video and check your answers in Activity 5.

7. Circle the correct answers.
   1. What is the main job of the people on the *Scotia*?
      a. To catch lots of fish.
      b. To get information about fish.
   2. Why was the *Explorer* an important ship?
      a. She carried lots of scientists.
      b. She had new electronic equipment.

EXPLORE MORE

8. Work in pairs. Do you think life on the *Explorer* was interesting? Why?/Why not?

9. ▶ 16 Watch the video again and correct the information in sentences 1–4 in your notebook.
   1. Ullapool is in England.
   2. They check the fish twice a year.
   3. They built the *Explorer* in 1966.
   4. On the *Explorer*, the scientists had to write everything.

10. ▶ 17 Watch Part 2 of the video and answer the questions.
    1. Check (✓) the information a–e that the scientists need about the fish.
       a. [✓] how many there are
       b. [ ] how big they are
       c. [ ] how old they are
       d. [ ] how fast they swim
       e. [ ] how deep they live
    2. Why do they look at a fish's ear bone?
    3. Why do normal fishermen and the *Scotia* travel to different parts of the ocean?
    4. What do the results today show?

11. Work in pairs. Do you think the future for fish is good or bad? Why?

    I think it's good because scientists can change things.
    I think it's bad because people are very greedy.

YOU EXPLORE

12. **CULTURE PROJECT** In small groups, create a presentation about an environmental problem.
    1. Use the internet to research a problem connected with the sea (or an area of natural beauty) in your country.
    2. Find out what people are doing about the problem.
    3. Write a short script and include some pictures or videos.
    4. Share your presentation with the class.

GRAMMAR TIME

1.2 Simple Present: affirmative and negative | Adverbs of frequency

We use the Simple Present for facts and routines.

+	I/You/We/They	live	in a small town.
	He/She/It	watches	movies on TV.
–	I/You/We/They	don't (do not) live	in a small town.
	He/She/It	doesn't (does not) watch	movies on TV.

Spelling rules
With *He/She/It* we add *-s*, *-es* or *-ies* to the verb:
- Most verbs, add *-s*: live – live**s**
- Verbs ending in *-o*, *-ch*, *-sh*, *-ss* and *-x*, add *-es*: go – go**es**, watch – watch**es**, wash – wash**es**
- Verbs ending in consonant + *-y*, cut *-y* and add *-ies*: study – stud**ies**

Adverbs of frequency
We place adverbs of frequency before the main verb in the Simple Present, but after the verb *to be*.

always   usually   often   sometimes   never

I **always** listen to music on my cell phone.
We don't **often** watch movies at school.

1 In your notebook, order the words to make sentences.
1. the guitar / a rock group / I / in / play
   I play the guitar in a rock group.
2. American / movies / often / watch / we
3. busy / she / always / is
4. go out / don't / on Mondays / usually / I
5. comics / doesn't / my / read / sister

2 Complete the text with the correct form of the words in parentheses.

Sandi has a very unusual life ...

Sandi ¹ *lives* (live) in an igloo in the Arctic. She ² _____ (get) up at 4 a.m. every day. She ³ _____ (often/eat) pizza for breakfast. She ⁴ _____ (fly) to school in a helicopter every day. After school, she ⁵ _____ (study) car mechanics. She ⁶ _____ (always/go) to bed at 7 p.m.

1.2 Simple Present: questions and answers

***Yes/No* questions and short answers**

| ? | Do | I/you/we/they | read novels? | Yes, I/you/we/they do. No, I/you/we/they don't. |
| | Does | he/she/it | live in Hollywood? | Yes, he/she/it does. No, he/she/it doesn't. |

***Wh-* questions and answers**
How often **do** you **go** to the movies?
Every Sunday. / I **go** to the movies every Sunday.
What time **does** the movie **start**?
At 8 p.m. / It **starts** at 8 p.m.
Where do they live?
In Chicago. / They **live** in Chicago.

Time expressions
every day/week/month
once/twice/three times a month
in the morning/afternoon/evening
on the weekend
at 8 o'clock Mondays

1 In your notebook, write *Yes/No* questions in the Simple Present. Then ask and answer the questions in pairs.
1. like / taking pictures / you / ?
2. songs / write / your favorite singer / ?
3. online videos / watch / your parents / ?
4. dancing / like / you and your friends / ?
5. draw / sometimes / on the board / pictures / your English teacher / ?

A: *Do you like taking pictures?*
B: *Yes, I do.*

2 In your notebook, write questions for these answers. Sometimes there is more than one possible question.
1. *Where does your aunt live?*
   My aunt lives <u>in Italy</u>.
2. The concert finishes <u>at 11:30</u>.
3. My parents <u>never</u> go dancing.
4. <u>No</u>, I don't.
5. <u>Yes</u>, she does.

GRAMMAR TIME

1.4 Present Continuous

We use the Present Continuous for things that are happening at or around the moment of speaking.

+	I	'm (am) reading a book.
	You/We/They	're (are) playing a game.
	He/She/It	's (is) sleeping.
–	I	'm not (am not) reading a book.
	You/We/They	aren't (are not) playing a game.
	He/She/It	isn't (is not) sleeping.
?	Am	I	reading a book?	Yes, I am. No, I'm not.
	Are	you/we/they	playing a game?	Yes, you/we/they are. No, you/we/they aren't.
	Is	he/she/it	sleeping?	Yes, he/she/it is. No, he/she/it isn't.
	Where	are	you	going?
	What	is	he	doing?

Spelling rules
- Most verbs, add *-ing*: go – going, look – looking
- Verbs ending in *-e*, cut *-e* and add *-ing*: live – living
- Short verbs that end with consonant + vowel + consonant, double the last consonant: sit – sitting, swim – swimming

Time expressions

now   at the moment
right now   today

1 Complete the dialogue with the Present Continuous form of the verbs in parentheses.

Mom: Tom! Where are you?
Tom: Hi, Mom. I ¹ _'m sitting_ (sit) in the park.
Mom: What ² _____ (you/do)?
       ³ _____ (you/have) fun?
Tom: No, I ⁴ _____ . I ⁵ _____ (study) for a test.
Mom: I can hear Matt! ⁶ _____ (he/study), too?
Tom: Yes, he ⁷ _____ .
Mom: Really? We ⁸ _____ (drive) past the park now. You ⁹ _____ (not read)!
       You ¹⁰ _____ (play) soccer!
Tom: Yes, we ¹¹ _____ (get) ready for our PE test!

2 Imagine you are having a party. In your notebook, use the Present Continuous to write ten sentences about what is happening.

I'm sitting on the couch with my friend Joanna.

1.4 Simple Present and Present Continuous

- We use the **Simple Present** for facts and routines.
  Bro lives in Hollywood.
  Lee plays his guitar every day.
  Amy doesn't clean her room.
  What time do you get up?

- We use the **Present Continuous** for something happening at the moment of speaking.
  What are you doing under the table?
  I'm looking for my earring!

- We also use the **Present Continuous** for something happening around now, but maybe not at the moment of speaking.
  Is she enjoying school at the moment?
  He isn't talking to his dad these days.
  Time expressions: these days, at the moment, this week/month

1 Complete the sentences with the correct form of the words in parentheses.

1 Oh no, it _'s raining_ (rain) again!
2 I _____ (live) in Berlin, but I _____ (visit) London now.
3 He _____ (save) money at the moment to buy a leather jacket.
4 Gemma _____ (often/go) to Miami on vacation.
5 Jim _____ (not speak) Italian, but he _____ (know) a little Chinese.

2 In your notebook, use the Simple Present to write about your typical Sunday afternoon.

On a typical Sunday afternoon, I usually sit on the couch at home and …

3 Now imagine you are spending an unusual Sunday afternoon. In your notebook, use the Present Continuous to write about it.

This is an unusual Sunday afternoon. I'm not sitting on the couch at home, I'm …

GRAMMAR TIME

2.2 Simple Past: was/were

We use the Simple Past to talk about finished events and situations in the past. The Simple Past of *to be* is *was/were*.

+	I/He/She/It You/We/They	was at school. were at home.	
−	I/He/She/It You/We/They	wasn't (was not) hungry. weren't (were not) late.	
?	Was	I/he/she/it	hungry?	Yes, I/he/she/it was. No, I/he/she/it wasn't.
	Were	you/we/they	tired?	Yes, you/we/they were. No, you/we/they weren't.
	When Where	was were	she born? you yesterday?	

The Simple Past of *there is/there are* is **there was/there were**.

Time expressions
yesterday
last Tuesday/week/month/year
two days/a week ago
this evening/tonight
at one o'clock
in June/2004

1 Complete the questions with *was/were*. Then ask and answer in pairs.

1 How _was_ your last English test?
2 _____ it cold yesterday?
3 Where _____ you born?
4 _____ you at a party last weekend?
5 Where _____ you five hours ago?
6 How old _____ you in 2015?
7 _____ you late for school this morning?

A: *How was your last English test?*
B: *It was easy!*

2 In your notebook, rewrite the sentences in the Simple Past.

1 "Are you bored?" "Yes, I am."
  "Were you bored?" "Yes, I was."
2 "Is it cold?" "Yes, it is."
3 "Are you at home?" "No, I'm not."
4 "Is there a letter for me?" "No, there isn't".
5 We aren't very hungry.
6 There aren't any tickets.

3 In your notebook, write ten sentences about a recent day out.

*Last Saturday I was at a Coldplay concert. I was with … It was at …
There were hundreds of fans.*

2.4 Simple Past: regular verbs

+	I/You/He/She/It/We/They	watched TV.	
−	I/You/He/She/It/We/They	didn't (did not) read.	
?	Did	I/you/he/she/it/we/they	sleep?	Yes, I/you/he/she/it/we/they did. No, I/you/he/she/it/we/they didn't.
	When did	he	arrive?	
	What did	they	watch?	

Spelling rules
- Most regular verbs, add *-ed*: watch – watch**ed**
- Verbs ending with *-e*, add *-d*: live – live**d**
- Verbs ending with consonant +*y*, cut *-y* and add *-ied*:
  try – tr**ied**
- One-syllable verbs ending with vowel + consonant, double the consonant and add *-ed*:
  stop – stop**ped**

1 Write the past form of the verbs below.

1 cook – _cooked_
2 carry – _____
3 play – _____
4 help – _____
5 drop – _____
6 marry – _____

2 Complete the sentences with the Simple Past form of the verbs in parentheses.

1 Mel _cleaned_ (clean) her room.
2 "_____ (they/like) the movie?"
  "No, they _____."
3 I _____ (not watch) TV last night.
4 "_____ (you/finish) your work?"
  "Yes, I _____."
5 He _____ (drop) his cell phone and it _____ (stop) working.

3 Work in pairs. Use the ideas below to ask and answer questions about your classmate's day yesterday.

clean your room   listen to music
wash your hair   rest   study English
watch a movie   call a friend

A: *Did you clean your room yesterday?*
B: *No, I didn't.*

GRAMMAR TIME

3.2 Simple Past: irregular verbs

+	I/You/He/She/It/We/They	took my camera.	
−	I/You/He/She/It/We/They	didn't (did not) take my camera.	
?	Did	I/you/he/she/it/we/they	take the camera?	Yes, I/you/he/she/it/we/they did. No, I/you/he/she/it/we/they didn't.
	Where	did	you	put it?

1 Write the past form of the verbs below.
1. come – *came*
2. drink – _____
3. drive – _____
4. eat – _____
5. find – _____
6. go – _____
7. leave – _____
8. make – _____
9. meet – _____
10. read – _____
11. run – _____
12. speak – _____
13. take – _____
14. write – _____

2 Use the verbs in Activity 1 to write six sentences about last weekend. Write them in your notebook.
1. *Last weekend I spoke to my grandpa on the phone.*

3 In pairs, use your sentences to ask questions.
A: *Did you speak to your grandpa on the phone last weekend?*
B: *No, I didn't. But we went to his house on Saturday.*

4 Complete Amy's story with the Simple Past form of the verbs below.

fall   feel   get   ~~have~~   hit   hurt   sit

I was in the bathroom. I ¹ *had* my cell phone with me. On the way out, I ² _____ my head on the door. It really ³ _____ .
I ⁴ _____ bad, so I ⁵ _____ down on the bathtub and my cell phone ⁶ _____ in the toilet! I didn't want to put my hand in the water, so I called my dad and he ⁷ _____ it out for me.

3.4 Relative Clauses

We use relative clauses to say which person, thing, or place we are talking about.
- We use **who** or **that** for people.
  A teacher is a person who/that works in a school.
- We use **which** or **that** for things.
  That is the book machine which/that my mom wrote about.
- We use **where** for places.
  We are in the room where they found the treasure.

1 Circle the correct option to complete the sentences.
1. The Taj Mahal is a building who / (where) many tourists take pictures.
2. My aunt is someone who / which I love spending time with.
3. Pumpkin soup is a food where / that I can't stand!
4. The lake near town is that / where I feel most relaxed.
5. English is a language that / who will help me a lot in the future.

2 Match 1-4 to a-d and rewrite the sentences using a relative pronoun.
1. Spain is a country
2. Steve Jobs was an inventor
3. Parma ham is a type of meat
4. Drones are a gadget

a. who changed the world
b. where I could go to learn Spanish.
c. that can fly.
d. which is popular in Italy.

1. [b] *Spain is a country where I could go to learn another language.*
2. [ ] _____
3. [ ] _____
4. [ ] _____

3 In your notebook, write four more sentences using relative pronouns. Use the idea's below.
- A person you admire
- Your favorite gadget
- A place you really like

I really like Angelina Jolie. She is an actress who works with a lot of charities.

Grammar Time 109

GRAMMAR TIME

4.2 Adverbs of manner

We use adjectives with nouns and adverbs with verbs.
- We can add *-ly* to most adjectives to make an adverb:
  She is quiet. She speaks quiet*ly*.
- With adjectives ending with *-y*, we cut the *-y* and add *-ily*:
  The rain is heavy. It's raining heav*ily*.
- Irregular adverbs have the same form as adjectives:
  hard, fast, right, wrong, early, late, high, last, best, wide
  He's a fast runner. He runs fast.
- The adverb for *good* is well.

We use *very*, *really*, and *so* before adjectives and adverbs.
She is very slow.
Children learn really quickly.
She wakes up so slowly.

1 Complete the sentences with the correct form of the adjectives in parentheses. Then, in pairs, complete the sentences with the name of someone you both know.

1 _Chris_ always speaks very _quickly_ (quick).
2 _____ speaks English really _____ (good).
3 _____ often laughs _____ (noisy).
4 _____ speaks _____ (quiet).
5 _____ often comes to class _____ (late).

2 Complete the sentences with the adjective in parentheses. Then use it as an adverb or to form an adverb.

1 I'm a _bad_ dancer. I dance so _badly_ ! (bad)
2 Sarah's a _____ singer. She sings really _____ . (good)
3 I'm sure Tim will arrive _____ . He's always _____ . (early)
4 The boys are very _____ to Eva. They always laugh _____ at her. (unkind)
5 It's snowing really _____ . The snow isn't usually so _____ . (heavy)

4.4 Modal verbs: *can*, *have to*, and *must*

Can
We use **can** to talk about things we are allowed/not allowed to do
I can go online when I want. (*It's OK/allowed.*)
I can't watch TV after 10 p.m. (*It isn't OK/allowed.*)
Can you invite friends to stay? (*Is it OK?*)

Have to
We use **have to** to say that something is necessary and **don't have to** to say that something isn't necessary.
You have to come home straight after school. (*It's necessary.*)
You don't have to come home straight after school. (*It isn't necessary.*)
Do I have to come home straight after school? (*Is it necessary?*)

Must
Must has a similar meaning to *have to*, but *have to* is more common.
I have to/must cook dinner.

We use **must not** to talk about what you're not allowed to do.
You must not stay up late. (*Don't!*)

Don't have to and **must not** have different meanings.
You don't have to go there. (*You can, but it's not necessary.*)
You must not go there. (*Don't!*)

1 In pairs, say where you can find these signs. Then write sentences in your notebook with *you have to* or *you must not* for each sign.

You must not park here.

1 NO PARKING
2 (no phones)
3  PLEASE WAIT HERE
4 SILENCE No Talking!

GRAMMAR TIME

2 Work in pairs. Circle the modal verb which makes the sentence true for your school.

1 You *can / must not* borrow books from the library.
2 You *can / must not* run in the corridors.
3 You *have to / don't have to* learn two foreign languages.
4 You *can / must not* use a cell phone in class.
5 You *have to / don't have to* stand up when the teacher enters the room.

3 Choose one situation below and write six sentences with rules about what you *can*, *can't*, *have to*, and *must not* do. In your notebook, write rules:

- for a visitor to your country.
- for somebody playing your favorite video/computer game.
- for someone going on vacation with your family.

You don't have to have a visa.

5.2 Countable and uncountable nouns | Quantifiers

Countable	Uncountable
How many bottles of water do we have? I don't have many hobbies. There are too many olives on my pizza.	How much water is in that bottle? I don't have much time. There's too much ice in my drink.
I bought some bananas. We eat a lot of oranges. We don't eat a lot of apples.	She bought some popcorn. We eat a lot of cheese. We don't eat a lot of bread.
Are there any cookies? There aren't any eggs in the refrigerator.	Is there any juice? There isn't any milk in the refrigerator.

1 Circle the correct option to complete the sentences. Then answer them in pairs.

1 How (many) / much meals do you eat every day?
2 Do you think you eat too *many / much* unhealthy food?
3 Do you have *any / some* food in your backpack?
4 How *many / much* time do you have for lunch on schooldays?
5 There aren't *many / much* places to eat near our school. True or false?

2 Complete the restaurant review with *a lot of*, *any*, *many*, *much*, or *some*.

STEWIE'S STEAKHOUSE

Stewie's Steakhouse looks nice, but it's very small and there are too [1] *many* tables, so there isn't [2] _____ space – you feel that you're eating in a shoebox! There aren't [3] _____ things on the menu and they all have meat in them. There aren't [4] _____ dishes for vegetarians – there's no salad! The food wasn't great. I had a steak and [5] _____ cold French fries. There was [6] _____ meat on my plate (about a kilo!), but it wasn't very good. And there was too [7] _____ salt in every dish! Finally, they didn't have [8] _____ juice, only soda!

5.4 Past Continuous and Simple Past

We use the Past Continuous to say something was in progress at a certain moment in the past.

+	I/He/She/It You/We/They		was watching TV. were sleeping	
–	I/He/She/It You/We/They		wasn't (was not) watching TV. weren't (we`re not) sleeping	
?	Was	I/he/she/it	watching TV?	Yes, I/he/she/it was. No, I/he/she/it wasn't.
	Were	you/we/they	sleeping at 9 p.m.?	Yes, you/we/they were. No, you/we/they weren't.
	Where What	was were	he you	going? doing?

Time expressions
at three o'clock this morning / 5:15 last Tuesday
forty minutes ago

Past Continuous and Simple Past
We use the Simple Past for a short/complete action (e.g., *I broke my leg*) and the Past Continuous for a longer activity in progress at the same time (e.g., *I was playing soccer*).

To introduce the clause in the Past Continuous, we use *while* or *when*.

While/When I was playing soccer, I broke my leg.
I broke my leg while/when I was playing soccer.

To introduce the clause in the Simple Past, we normally use *when*.

What were you doing when the accident happened?
When the accident happened, what were you doing?

Grammar Time 111

GRAMMAR TIME

1 Complete the sentences with the Past Continuous form of the verbs in parentheses.
1. The phone rang while the Johnsons _were sleeping_ (sleep).
2. Anna _____ (not dance) at one o'clock in the morning.
3. Where _____ (Sue/go) when she fell?
4. I _____ (not listen) when the doctor told me his name.
5. What _____ (you/do) when you cut your finger?

2 Complete the story with the Simple Past or the Past Continuous form of the verbs in parentheses. Then compare with a classmate.

> Last Sunday afternoon I ¹ _was riding_ (ride) my bike. It ² _____ (rain) a lot, so I ³ _____ (put) up my umbrella. While I ⁴ _____ (go) past the station, I ⁵ _____ (see) Jennifer Lawrence! She ⁶ _____ (get) into a taxi. I ⁷ _____ (not look) where I ⁸ _____ (go), so I ⁹ _____ (ride) my bike into the back of a car! I ¹⁰ _____ (fall) and ¹¹ _____ (hit) my head. I was lucky I ¹² _____ (wear) a helmet.

6.2 Comparatives and superlatives of adjectives

We use the **comparative** form of adjectives with *than* to compare two people or things.
He's taller than me.

We use the **superlative** form of adjectives to compare one person or thing in a group with all the other people or things in that group.
She's the nicest person I know. (She's nicer than all the other people I know.)

Look at how we form the comparative and superlative of adjectives:

Adjectives	Adjective	Comparative	Superlative
with one syllable	near	nearer	the nearest
with one syllable ending with -e	wide	wider	the widest
with one syllable ending in vowel + consonant	hot	hotter	the hottest
ending in consonant + -y	lazy	lazier	the laziest
with two or more syllables	intelligent	more intelligent	the most intelligent
irregular	good bad	better worse	the best the worst

We usually use *the* before superlative adjectives. But we don't use *the* after my/your/his/her/its/our/their.
He's their youngest son. NOT ~~He's their the youngest son.~~

We can also compare things using (*not*) *as* ... *as*.
This book isn't as interesting as the first one.
(*The first one is more interesting than this book.*)

1 Write the comparative and superlative forms of the adjectives below.
1. fat – _fatter, the fattest_
2. easy – _____
3. late – _____
4. expensive – _____
5. young – _____

2 How much can you remember about last year? Complete the questions with the superlative form of the adjectives in parentheses. Then ask and answer the questions in pairs.
1. What was _the most beautiful_ (beautiful) place you visited?
2. What was _____ (happy) day you can remember?
3. What was _____ (long) trip you made?
4. What was _____ (tasty) meal you ate?
5. What was _____ (bad) movie you saw?

3 Do you prefer shopping in a mall or in small stores? Use the ideas below and, in your notebook, write five sentences to answer the question.

Price	low/high
Service	friendly/rude quick/slow
Other	busy/quiet relaxing/stressful cold/hot/warm/wet good/poor choice

I prefer shopping in a mall because the prices aren't as high as in small stores ...

Grammar Time

GRAMMAR TIME

6.4 *Going to* and the Present Continuous

We use *going to* or the **Present Continuous** to talk about intentions, plans, and arrangements in the future.

Going to
We use *going to* to talk about intentions and plans which might change in the future.

I'm going to get there early.
We're not going to invite them.
Are you going to watch the soccer?

+	I	'm (am) going to buy a new car.
	You/We/They	're (are) going to go shopping.
	He/She/It	's (is) going to come home.
−	I	'm not (am not) going to buy a new car.
	You/We/They	aren't (are not) going to go shopping.
	He/She/It	isn't (is not) going to come home.
?	Am	I	going to buy a motorcycle?	Yes, I am. / No, I'm not.
	Are	you/we/they	going to go to a party?	Yes, you/we/they are. / No, you/we/they aren't.
	Is	he/she/it	going to stay?	Yes, he/she/it is. / No, he/she/it isn't.
	When	are	they	going to visit us?

Present Continuous
We use the Present Continuous to talk about arrangements. We often mention a time and/or place to show that the plan is more than just an intention.
The game is starting at 2:00.

Time expressions:
tonight   next Monday/weekend
tomorrow   on Thursday morning/afternoon

1 Finish these New Year's resolutions with *going to* and the ideas below (or your own).

> buy   get up   spend less/more time
> study   take up

1 I missed the school bus again. Next year,
  I 'm going to get up earlier every morning.
2 I'm not fit. Next year,
  I _____
3 I was so mean to my sister last year. Next year,
  I _____
4 My school grades aren't very good. Next year,
  I _____
5 English is such a useful language. Next year,
  I _____

2 Complete the questions below with the Present Continuous form of the verbs in parentheses. Then use Ben's note to ask and answer in pairs.

> TRIP TO HOUSTON – Saturday
> • train from Conroe to Houston – leave 8:30 a.m. and arrive 9:40 a.m.
> • meet Aunty Hannah for lunch – National Gallery café, 12:30 p.m.
> • train to Conroe from Houston – 6:35 p.m.

1 What station **is Ben leaving** (Ben/leave) from?
  He's leaving from Conroe.
2 What time _____ (he/arrive) in Houston?
3 What time _____ (he/catch) the train home?
4 Who _____ (Ben/meet) in Houston?
5 What time _____ (he/meet) her?
6 Where _____ (they/have) lunch?

7.2 *Will* for future predictions

We use *will* to make predictions about the future.

+	I/You/He/She/It/We/They	'll (will) win the game.
−	I/You/He/She/It/We/They	won't (will not) lose.
?	Will	I/you/he/she/it/we/they	win?	Yes, I/you/he/she/it/we/they will. No, I/you/he/she/it/we/they won't.
	What time	will	the game	start?
	How	will	you	get there?

I think this will happen.
I don't think this will happen.
NOT ~~I think this won't happen~~.

Time expressions
tomorrow   next week/month/year
in 2035/twenty years/the future
by (= before) 2035/Christmas/my twentieth birthday/this time tomorrow/the end of the week

Grammar Time 113

GRAMMAR TIME

1 Complete the sentences with *will* or *won't* to make them true for you.

1. My country _won't_ win the next soccer World Cup.
2. It _____ be bright and sunny tomorrow.
3. I _____ become famous in the next fifteen years.
4. We _____ get a surprise English test by the end of the week.
5. The world _____ end in 2035.
6. A teacher _____ give us a test today.

2 In your notebook, write six sentences about life in 2035. Use the ideas below.

> classrooms   a typical school schedule
> popular gadgets   travel
> fashion   best and worst jobs

Classrooms will be very different in 2035. There won't be so many students and …

7.4   First Conditional

We use the First Conditional for things that will possibly or probably happen in the future if something happens in the present.

Simple Present	will + verb
If she studies hard,	she'll pass the test.
If you don't pass,	I'll be disappointed.
If he doesn't pass,	his mom won't be happy.

We can change the order of the clauses without changing the meaning. We don't use a comma if the *will/won't* clause comes first

will + verb	Simple Present
She'll pass the test	if she studies hard.
I'll be disappointed	if you don't pass.
His mom won't be happy	if he doesn't pass.

In questions, it's more usual to begin with *will*.

will + verb	Simple Present
Will you be angry	if you don't pass the test?
What will you do	if you get the best grade?

1 Use the verbs in parentheses to make First Conditional sentences.

1. If I _become_ (become) famous, I _won't forget_ (not forget) my friends.
2. I _____ (tell) Mom if you _____ (do) that again.
3. If my dad _____ (not get) a new job, we _____ (not move) to a new house.
4. You _____ (not pass) if you _____ (not do) any homework.
5. If Patrick _____ (help) me, I _____ (help) him.
6. If you _____ (not panic), you _____ (get) a good grade in the test.
7. How _____ (you/feel) if you _____ (not pass) the test?
8. _____ (she/help) me if I _____ (ask) her?

2 In pairs, use the ideas below to make First Conditional sentences. Write them in your notebook.

1. pass all my tests → have a party
   If I pass all my tests, I'll have a party.
2. we make a lot of noise → my parents tell us to be quiet
3. have a math test → stay home to study
4. get tired of studying → play a board game

8.2   Present Perfect – all forms

We use the Present Perfect to talk about completed actions in the past when we don't say when they happened.

+	I/You/We/They He/She/It	've (have) swum with dolphins. 's (has) visited Canada.	
–	I/You/We/They He/She/It	haven't (have not) swum with dolphins. hasn't (has not) visited Canada.	
?	Have	I/you/we/they	enjoyed it?	Yes, I/you/we/they have. No, I/you/we/they haven't.
	Has	he/she/it	learned a lot?	Yes, he/she/it has. No, he/she/it hasn't.
	Where	have	you	been?

To form the Present Perfect, we use *have/has* and the past participle.

For regular verbs, the past participle is the same as past form of verbs.

I have finished.   She hasn't tried.   We've stopped.

Many past participles are irregular (see verb list on page 118).

They have eaten.
He's gone.
Have you slept?

114 Grammar Time

GRAMMAR TIME

Present Perfect with *ever/never*

We often use the Present Perfect with ***ever*** in questions. It means "at any time before now."
Have you ever been to Spain?

We also use the Present Perfect with ***never***. It means "at no time before now."
No, I've never been to Spain.

1 Complete the text with the Present Perfect form of the verbs in parentheses.

ASK TODD!

Gemma ¹ *has written* (write) to ask me if it's better to travel with friends or family. Well, it depends. Some of my nicest travel experiences ² _____ (be) with my friends. My best friend, Scott, ³ _____ (travel) with me a lot, we ⁴ _____ (have) much fun, and we ⁵ _____ (not fall) out! But my sister ⁶ _____ (never/be) abroad with me because we always argue when we're traveling!

2 In your notebook, write questions with *ever* and the Present Perfect using the ideas below. Then ask and answer in pairs.

> travel alone
> go to a restaurant with friends
> go on a school trip abroad
> buy clothes without your parents
> meet someone from another continent

A: *Have you ever traveled alone?*
B: *No, I've never traveled alone. / Yes, I have.*

3 In your notebook, write five sentences about things you have never done, but hope to do in the future.

I've never been to New York – I hope to go there in the future.

8.4 Present Perfect with *already*, *just*, and *yet*

We use ***already*** and ***just*** in affirmative sentences with the Present Perfect. *Already* and *just* usually come immediately before the main verb.
He's just called. (= recently/a short time ago)
I've already checked the timetable. (= earlier than expected)

We use ***yet*** in negative sentences and questions with the Present Perfect. *Yet* usually comes at the end of the negative statements or questions.
We haven't bought all the food yet. (It hasn't happened, but will probably happen soon.)
Have you bought tickets yet?

1 Complete the sentences with *just* and the Present Perfect form of the verbs below.

> make   ~~go~~   clean   fix   miss   go

1 There's a lot of food in the refrigerator. I *'ve just gone* shopping.
2 I _____ my computer. It's working again!
3 Mia _____ lunch. It's on the table.
4 Rona _____ her bedroom. It's looking better now!
5 I'm afraid you can't speak to Mom now. She _____ to work.
6 We _____ the bus – we'll be late now!

2 In your notebook, rewrite the underlined sentences using *yet* or *already*.

1 Jason has arrived at the campsite. He's putting up his tent.
Jason has already arrived at the campsite.
2 I'm not hungry, thanks. I've had breakfast.
3 Hurry up! Have you finished?
4 Wow – you're slow! We've finished.
5 She can't come. She hasn't done her homework.
6 Have they gotten their final grades?

STUDENT ACTIVITIES

Unit 2 — Lesson 2.1, Activity 6

1 T
2 T
3 F
4 T
5 T
6 T

Unit 2 — Lesson 2.4, Activity 6

Use the prompts below to answer the questions in Activity 6, on page 24.

1 Lee / call / police ✓
2 police / help / them ✗
3 look downtown / then / return / park
4 dog / be / there ✗
5 he / start / panic / imagine / awful things

Unit 6 — Lesson 6.2, Activity 4

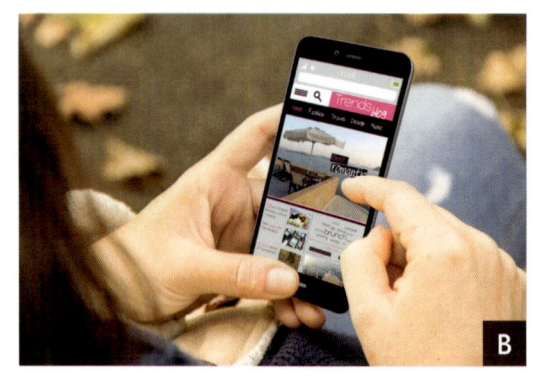

A

B

C

Unit 6 — Lesson 6.3, Activity 1

1 Why do they play music all the time?
 Because then people relax and stay longer.
2 Why is it hard to find the exit?
 Because if people can't get out easily, they stay longer and spend more money.
3 Why is it a long way from the up escalators to the down escalators?
 Because then shoppers walk past more stores.

Unit 6 — Lesson 6.5, Activity 5

How important is money to you?

Give yourself 2 points for every a) answer and 1 point for every b) answer.

5–6 points

For you, money is like water. When you're thirsty, you have to drink. When you have money, you have to spend it. You don't know how to save money.

7–8 points

For you, money is useful and important, but you don't worry about it all the time. You are generous, but intelligent with your money. You don't spend more than you have, but you don't try to save every cent.

9–10 points

For you, money is a wonderful thing. It is so wonderful that you don't want to spend it. Maybe you need to learn how to enjoy spending money.

Unit 8 — Lesson 8.6, Activity 7

Student A

1 You want to check a website. Your friend has his/her laptop with him/her.
2 You're on the bus. There's a free seat next to your friend.

Student B

1 You want to check a word. Your friend has a dictionary.
2 You're on the bus. A window's open and it's very cold.

STUDENT ACTIVITIES

Unit 1 — Self-check, Activity 7

Student B

You work at a movie theater. Use the information in the chart to answer Student A's questions.

FILMWORLD CINEPLEX	
Film	Time
X-Men: the End **Sold Out**	6:40 / 8:30
Up 2 **Row 7 – No, Row 6 – Yes**	6:50 / 8:40
Tickets	$6.95

Unit 2 — Self-check, Activity 6

Student B

1 Student A started the argument, but it was your fault, too. You like Student A a lot and want to stay friends with him/her. Accept Student A's apology.
2 You posted an embarrassing picture of Student A online. Now you feel bad about it. Apologize.

Unit 3 — Self-check, Activity 7

Student B

1 Listen to Student A's story.
2 Use phrases like *Awesome!/No way!*
3 Ask questions to show you are listening: *How did you feel? / What did you do? / Why did you do that?*, etc.

Unit 4 — Self-check, Activity 6

Student B

1 Give Student A advice on how to change the decoration in his/her bedroom. If he/she rejects your ideas, give him/her different advice.
2 You want to organize a surprise party for a friend. Ask Student A for advice. Then accept or reject the advice.

Unit 5 — Self-check, Activity 5

Student B

1 Answer Student A's question – you're unhappy because you have a bad toothache.
2 Listen to Student A's advice.
3 Thank Student A for his/her advice.

Unit 6 — Self-check, Activity 6

Student B

1 You are a salesclerk in a sports store. Help Student A buy a new sweatsuit.
2 You go to a shoe store to buy a new pair of shoes. You can't decide between boots or sneakers.

Unit 7 — Self-check, Activity 7

Student B

1 You are at a Student Careers office. You enjoy working with your hands, being creative, working alone, and being in contact with nature.
2 You're thinking of working as an accountant.
3 Listen to Student A's advice. Say which advice you agree with: *I probably won't enjoy … / I might/may be good at working as a …*

Unit 8 — Self-check, Activity 7

Student B

1 Student A wants to go mountain biking tomorrow and asks for permission to use your bike. Refuse permission. You want to use the bike yourself tomorrow. Then Student A asks for permission to borrow a helmet. Give permission. You have an extra helmet you never use.
2 You hear that Student A is going on a camping trip with his/her family. Ask for permission to go with him/her. If Student B agrees, say you don't have a tent and ask for permission to share Student A's tent.

IRREGULAR VERBS LIST

INFINITIVE	SIMPLE PAST	PAST PARTICIPLE
be	was/were	been
become	became	become
begin	began	begun
break	broke	broken
bring	brought	brought
build	built	built
burn	burned/burnt	burned/burnt
buy	bought	bought
can	could	been able to
catch	caught	caught
choose	chose	chosen
come	came	come
cost	cost	cost
cut	cut	cut
do	did	done
draw	drew	drawn
dream	dreamed/dreamt	dreamed/dreamt
drink	drank	drunk
drive	drove	driven
eat	ate	eaten
fall	fell	fallen
feed	fed	fed
feel	felt	felt
fight	fought	fought
find	found	found
fly	flew	flown
forget	forgot	forgotten
forgive	forgave	forgiven
get	got	got
give	gave	given
go	went	gone
grow	grew	grown
hang	hung	hung
have	had	had
hear	heard	heard
hide	hid	hidden
hit	hit	hit
hold	held	held
hurt	hurt	hurt
keep	kept	kept

INFINITIVE	SIMPLE PAST	PAST PARTICIPLE
know	knew	known
learn	learned/learnt	learned/learnt
leave	left	left
lend	lent	lent
let	let	let
lie	lay	lain
lose	lost	lost
make	made	made
meet	met	met
pay	paid	paid
put	put	put
read	read	read
ride	rode	ridden
ring	rang	rung
run	ran	run
say	said	said
see	saw	seen
sell	sold	sold
send	sent	sent
set	set	set
shine	shone	shone
sing	sang	sung
sit	sat	sat
sleep	slept	slept
speak	spoke	spoken
spell	spelled/spelt	spelled/spelt
spend	spent	spent
stand	stood	stood
steal	stole	stolen
sweep	swept	swept
swim	swam	swum
take	took	taken
teach	taught	taught
tell	told	told
think	thought	thought
understand	understood	understood
wake	woke	woken
wear	wore	worn
win	won	won
write	wrote	written

Irregular verbs list

WORKBOOK

W WELCOME TO CHESTERTON

1 Complete the words from the descriptions.

1 Your father's sister is your:
a <u>u n t</u>
2 Your father's sister's child is your:
c _ _ _ _ _ _
3 Your father's father is your:
g _ _ _ _ _ _ _ _ _ _ _
4 Your father's brother is your:
u _ _ _ _
5 Your brother is your father's:
s _ _

2 Complete the sentences with the correct possessive adjectives.

1 Hi! I'm Lucas and this is ___my___ brother. _____ name is Fernando.
2 Hi! My name is Petra and this is _____ cousin. _____ name is Ana.
3 Penelope and I are sisters. _____ last name is Souza.
4 My parents have a car. _____ car is blue.
5 Hi! Is _____ name Mark?

3 Circle the correct option.

1 The (boy's) / boys name is Gary.
2 My cousin's / cousins are Tina and Tom.
3 My parents / parents' dog is Rusty.
4 Pam is the children's / childrens' mom.
5 Harry and Jan's / Harry's and Jan's house is in Cape Town.

4 Write the dates in words.

1 2/11   _February eleventh_
2 6/15   _____
3 11/26 _____
4 4/02   _____
5 7/30   _____

5 **WORD FRIENDS** Match words 1-9 to words and phrases a-i to make Word Friends.

1 [e] listening   a TV
2 [ ] playing   b photos
3 [ ] surfing   c relatives
4 [ ] watching   d to the movies
5 [ ] going   e to music
6 [ ] doing   f a book
7 [ ] taking   g video games
8 [ ] visiting   h nothing
9 [ ] reading   i the internet

6 Match sports 1-8 to pictures A-H.

1 [E] cycling   5 [ ] volleyball
2 [ ] swimming   6 [ ] soccer
3 [ ] tennis   7 [ ] running
4 [ ] basketball   8 [ ] judo

7 Match words 1-6 to pictures A-F.

1 [F] sneakers   4 [ ] a backpack
2 [ ] a pencil case 5 [ ] keys
3 [ ] a helmet   6 [ ] sunglasses

Welcome!

8 Use the picture clues to complete the crossword with the school subjects.

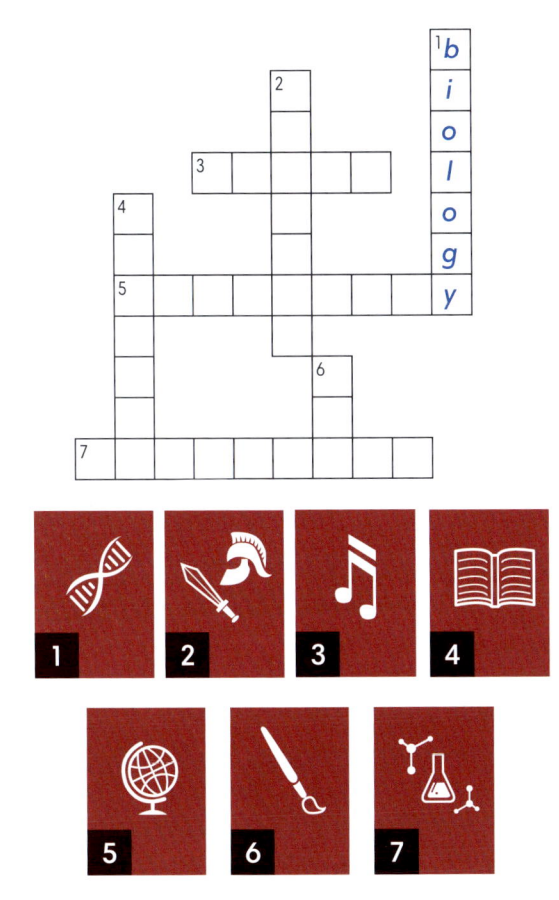

9 Write affirmative and negative sentences and questions with *there is/there are*.

1 a TV / in your bedroom **?**
  Is there a TV in your bedroom?

2 books / in the kitchen ✗

3 posters / in the classroom ✓

4 sneakers / in your sports bag **?**

5 a game / on the computer ✓

6 a dictionary / in the classroom ✗

7 a cell phone / in your backpack **?**

10 Use the pictures and the verbs below to complete sentences 1–8 about the people's abilities.

| drive play repair speak ~~shoot~~ bake read draw |

1 Dan   *can shoot a basketball.*
2 Joe
3 Peter
4 Chris
5 Helen
6 Ben
7 Jenna
8 Beth

11 Write questions and short answers for the sentences in Activity 10.

1 A: *Can Dan shoot a basketball?*
  B: *Yes, he can.*
2
3
4
5
6
7
8

12 Circle the correct option.

1 *Have /* (*Are*) *you sixteen?*
2 *Do / Does you have any brothers?*
3 *Are / Is there a café near your school?*
4 *Is / Are there any posters in your room?*
5 *Is / Can your sister drive a car?*
6 *Does / Is your dad use social media?*
7 *Are / Can you speak Italian?*

Welcome! 121

1 TIME FOR CULTURE

1 Complete the words in the sentences.

1 My friend, Hannah, is an amazing d <u>a n c e r</u>.
2 My sister is a great _ u _ i _ _ _. She can play the piano really well.
3 My favorite w _ _ t _ _ is J. K. Rowling.
4 My brother's a good p _ o _ o _ _ a _ h _ _ _. He has a cool camera!
5 I don't really like modern art, but I really like old _ r _ _ s _ s like Leonardo Da Vinci.
6 I think Mark Ruffalo is a very good _ c _ _ _. He's in lots of great movies.

2 Complete the sentences with the correct words.

| don't   hate   really   into   ~~love~~   interested |

1 I <u>love</u> samba. It's cool!
2 I'm not _____ in graphic novels.
3 I'm _____ acting. I'd love to be an actor.
4 I _____ documentaries. They're so boring!
5 I _____ like dancing much.
6 I'm _____ interested in drawing. I like art.

3 **WORD FRIENDS** Match the parts of the sentences.

1 [d] I like playing   a faces.
2 [ ] I like listening   b comic books.
3 [ ] I like drawing   c pictures.
4 [ ] I like reading   d the violin.
5 [ ] I like watching   e to hip-hop.
6 [ ] I like taking   f cartoons.

4 Complete the words from the descriptions.

1 You can watch movies in this place: m <u>o v i e   t h e a t e r</u>
2 This person can paint pictures very well: a _____
3 This is a musical instrument: v _____
4 This is a scary movie: h _____ m _____
5 This is a funny movie: c _____
6 You can do this if you have a camera: p _____
7 This is a classical type of dancing: b _____
8 You can read this: n _____

5 Complete the sentences with the correct words.

| piano   salsa   director   ~~comedy~~   short stories   rock |

1 This is my favorite <u>comedy</u>. It's really funny.
2 I want to learn to play the _____.
3 I have a really good book of _____. I read one every day.
4 I know all the actors in the movie, but not the _____.
5 I want to go to _____ classes. It's a great dance!
6 I love _____ music and I always listen to it in my room.

6 Use the letters to write the correct words.

1 I like TRACIMON <u>romantic</u> movies, but I prefer DEMISOEC _____.
2 I'm really into NICNAGD _____ and I'd like to go to TEBLAL _____ classes.
3 Our teacher is a great ISNAUMIC _____ and he can play the RIGTUA _____.
4 People who are good at GRINDAW _____ can make TROCNOA _____ movies.
5 I'm not into DREGANI _____, but I like TWICGAHN _____ movies.

7 Circle the correct option.

whatareyouinto.com

TV, MUSIC, ART, ACTING??
What are YOU into?

guy15   24 Aug 11:05

I ¹(really) / very love books and I am reading a ²cartoon / graphic novel at the moment. The ³writer / director is a good ⁴musician / artist, too and the pictures are great. There's a ⁵documentary / fantasy movie of the book and I want to see it at the ⁶movie theater / concert. I'm ⁷love / interested in drawing and ⁸taking / making pictures, too. Maybe I can write a novel like this! But I'm also ⁹in / into acting in plays so maybe I can be a(n) ¹⁰actor / photographer! Who knows?

Tweet 13   Like 4

Unit 1

8 Complete the sentences with the correct affirmative form of the Simple Present of the verbs in parentheses.
1. My brother _likes_ (like) hip-hop.
2. My friends _____ (go) to a café after school.
3. I _____ (play) video games.
4. My teacher _____ (write) poems.
5. I _____ (speak) English.
6. My English friend _____ (live) in London.

9 Rewrite the sentences in Activity 8 in the negative form.
1. *My brother doesn't like hip-hop.*
2. _____
3. _____
4. _____
5. _____
6. _____

10 Write the adverbs of frequency in parentheses in the correct place in the sentences.
1. We go to the movies. (never)
   We never go to the movies.
2. I read short stories. (sometimes)
   _____
3. My brother is in his room. (always)
   _____
4. I'm interested in new songs. (always)
   _____
5. My mom goes to salsa classes on Mondays. (usually)
   _____
6. My classmates are bored in Mr. Tutt's classes! (never)
   _____

11 Order the words to make sentences or questions.
1. like / Hannah / reading / does / ?
   Does Hannah like reading?
2. video / with / often / friends / I / my / games / play
   _____
3. understand / you / Spanish / do / ?
   _____
4. don't / buy / online / I / clothes / usually
   _____
5. teacher / car / drive / doesn't / our / a
   _____
6. never / for / Tom / class / late / is
   _____

12 Complete the text with the correct form of the verbs in parentheses.

I often ¹ _go_ (go) to the movies with my friends on the weekend. We ² _____ (not go) in the evenings because we ³ _____ (do) our homework then. Our teacher ⁴ _____ (not be) happy if we ⁵ _____ (hand) homework in late! What kind of movies ⁶ _____ (we/watch)? Action movies, because they're exciting! I like romantic movies, but my best friend ⁷ _____ (not like) them, so sometimes my sister and I ⁸ _____ (watch) romantic movies at home. It's always nice to watch a movie with someone else! ⁹ _____ (your sister/watch) movies with you?

Unit 1

1 TIME FOR CULTURE

13 Read the article. Match paragraphs 1–4 to headings a–e. There is one extra heading.

a The right time for you
b A new way to watch TV
c Marathon TV
d Too much choice?
e With others or alone?

PEOPLE TODAY WATCH TV IN DIFFERENT WAYS

OUR READERS TELL US ABOUT HOW THEY AND THEIR FAMILIES WATCH TV.

Jake, 14, from New Zealand

1 [e] I usually watch TV shows on my laptop in my room, but sometimes I watch them with my family. There is a smart TV in our living room. That's good because we don't often spend a lot of time together. Also we can talk about the movie or TV show and sometimes have arguments! But one problem is that my family often disagrees about what they want to watch! In my room I can choose my own shows.

2 When we're not at home, my mom records our favorite shows on our smart TV and we all watch them together later. That way we can cut all the commercials – which is great! I like to watch movies and series online, too. You can watch anything, even really old TV series! But you get the commercials, too.

3 My brother never watches much TV because he spends all his time checking different channels. He watches for a few minutes and then gets bored and looks for another show! In the end he never watches a complete show.

4 My dad doesn't have much time to watch TV during the week, so on weekends he watches about four hours of shows like *Downton Abbey* using a streamling platform. They say teenagers watch a lot of TV, but in our family, it's my dad!

14 Read the article again. Mark the sentences ✓ (right), ✗ (wrong), or ? (doesn't say).

1 [✗] Jake's family does a lot of things together.
2 [ ] They usually have the same opinions.
3 [ ] Jake prefers shows without breaks.
4 [ ] Jake's brother doesn't like watching TV.
5 [ ] Jake likes *Downton Abbey.*
6 [ ] Jake's father works in the evenings.

15 Complete the sentences with the correct words from the text.

| live   online   ~~channel~~   commercials

1 I want to watch the new documentary tonight. Which _channel_ is it on?
2 I often watch series _____ because I'm out a lot in the evenings.
3 When I watch a movie and the _____ come on, I go out and get a glass of water or something!
4 My dad never records programs. He always watches _____ TV.

16 Circle the correct option.

1 My grandparents are *teenagers /* (*older people*) and they often watch TV during the day.
2 My brother is a *teenager / kid* and watches a lot of children's shows and cartoons.
3 *Teenagers / Adults* can't watch too much TV when they have school tests.
4 There are many news shows on TV in the evening. A lot of *kids / adults* watch them.

17 Decide if the verbs in the sentences show a fact (F), a routine (R), something happening during a period of time (P), or something happening right now (N).

1 [F] My mom works in a hospital.
2 [ ] She always gets up at 6:30 a.m. and takes a taxi to work.
3 [ ] Today she is feeling sick, so she's staying at home.
4 [ ] At the moment she's sitting in bed and sending some emails.
5 [ ] She has friends in lots of different countries.
6 [ ] She's working with a new team of doctors this week.
7 [ ] She usually finishes work at 6:00 p.m.
8 [ ] Oh – the phone is ringing. Maybe it's the hospital.

Unit 1

18 Match the parts of the sentences.
1. [c] Cathy doesn't usually go to bed late,
2. [ ] She really enjoys TV series,
3. [ ] She knows a lot of languages,
4. [ ] She usually goes to other countries on vacation,
5. [ ] She sometimes plays the guitar in a band,
6. [ ] She doesn't often go out during the week,

a but she hates game shows.
b but she's staying home this week.
c but she's watching a movie right now and it's already midnight!
d but this week she's playing the drums.
e but she's hanging out at the snack bar with us right now.
f but she doesn't speak Italian.

19 Complete the sentences with the correct present form of the verbs.
1. I usually have cereal for breakfast. Today, I'm _having_ some fruit, too.
2. Danny doesn't always come to extra math classes after school. He _____ this week because his grades are getting worse!
3. It always _____ when I'm on vacation and look – it's raining now!
4. I know you play tennis a lot. _____ this weekend?
5. My brother usually watches game shows, but tonight he _____ a news show.

20 Circle the correct option.
1. We (usually study) / are usually studying math on Mondays, but today we *take* / *'re taking* a test.
2. Jenna's listening to some music *and* / *but* she's watching TV at the same time! How?
3. I *don't do* / *'m not doing* my online homework at the moment because my laptop *doesn't work* / *isn't working*.
4. Harry is waiting for Lisa outside school, *and* / *but* she doesn't want to see him.
5. *Do you always have* / *Are you always having* a big breakfast before school? No, I *don't* / *'m not*.
6. My sister *usually wears* / *is usually wearing* jeans and a T-shirt, *and* / *but* today she *wears* / *'s wearing* a skirt and a jacket.

21 Complete the text with the correct form of the verbs.

play   sing (x3)   not get   hear
love   ~~have~~   enjoy

My friend Mia is amazing. She's only fifteen, but she ¹ _has_ an awesome part-time job. Every Friday and Saturday night she ² _____ with a band. She has a beautiful voice. Her brother ³ _____ the guitar. They're both really good musicians. They ⁴ _____ a lot of money, but they ⁵ _____ it. The band always ⁶ _____ in our classroom during the lunch break and I can ⁷ _____ them now. Mia ⁸ _____ an Ellie Goulding song and it's beautiful! I ⁹ _____ their music!

22 Match the types of media and TV shows 1–7 to pictures A–G.
1. [B] talk show
2. [ ] news show
3. [ ] documentary
4. [ ] TV series
5. [ ] reality show
6. [ ] game show
7. [ ] weather forecast

Unit 1

1 TIME FOR CULTURE

23 Match comments 1–7 to the types of media and TV shows from Activity 22.
1. I know all the answers. _game show_
2. That singer is awesome! ____
3. It's really interesting and the photography is beautiful. You can learn a lot. ____
4. That's the man's girlfriend. They're always arguing. ____
5. That's my favorite athlete. They also have my favorite actor and comedian on today. ____
6. Yes, it's sunny all week! ____
7. That's awful! I hope the people are all right. ____

24 Match questions 1–4 to answers a–d.
1. [c] What's on?
2. [ ] Can I have three tickets for *True Blue*?
3. [ ] How much is that?
4. [ ] Here you are.

a. That's $20.
b. Thanks. Enjoy the movie.
c. A fantasy movie, *True Blue*.
d. Sure, which screening?

25 Complete the dialogue with the correct phrases.

> No way   Here you are   which screening
> I'd like   That's   Enjoy the movie   ~~Let's go~~
> What's on   Can I have   Come on

A: ¹ _Let's go_ to the movies.
B: OK. ² _____?
A: Well, there's *Five Lives*. That's a horror movie.
B: ³ _____! I don't like horror movies.
A: ⁴ _____!
B: Well, OK. ⁵ _____ two tickets for *Five Lives*, please?
C: Sure, ⁶ _____?
B: The 7:30.
C: I'm sorry, it's sold out … Oh, no, hold on! There are two seats in the front row.
B: OK. ⁷ _____ two tickets, please. How much is that?
C: ⁸ _____ $16.80, please.
B: ⁹ _____.
C: Thank you. ¹⁰ _____.

26 Decide if the sentences give us personal information (P), information about hobbies/interests (H), or information about routines (R).
1. [P] I have one sister and two brothers.
2. [ ] I go to school by bus every day.
3. [ ] My big passion is books.
4. [ ] My best friend is Patsy.
5. [ ] I live in Marchwood.
6. [ ] I'm really into tennis and I'm good at it.
7. [ ] I'm in 8th grade at Brooklyn Middle School.

SELF-ASSESSMENT

Vocabulary

1 Complete the words in the sentences.

0 My brother plays the **d** _r u m s_ in a band.
1 I don't enjoy **c**_____ music, like Mozart or Beethoven.
2 My cousin is a **p**_____. She takes beautiful pictures.
3 I often watch **r**_____ movies where people are in love.
4 A lot of children love watching **c**_____, like *The Powerpuff Girls* or *Ben 10*.
5 **T**_____ music in my country uses hand clapping and wooden instruments.

/5

2 Complete the sentences with the correct words.

> listening   painting   ~~playing~~
> reading   taking   watching

0 We have a piano, but I hate _playing_ it.
1 My dad is crazy about _____ to old music.
2 My mom is really into _____ selfies.
3 I like _____ reviews about new movies.
4 Our family loves _____ TV series together.
5 I don't like _____ pictures in art classes at school.

/5

Grammar

3 Complete the dialogue with *do*, *does*, *don't*, or *doesn't*.

A: 0 _Do_ you like classical music?
B: No, I 1_____, but my sister 2_____.
A: 3_____ she like hip-hop music, too?
B: No, she 4_____, but I 5_____!

/5

4 Make sentences or questions from the prompts.

0 I / not / like / documentaries
 I don't like documentaries.
1 you / want / to go to the movies / ?
 _____
2 my friend / not / live / near me
 _____
3 Jack / speak / English and French
 _____
4 our teacher / usually / give / us a lot of homework
 _____
5 what time / you / go to bed on Fridays / ?
 _____

/5

5 Circle the correct option.

To: eva@hellomail.com
Subject: I need new clothes!

Hi Eva,
What 0(are you doing)/ do you do? I'm sure you 1're reading / read a book. You 2are reading / read every evening! I 3'm sitting / sit in my room at the moment. I 4'm trying / try to choose a dress to wear to the concert tonight. I need to buy some new clothes! 5Are you wanting / Do you want to come shopping with me on Saturday?
Anyway – see you later!
Jess

/5

Speaking language practice

6 Complete the dialogue.

A: What's 0 _on_ today?
B: There's a horror movie and a comedy.
A: 1_____ I have a ticket for the horror movie, please?
B: Is that for the 5:00 or the 6:00 2_____?
A: The five o'clock, please.
B: Sorry, it's 3_____ out.
A: OK, for the six o'clock, please.
B: There's a 4_____ in the front row.
A: How 5_____ is that?
B: That's $20, please.

/5

Vocabulary /10
Grammar /15
Speaking language practice /5
Your total score /30

Unit 1

2 ANIMAL MAGIC

1 Complete the names of the animals.
1. sh _a_ _r_ k
2. b u _ _ _ _ _ _ y
3. s p _ _ _ _ r
4. g i _ _ _ _ e
5. k a _ _ _ _ _ o
6. s n _ _ e
7. m o _ _ _ y
8. c h _ _ _ _ n

2 Find the animals from Activity 1 in the word search.

C	S	C	A	I	J	T	H	X	B	E	Y
H	V	W	A	A	E	Y	T	Y	O	E	P
I	O	C	L	T	F	S	L	O	K	S	N
C	G	I	R	A	F	F	E	N	P	N	E
K	A	N	G	A	R	O	O	F	N	Z	A
E	X	H	E	E	N	M	M	S	D	U	X
N	S	S	T	M	T	J	T	P	T	X	Y
S	V	T	B	W	S	F	X	I	L	S	E
O	U	H	C	Y	N	H	O	D	E	H	R
B	H	S	N	O	A	D	A	E	P	S	C
D	U	R	I	V	K	M	E	R	X	L	Q
S	R	O	T	S	E	C	D	B	K	L	S

3 Decide if the animals below are farm animals (F), wild animals (W), or insects (I).
1. [W] tiger
2. [ ] bear
3. [ ] ant
4. [ ] sheep
5. [ ] chimp
6. [ ] donkey
7. [ ] duck
8. [ ] chicken
9. [ ] spider
10. [ ] dolphin
11. [ ] cow
12. [ ] bee
13. [ ] monkey
14. [ ] fly
15. [ ] butterfly

4 Match descriptions 1–8 to animals a–h.
1. [g] It's very slow.
2. [ ] It's black and white.
3. [ ] It lives in the sea.
4. [ ] It visits flowers.
5. [ ] It's very, very big.
6. [ ] It gives us milk.
7. [ ] It can sometimes talk.
8. [ ] It has very long ears.

a parrot
b cow
c rabbit
d zebra
e dolphin
f bee
g tortoise
h elephant

5 Circle the correct answer.
1. Which animal doesn't have a tail?
   a butterfly (circled)
   b rabbit
   c zebra
2. Which animal doesn't have fur?
   a snake
   b chimp
   c tiger
3. Which animal doesn't have wings?
   a bee
   b dolphin
   c parrot
4. Which animal doesn't have feathers?
   a duck
   b parrot
   c ant
5. Which animal doesn't have claws?
   a rabbit
   b cow
   c bear

6 Complete the sentences with the correct words.

| tails   wings x2   ~~feathers~~   claws   fur |

1. Parrots have brightly colored _feathers_.
2. Monkeys use their _____ to hold onto trees when they jump.
3. Bears have different colored _____. Sometimes it's brown, sometimes white, and sometimes black.
4. Ducks have _____ and can fly when they want to.
5. Our dog has long _____ and we have to cut them from time to time.
6. The _____ of a butterfly are usually very pretty.

7 Circle the correct option.
1. A bee *swims* / *flies* (circled) and has *wings* / *claws*.
2. A duck *climbs* / *swims* and has *claws* / *feathers*.
3. A monkey *climbs* / *flies* and has *feathers* / *a tail*.
4. A tiger eats *vegetables* / *meat* and has *wings* / *claws*.
5. A rabbit *jumps* / *swims* and has *feathers* / *fur*.
6. A shark *walks* / *bites* and lives in the *forest* / *sea*.

Unit 2

8 Complete the email with the correct words.

> ducks   rabbits   ~~butterflies~~   sheep   tails
> wings   tortoise   claws

To: emma@fastmessage.com

Hi Emma,

When you're on vacation you have to visit the Wildlife Center. It's incredible! They have a special room with beautiful ¹ *butterflies* . They have very pretty ² _____ and there are hundreds of them flying all over the place. Sometimes they land on your arm or head! If you have your little sister with you, she can go to the petting zoo. They usually have some baby animals there. She can pick up the baby ³ _____ – their mothers are out in the field with their long woolly coats eating grass! And there are a lot of ⁴ _____ with their little round white fluffy ⁵ _____ . She can pick them up, but be careful because their ⁶ _____ can be quite sharp! If you want a new pet, you can buy one to take home! The center also sells their wooden houses to keep in the garden. The baby ⁷ _____ are really cute, too. They follow their mother in a long line to the river for a swim! And there's a ⁸ _____ that is nearly a hundred years old at the center, too! It lives in a warm box in the winter, but in the summer you can see it walking very, very slowly across the grass!

Have fun!
Chris

9 Complete the sentences with *was*, *wasn't*, *were*, and *weren't*.

1 I *wasn't* at school last week because I _____ on vacation with my parents.
2 We _____ in Spain, on the south coast.
3 We _____ in a very expensive hotel because dad wanted a cheap vacation! But it _____ nice and there _____ a lot of teenagers there – cool for me!
4 Our hotel _____ on the beach and I _____ in the water every day!
5 It _____ very hot, but the sea _____ quite warm and good for swimming.
6 There _____ an aquarium near the hotel and there _____ some interesting fish! There _____ any sharks or dolphins – just small fish.

10 Order the words to write questions.

1 after / you / soccer practice / tired / yesterday / were / ?
    Were you tired after soccer practice yesterday?
2 your / Saturday / party / were / at / the / friends / last /?
    _____
3 morning / Marie and Tim / class / were / this / in / ?
    _____
4 open / evening / mall / was / yesterday / the / ?
    _____
5 the / interesting / movie / was / ?
    _____
6 house / Jake / last / was / night / your / at / ?
    _____

11 Write short answers for the questions in Activity 10.

1 Yes, *I was* .
2 No, _____ .
3 Yes, _____ .
4 Yes, _____ .
5 No, _____ .
6 No, _____ .

12 Circle the correct option.

1 I was (in)/ on England in the summer.
2 We were *in* / *at* the movies on Saturday.
3 I was *at* / *on* home this morning.
4 Were you *at* / *in* Rob's party?
5 They weren't *in* / *at* the classroom at 9:15. It was empty.
6 The dog was *at* / *in* the park this afternoon.

Unit 2 129

2 ANIMAL MAGIC

13 Read the sentences and write questions about the underlined words.

1. We were in Switzerland <u>last week</u>.
   When were you in Switzerland?
2. They were <u>in the park</u> at lunch.
   _____
3. The weather was <u>hot</u> in Italy.
   _____
4. The movie was on TV <u>at 7:30</u>.
   _____
5. <u>Jessie</u> was on the phone.
   _____

14 Complete the dialogue with the correct words.

A: Hi! ¹ *Where* were you after school? You ² _____ at the café.
B: No, I ³ _____ . I was ⁴ _____ the park with my dog. The weather ⁵ _____ beautiful. There ⁶ _____ a lot of rabbits and she was very happy! ⁷ _____ Mark at the café?
A: Yes, he ⁸ _____ . He was with Sally from 8th grade. Later they ⁹ _____ at the movies together, too! I was there with Jenny.
B: ¹⁰ _____ was the movie?
A: *True Love!*
B: Ahhh! ¹¹ _____ it good?
A: It ¹² _____ very good, but Mark and Sally were happy. "True Love" I think!

15 Complete the words from the descriptions.

1. This is someone who can't remember things: f o r g e t f u l
2. This is someone who is cute and other people like a lot: l _ _ _ _ _
3. This is someone who gets angry and fights a lot: a _ _ _ _ _ _ _ _
4. This is someone who likes doing new and dangerous things: a _ _ _ _ _ _ _ _ _
5. This is someone who does things quickly without thinking: i _ _ _ _ _ _ _ _

16 Read the article below. Mark the sentences right (✓), wrong (✗), or doesn't say (?).

1. [?] All animals need to live with both parents for a short time.
2. [ ] There are some similarities between orangutan and human babies.
3. [ ] The orangutans' home is disappearing.
4. [ ] In school, baby orangutans learn different subjects from humans.
5. [ ] Orphaned orangutans always return to the jungle.
6. [ ] The International Animal Rescue charity can't save all the orphans.

School for Orangutans!

Everyone needs to go to school. We need to learn things that can help us when we grow up. But what about animals?

People say that animals are born with instincts and know naturally how to survive. However, that is not exactly true.

Animals depend a lot on their mothers, at least for a short time, to teach them different skills. So, what happens when they have no mothers? For many baby orangutans in Borneo this is an enormous problem. Young orangutans are like human babies because they stay with their mothers for a long time. They learn lots of skills from their mothers before they can live by themselves. But a lot of orangutans are dying in Borneo because people are cutting down the rainforests where they live. Babies are losing their mothers and it is impossible for them to survive. The charity International Animal Rescue tries to save them.

Today in Borneo there is a special school for orphaned baby orangutans! Volunteers teach them all the things they need to learn. In Baby School they learn how to climb trees, what to eat, and where to build nests to sleep safely. The good students go on to Forest School and later they return to the jungle. Humans aren't the same as mother orangutans, but they give these lovable babies a real chance to live.

17 Complete the sentences with the Simple Past form of the verbs.

help   walk   ~~want~~   arrive   decide   look

1 Olly ___wanted___ to be a vet when he was younger.
2 Jack _____ me with my animal project last night.
3 We _____ at pictures of Annie's cat this morning.
4 I _____ to take my sister Tilly to the zoo for her birthday.
5 Megan and Bree _____ late for class this morning.
6 The penguins at the zoo _____ in a funny way!

18 Complete the sentences with the negative form of the verbs.

1 I needed some paper. I ___didn't need___ a pen.
2 Harry called Leo. He _____ me.
3 We studied vocabulary. We _____ grammar.
4 They walked on the beach. They _____ in the park.
5 Dad promised to get us a cat. He _____ to get us a dog.
6 We watched a movie on TV. We _____ a movie online.

19 Order the words to write questions. Then write short answers.

1 you / did / yesterday / call / he / ?
   ___Did he call you yesterday?___
   Yes, ___he did___.
2 answer / question / teacher's / you / the / did / ?
   _____
   No, _____.
3 walk / party / they / to / did / the / ?
   _____
   Yes, _____.
4 police / did / dog / look / the / for / the / ?
   _____
   No, _____.
5 the / at / finish / 9:30 / TV / did / show / ?
   _____
   No, _____.

20 Complete the dialogues with the correct Simple Past form of the verbs.

1 (watch)
   A: ___Did you watch___ the documentary about wild animals last night?
   B: No, I ___didn't watch___ the documentary, but I ___watched___ a game show.
2 (call)
   A: When _____ Hannah?
   B: I _____ her at 7:30, but she wasn't at home.
3 (listen)
   A: _____ to Taylor Swift's new song?
   B: Yes, I _____ to it last night. It was brilliant.
4 (end)
   A: When _____?
   B: The movie _____ after midnight! It was late.
5 (play)
   A: What _____ at the concert?
   B: The band _____ their new song, but they _____ all their old ones.
6 (rain)
   A: _____ while you were on vacation?
   B: No, it _____. It was sunny every day.

21 Complete the dialogue with the correct form of the verbs.

print   change   play   promise   ~~ask~~
not play   look   not finish   decide

A: Did you start the animal project last night?
B: Yes, I did. I ¹ ___asked___ Andy to help me.
A: But he ² _____ tennis last night.
B: He ³ _____ his plans.
   He ⁴ _____ tennis.
   He ⁵ _____ to help me instead!
A: That was really nice of him!
B: I know. We ⁶ _____ online and
   ⁷ _____ some interesting articles about wildlife in Africa.
   We ⁸ _____, but he ⁹ _____ to help me again tonight.

2 ANIMAL MAGIC

22 **WORD FRIENDS** Match the parts of the sentences. Then match sentences 1–6 to pictures A–F.

1. [d] Cats often give
2. [ ] I brush
3. [ ] I have to empty
4. [ ] I usually take
5. [ ] Our cat scratches
6. [ ] If you get a big dog, it can protect

a our furniture and mom gets mad.
b my dog for a walk after school.
c your home.
d people allergies.
e my dog's fur every day.
f our cat's litter box because it smells!

A
B
C
D
E (1)
F

23 Complete the chart with the phrases.

> ~~It's all my fault.~~   I'm so sorry.
> These things happen.
> I'm really angry about this.   No problem.

Apologizing	I apologize. / I feel terrible. It was an accident. *It's all my fault.*
Accepting apologies	It's not your fault. Never mind. I totally understand.
Not accepting apologies	You promised to. You can't be serious! How could you be so careless?

24 Circle the correct response.

1. I'm sorry I'm late.
   a Good for you!
   b Here you are.
   c No problem. ⓒ
2. I'm sorry – I dropped your book in the bathtub.
   a Oh, come on, please!
   b It's all my fault.
   c These things happen.
3. I'm sorry, I didn't remember to bring your book.
   a Never mind.
   b Here you are.
   c Good job.
4. I'm sorry I knocked your tortoise off the table.
   a That's amazing!
   b What's wrong?
   c How could you be so careless!
5. I'm sorry I burned the dinner.
   a I don't get it!
   b These things happen.
   c How much is that?

25 Complete the sentences with *in*, *on*, or *at*.

1. Taylor Swift was born ___in___ 1989. She's my favorite singer.
2. Do you take your dog for a walk _____ the morning?
3. Dad took our cat to the vet _____ Monday.
4. What did you do _____ New Year's Day?
5. They finished the English test _____ 11:15. It was a difficult test.
6. Marissa celebrated her birthday with a big party _____ the weekend.
7. My grandparents often go out _____ night. They never go to bed early.
8. The Taylors didn't travel _____ July, but they had a lot of fun.

132 Unit 2

SELF-ASSESSMENT

Vocabulary

1 Circle the odd one out.

0 **Insects:**
beetle (snake) ant
1 **Farm animals:**
cow   sheep   bear
2 **Water animals:**
monkey   dolphin   shark
3 **Large animals:**
giraffe   duck   elephant
4 **Flying animals:**
butterfly   rabbit   parrot
5 **Animal skin:**
fur   feather   claw

/5

2 Complete the sentences with the correct adjective.

| adventurous   ~~aggressive~~   careless |
| forgetful   impulsive   shy |

0 Someone who likes to fight and shout is _aggressive_.
1 Someone who doesn't like talking or meeting people is _____.
2 Someone who can't remember things is _____.
3 Someone who does things without thinking for a long time is _____.
4 Someone who likes trying new things is _____.
5 Someone who isn't careful is _____.

/5

3 Circle the correct option.

0 A big dog can (protect) / feed your home.
1 I *take* / *brush* my dog's fur every day.
2 My brother's job is to *scratch* / *empty* his cat's litter tray in the morning.
3 Cats *make* / *give* my sister allergies.
4 Don't allow your pets to *brush* / *scratch* the furniture.
5 How often do you *go* / *take* your dog for a walk?

/5

Grammar

4 Write sentences using the correct past form of *be*.

0 I / in bed early last night [✓]
I was in bed early last night.
1 your parents / at the concert on Saturday [?]
_____
2 That documentary / very interesting [✗]
_____
3 Tom / at your party [?]
_____
4 What / your favorite movie last year [?]
_____
5 There / any monkeys at the safari park [✗]
_____

/5

5 Complete the sentences using the correct Simple Past form of the verbs in parentheses.

- When I ⁰ _was_ (be) younger I ¹ _____ (not like) classical music.
- Where ² _____ (you/live) before you ³ _____ (move) here last year?
- My dad ⁴ _____ (not work) last month because he ⁵ _____ (be) sick.

/5

Speaking language practice

6 Complete the dialogues with the correct words.

| accident   all   angry   can't   could   ~~so~~   totally |

- A: I'm ⁰ _so_ sorry. It's ¹ _____ my fault.
  B: Never mind. I ² _____ understand.
- A: I apologize. It was an ³ _____.
  B: How ⁴ _____ you be so careless? I'm really ⁵ _____ about this!

/5

Vocabulary /15
Grammar /10
Speaking language practice /5
Your total score /30

Unit 2

3 NEW TECHNOLOGY

1 Label pictures 1–8 with the correct words.

drone   smartphone   tablet   stylus   e-reader
digital camera   smart TV   ~~games console~~

1 _____
2 _____
3 _____
4 *games console*
5 _____
6 _____
7 _____
8 _____

2 Complete the sentences with the correct words from Activity 1.

1 My best gift ever was a __*games console*__. I play on it a lot with my friends.
2 My dad doesn't like my _____. He says he likes to turn over real pages!
3 I use my _____ for everything – to take pictures, listen to music, watch videos … good thing it fits in my pocket!
4 My brother loves flying his _____, but I think it's annoying!
5 My grandma plays card games online on her _____. She loves it!
6 On Friday nights, my family sits in the living room to watch movies on our _____.
7 My sister takes lots of pictures and my dad gave her a cool _____ for her birthday.

3 **WORD FRIENDS** Complete the words in the sentences.

1 I l_i s t e n_ to music on the bus.
2 I s __ r __ the internet every day.
3 I t _____ pictures with my digital camera.
4 I r __ a __ books on my e-reader.
5 I w __ t _____ movies on my tablet.
6 I c _____ c __ emails on my smartphone.
7 I m _____ videos on my computer.
8 I p __ a __ games on my games console.

4 Match the parts of the sentences.

1 [h] I always listen
2 [ ] We're reading
3 [ ] My friend checks
4 [ ] My dad downloads
5 [ ] I like sending
6 [ ] My mom's phone doesn't take
7 [ ] Some friends and I made
8 [ ] After school I often surf

a a good book in our English classes this term.
b the internet for hours.
c text messages in class and the teacher gets angry with her.
d a video and uploaded it to YouTube.
e programs regularly for his work.
f messages because it's quick.
g pictures because it's really old!
h to music when I'm traveling.

5 Complete the sentences with the correct words.

~~battery~~   flash drive   USB ports   memory
keyboard   joystick

1 I need to get a new __*battery*__ for my digital camera.
2 I can't read the letter "E" on my _____ anymore!
3 The _____ for my games console is broken.
4 My cell phone doesn't have enough _____ to download all the pictures.
5 There are several _____ on my laptop – they're really useful.
6 How much is a _____? I'd like to store my pictures on one.

134 Unit 3

6 Circle the correct answer.
1 My friend is making a _____ of her dog to post online.
   a memory   **b** video   c text
2 My _____ isn't working and I can't listen to my favorite music.
   a message   b tablet   c console
3 If your cell phone _____ is full, you can't download any more pictures.
   a file   b joystick   c memory
4 You plug this into your _____ and then you can store files on it.
   a flash drive   b battery   c USB port
5 How often do you _____ your emails?
   a surf   b check   c watch

7 Complete the blog with the correct words.

My blog

ABOUT ME | NEW POSTS | CONTACT ME

computerfan100 6:45 p.m.

I guess I'm addicted to the internet! I'm always on my computer and I love my gadgets! When I wake up, I ¹ _check_ my emails and texts. While I'm having breakfast, I listen to music on my smartphone and send some ² _____ to my best friend. I don't often call her because it's quicker and easier to speak online! I take my ³ _____ in my pocket with me everywhere – even to class. I can go online and ⁴ _____ the internet for information – that's educational! At recess and after school, I ⁵ _____ games on my phone. In the evening I sometimes turn on the ⁶ _____ and watch a movie on our big screen. I don't have many printed books because I read them on an ⁷ _____ and I keep all my pictures on a really small ⁸ _____, which I keep in my pocket. At the end of the day, my phone and tablet batteries are down, so I ⁹ _____ them before I go to bed. I can't imagine living without my gadgets!

COMMENTS 0 | LIKES

8 Write the Simple Past forms of the irregular verbs.
1 cost _cost_   5 forget _____
2 buy _____   6 go _____
3 lose _____   7 take _____
4 do _____   8 find _____

9 Find the irregular Simple Past forms of the verbs in the word search.

~~eat~~ have put send leave do
see get steal give

A	T	O	S	C	N	P	T	E	P
N	T	V	R	Q	A	U	G	Y	A
C	D	I	R	D	E	T	L	O	I
T	I	S	A	I	W	S	E	N	T
T	S	H	E	D	T	T	F	E	M
A	N	D	E	N	N	O	T	H	E
G	O	L	P	N	P	L	S	V	W
D	I	E	O	T	F	E	A	H	W
D	A	P	P	X	R	G	W	Z	Q
Z	I	G	T	C	S	C	E	R	N

10 Complete the sentences with the Simple Past form of the verbs.

put send steal cost ask ~~get~~
forget see give

1 Harry _got_ a new laptop for his birthday last month.
2 A thief _____ Rianna's cell phone and her tablet during lunchbreak.
3 I _____ Katy some help in class today.
4 Sorry, I _____ to bring your book back today.
5 Dan _____ me three messages about the party last night!
6 My new watch _____ a lot of money, but I love it.
7 I _____ Amy this morning and she _____ for your email address.
8 I'm sure I _____ my homework here on the table this morning. Where is it?

Unit 3   135

3 NEW TECHNOLOGY

11 Complete the dialogues with the correct Simple Past form of the verbs.

1 see
A: I _saw_ a new movie yesterday.
B: Oh, _____ Magic Men?
A: No, I _____ Magic Men. I _____ Heroes.

2 buy
A: Mom and Dad _____ a new TV last week.
B: Oh, _____ a smart TV?
A: No, they _____ a smart TV. They _____ a normal flat screen.

3 give
A: The teacher _____ us a test in class today.
B: Oh, _____ you a long test?
A: No, she _____ us a long test. She _____ us a VERY long test!

4 leave
A: Mack and Lily _____ school early today.
B: Oh, _____ after lunch?
A: No, they _____ after lunch. They _____ after math class.

12 Use the prompts to write a dialogue.

A: the new electronics store / open / yesterday; you / go?
¹ _The new electronics store opened yesterday. Did you go?_

B: Yeah; I / go / with Tina; we / arrange / to meet at the store
² _____

A: where / you / go / ?
³ _____

B: we / find / a table / at Marco's
⁴ _____

A: what / you / have / ?
⁵ _____

B: I / have / pizza; Tina / not eat / anything; she / not be / hungry
⁶ _____

A: and how many / gadgets / you / buy / ?
⁷ _____

B: I / not buy / any / ! ; we / not stay / long; it / be / very crowded / !
⁸ _____

13 Complete the advice with the correct verbs.

look   turn   ~~keep~~   hang   check   give

1 A: Great to see you! Goodbye! | B: Please _keep_ in touch.
2 A: My computer isn't working! | B: Did you _____ it on?
3 A: Someone keeps calling me and never says anything! | B: _____ up right away.
4 A: I can't do this activity. It's too hard. | B: Don't _____ up. You can do it.
5 A: No one sent me a birthday card! | B: _____ out your timeline on Facebook!
6 A: Where's your house? I'm on your street. | B: _____ for a house with a red door. That's ours!

14 Read the conversation on page 137 and complete blanks 1–5 with sentences a–f. There is one extra sentence.

a It even told you what activity you needed to do.
b I lost it when we were on vacation in Greece.
c You're right – some of those gadgets were awesome!
d And it was pretty heavy and big.
e You can wear it in the water.
f It was on at 6:30.

Carrie
Did you see the TV show last night about new gadgets? [1] _f_
I watched it with my brother and we both made a list of gifts for next year!

Marlon
I got back from soccer a little late last night. So I didn't see it at 6:30, but I watched it online later.
[2] _____ I want the new smartwatch they showed. It's awesome!

Carrie
But you got a smartwatch last Christmas. I remember! You were really proud of it! It gave you lots of interesting information. [3] _____ You got emails and everything on it.

Marlon
I know. It was cool. But I didn't like its appearance very much. [4] _____ Now – this new one … it does everything AND it looks good. Besides, I don't have that watch anymore. [5] _____ We went on a boat and it fell into the water.

Carrie
What a shame!

Marlon
Yes, I was really upset then. But at least now I can ask my parents for a new one for this Christmas.

15 Mark the sentences ✓ (right), ✗ (wrong), or ? (doesn't say).
1 ✓ Carrie watched the TV show before Marlon.
2 ☐ Marlon agrees with Carrie about the TV show.
3 ☐ Marlon liked his watch because it looked good.
4 ☐ Carrie lost her watch, too.
5 ☐ Marlon dropped his watch in a swimming pool.

16 Match the parts of the sentences.
1 _b_ That's the teacher
2 ☐ That's the picture
3 ☐ That's the town
4 ☐ That's a picture of the singer
5 ☐ That's the book
6 ☐ That's the actress

a that I borrowed from Lara.
b who taught me math in sixth grade.
c where we went on vacation last summer.
d who recorded the song *My Time*.
e that I painted.
f who was really good in the movie *The Maze Runner*.

17 Use the clues to complete the crossword.

Across
2 It's a group of online pages that are about the same topic.
3 It's something that we download regularly to make computers and cell phones work better.
6 It's any new electronic machine which is useful.

Down
1 It's something bad that can hurt a computer.
4 It's something that we send to a friend on a phone.
5 It's something that we use to click on things on a computer screen.
7 It's a program with a specific purpose that we download to a cell phone.

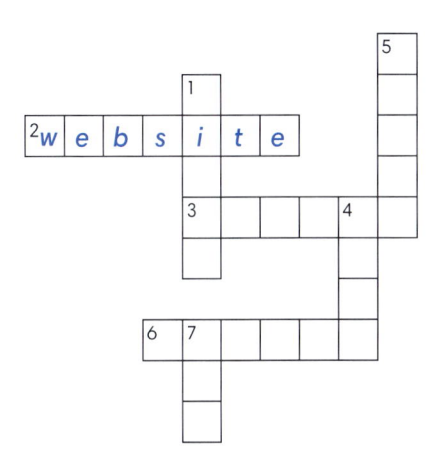

² w e b s i t e

3 NEW TECHNOLOGY

18 Complete the email with the correct words.

We have a teacher at school ¹ _who_ knows a lot about computers. She told us about a computer course ² _____ we can take online. Yesterday I had my first class, ³ _____ was all about writing code. We learn things ⁴ _____ are really interesting. There's a teacher ⁵ _____ can answer our text messages if we have a problem. He told us about a website ⁶ _____ we can buy a special book for the course.

19 WORD FRIENDS Complete the sentences with the correct verbs.

| upload   click   download   share   ~~search~~   chat |

1 I often _search_ the web for information.
2 I make a lot of videos and I like to _____ them with my friends online.
3 Did you _____ that video of the eagle on the Burj Khalifa from the link I sent you?
4 I often _____ online with my best friend.
5 _____ on the link in this email and you can see the website I told you about.
6 I often _____ pictures to share with my friends online.

20 WORD FRIENDS Complete the sentences with the correct words.

| give   crashed   ~~connect~~   program
working   died   virus   up |

1 I can't _connect_ a microphone to my PC. Could you _____ me a hand?
2 A: Hi – what's _____ ?
   B: My computer _____ yesterday and I can't get online.
3 Do you want to come over to help me with my computer? It got a _____ !
4 Sorry I couldn't call earlier. The battery in my phone _____ .
5 Help! My internet connection stopped _____ this morning! Can I come to your house and use your computer?
6 I tried to download the _____ last night, but I think it was too big. Did you manage to download it?

21 Complete the sentences with the correct words.

| suddenly   end   that   finally
~~first~~   later   then   all |

1 My phone rang. At _first_ , there was silence. _____ my uncle said, "Hi Brian!"
2 I turned on my hair dryer. First of _____ , there was a strange noise. A few moments _____ it stopped working.
3 I was on my computer when _____ I smelled smoke!
4 I spent hours on my essay last night. I _____ finished it at midnight.
5 Just before class I called my mom on the phone. After _____ , I turned it off.
6 I tried to fix the problem on my laptop, but in the _____ I asked my smart friend Dave to help!

22 Put the events in the correct order. Then add the time words to the beginning of the sentences.

A ~~At first~~ / Then / Finally
 a ☐ _At first_ , I really enjoyed checking posts.
 b [1] I started using Facebook a year ago.
 c ☐ _____ , I stopped using it completely and started using Twitter.
 d ☐ _____ I got a little bored.

B First of all / Next / In the end
 a ☐ _____ , we had to tell the class our answers.
 b ☐ We had an interesting computer lesson today.
 c ☐ _____ , she put us in small groups to compare our answers.
 d ☐ _____ , the teacher gave us a questionnaire to fill in.

C First / After that / Finally
 a ☐ _____ we learned to write simple programs.
 b ☐ _____ , we took a test and we all passed.
 c ☐ _____ we did more difficult things.
 d ☐ I started learning to code when I was ten.

Unit 3

SELF-ASSESSMENT

Vocabulary

1 Complete the words from the descriptions.

0 We play games on this:
c o n s o l e
1 A digital camera doesn't work without this:
b _ _ _ _ _ _ _
2 You can copy files onto this:
f _ _ _ _ _   d _ _ _
3 You type on this: k _ _ _ _ _ _ _
4 You take aerial pictures with this:
d _ _ _ _
5 You can carry this small computer easily:
t _ _ _ _ _

[ ]/5

2 Complete the sentences with the correct words.

| chat   charge   check   click   make   text |

0 I _check_ my emails every hour.
1 My friend and I _____ online after school.
2 I sometimes _____ my friends during classes!
3 You need to _____ your phone every night.
4 We often _____ videos and upload them.
5 You must _____ on this link to get to the website.

[ ]/5

3 Circle the correct option.

0 Can you help me *put* / (*connect*) the microphone?
1 My computer *fell* / *crashed* yesterday so I didn't do any work.
2 The battery in my camera *died* / *emptied* and I couldn't take any pictures.
3 Our internet connection *stopped* / *finished* working and I had to go to Lucy's house to download the homework files.
4 My cell phone didn't have enough memory to *remember* / *download* the app.
5 Don't open that email or you might get a(n) *illness* / *virus*.

[ ]/5

Grammar

4 Complete the sentences with the correct past form of the verbs in parentheses.

0 I _forgot_ to do my homework last night. (forget)
1 I _____ my book on the bus this morning. (leave)
2 The teacher _____ us a lot of work in class today. (not give)
3 _____ the computer _____ a lot of money? (cost)
4 My brother _____ the dog for a walk early today. (take)
5 Someone _____ my dad's car last week. (steal)

[ ]/5

5 Complete the sentences with *who*, *which*, or *where*.

0 Mia was the person _who_ helped me.
1 The place _____ we met was the library.
2 That's the book _____ you gave me for my birthday.
3 That's the office _____ my dad works.
4 This is the restaurant _____ Ronnie recommended.
5 That's the teacher _____ first taught me English.

[ ]/5

Speaking language practice

6 Complete the text with the words below.

| after   ago   all   at   end   later |

Two days ⁰ _ago_ we went to a store to buy a laptop. First of ¹ _____, we looked at a very new one. ² _____ first, we couldn't see the price, but then we saw it on the shelf. It was very expensive! We checked other laptops and ³ _____ that we left the store. Half an hour ⁴ _____, we went back. In the ⁵ _____, we decided to buy the first one!

[ ]/5

Vocabulary	[ ]/15
Grammar	[ ]/10
Speaking language practice	[ ]/5
Your total score	[ ]/30

4 MY HOME, MY TOWN

1 Circle the odd one out.
1. stove   sink   (fireplace)   faucet
2. armchair   toilet   rug   coffee table
3. chair   bed   washing machine   closet
4. shower   bathtub   washbasin   couch
5. wall   switch   floor   ceiling
6. bedroom   bathroom   mirror   kitchen

2 Find eight words from Activity 1 in the word search.

S	S	S	M	Y	W	C	G	F	B
W	M	H	D	S	A	A	M	A	E
I	I	K	R	A	S	B	T	U	P
T	R	S	M	R	H	I	T	C	X
C	R	A	O	M	B	N	X	E	T
H	O	V	I	C	A	E	K	T	O
R	R	U	X	H	S	T	F	L	I
D	D	L	V	A	I	D	L	P	L
N	K	B	G	I	N	A	Q	N	E
P	N	F	A	R	W	V	B	N	T

3 Complete the sentences with the correct words.

curtains   faucet   mirror   floor   ~~closet~~   lamp

1. I need a new _closet_ to put all my clothes in.
2. I often turn on the _____ by my bed and read before I go to sleep.
3. I looked in the _____ and saw that my hair was a mess.
4. Can I have different colored _____ in my bedroom? These striped ones are old!
5. The _____ in the bathroom isn't working. I can't get any water.
6. When I walk on my bedroom _____, it makes a squeaky noise!

4 Complete the words from the descriptions.
1. You wash yourself in here: s h o w e r
2. You put dirty clothes in this: w _ _ _ _ _ _ _ m _ _ _ _ _ _ _
3. You turn this on to get water: f _ _ _ _ _ _
4. You sit and lie down on this: c _ _ _ _
5. You keep packages of food in this: c _ _ _ _ _ _
6. You look in this to see your face: m _ _ _ _ _
7. You have these on your window: c _ _ _ _ _ _ _
8. This gives you light: l _ _ _

5 Look at the picture above and complete the sentences with the correct words or phrases.

under   in front of   opposite   next to
behind   above   ~~on~~   between

1. The cat is lying _on_ the rug.
2. The dog is _____ to the cat.
3. They are _____ the fireplace.
4. The fireplace is _____ the two cabinets.
5. A clock is _____ the fireplace.
6. A letter is _____ the clock.
7. My backpack is _____ the table.
8. The table is _____ the couch.

6 Circle the correct answer.
1. Are those your dirty plates in the _____?
   a desk
   (b) sink
   c cabinet
2. I left my book on the _____.
   a faucet
   b nightstand
   c mirror
3. I want to buy a new _____ for the bedroom floor.
   a lamp
   b bed
   c rug
4. Come here and sit _____ me on the couch.
   a next to
   b between
   c above
5. I sat _____ Tim at dinner.
   a opposite
   b above
   c between

140   Unit 4

7 Complete the email with the correct words.

To: bella@hello.com

Hi, Bella,
We moved to a new house last week. It's really big. There's a nice ¹ _kitchen_ with a very modern stove. There's a big ² _____ above the ³ _____, so you can look at the yard while you're washing the dishes! The ⁴ _____ room is very big, so we need a bigger ⁵ _____ to sit on while we watch TV. I have a nice bedroom. Mom and Dad bought me a new ⁶ _____ for my clothes and a nice red ⁷ _____ to put on the floor. At the moment, the ⁸ _____ are green, but I want to paint them white. In my room there is a door which leads into my own ⁹ _____ with a shower and toilet. It's awesome! Now I also have a puppy. His name is Fred! Here is his picture.

Take care,

Lucas

8 **WORD FRIENDS** Complete the sentences with the correct verbs.

set ~~do~~ make dry load sweep take clean

1 Mom and Dad __do__ the grocery shopping every Saturday morning.
2 Can you _____ the dishwasher while I _____ out the trash?
3 My brother didn't _____ his bed this morning and his room's a mess.
4 We have to _____ the floor every day because of our dog's hairs!
5 I usually _____ my room on the weekend.
6 I can wash the dishes if you _____ them.
7 I need to _____ the table for five people.

9 Circle the correct option.

1 I usually eat my breakfast very quick /(quickly).
2 My young sister is a very happy / happily little girl.
3 Jack waved to me cheerful / cheerfully when I saw him this morning.
4 The man shouted at the dog angry / angrily.
5 The students chatted noisy / noisily while they waited for the teacher.
6 Paul is a really bad / badly tennis player and no one wants to play with him!

10 Make adverbs from the adjectives. Then complete the chart with the adverbs.

~~fast~~ ~~careful~~ angry late bad
hard slow cheerful early right
noisy sad wrong quick

A Adjectives that take –ly ending for adverbs:
carefully

B Adjectives that stay the same when adverbs:
fast

11 Complete the sentences with the correct adverbs.

1 She's a slow driver. She drives _slowly_.
2 He's a fast learner. He learns _____.
3 My dad's a hard worker. He works _____.
4 He's a good soccer player. He plays soccer _____.
5 I gave the wrong answer. I got the answer _____.
6 I was late for the meeting. I arrived _____.
7 My sister's a bad cook. She cooks _____.

12 Match the parts of the sentences.

1 _c_ Jack spoke so quietly that
2 ☐ The party was so noisy that
3 ☐ Mike drove so fast that
4 ☐ Tom's results were so good that
5 ☐ Dave ran so slowly that
6 ☐ My dad got up so early that

a Leo's neighbor complained.
b he was last in the race.
c the teacher didn't hear him.
d he was tired by lunch.
e he arrived very early.
f his parents gave him a gift.

4 MY HOME, MY TOWN

13 Circle the correct option.

---

myblogpage.com

I had a really ¹**bad** / *badly* day yesterday. First, I got up ²*late* / *lately* and I didn't have time for a shower. Then I ate my breakfast ³*so* / *very* quickly and I felt sick on the bus to school. I forgot to ⁴*take* / *make* out the trash and my dad was ⁵*angry* / *angrily*. In math, I got all the test questions ⁶*wrong* / *wrongly* and the teacher gave me extra work. I tried to do my history homework in the evening, but my computer was ⁷*so* / *very* slow that I gave up. It was my turn to ⁸*clean* / *set* the living room, but I didn't do the vacuuming ⁹*careful* / *carefully* and my mom told me to do it again. Then something went ¹⁰*right* / *rightly*! I watched a ¹¹*late* / *lately* soccer game on TV. My favorite team played very ¹²*good* / *well* and they won. But I shouted so loudly ¹³*than* / *that* my mom sent me to my room. Oops …

---

14 Complete the sentences with the correct adjectives.

> messy   large   narrow   ~~bright~~
> cozy   modern

1 My bedroom is quite dark, but your room is lovely and ___bright___.
2 The couch we had in our previous house was big and uncomfortable, but this one is nice and _____.
3 The hotel had wide corridors downstairs, but upstairs they were very _____.
4 This closet is too small for all my dresses and I need a _____ one.
5 My mom likes old-fashioned furniture, but my dad prefers _____ things.
6 These days my room is always clean, but when I was younger it was very _____.

15 Read the story. Mark the sentences ✓ (right), ✗ (wrong), or ? (doesn't say).

1 ✗ The girl listened to a story on her earphones.
2 ☐ The girl did the same things every night.
3 ☐ She heard a man's voice.
4 ☐ She felt scared in her room.
5 ☐ The girl has two sisters.
6 ☐ The house shook when the tree fell.
7 ☐ The tree fell because it was old.
8 ☐ Josh called the girl on her cell phone.

An **important** message

It was quite late and I was in bed. Outside it was very dark and the weather was bad. The wind was loud in the trees, but my bedroom was warm and cozy. I put my earphones on to listen to my favorite music and started to read my book. I always listened to music and read before I went to sleep.

Suddenly the music stopped. I looked at my cell phone. It was still turned on and it was ringing. The caller was unknown. When I answered the call, a voice spoke quietly in my earphones. "Get out of your bedroom. Now." I felt a little frightened. Who was it? My door was closed … everyone was asleep, the house was quiet.

Then the voice on the phone spoke again. "Get out. Now!" I was so scared that I dropped my book on the floor. Suddenly, my room didn't feel warm and cozy. It felt scary.

"Now!" this time the voice shouted loudly. I pulled out my earphones quickly and jumped out of bed. I ran to the door and opened it. Behind me there was a very loud noise. I didn't look back. I ran down the corridor and down the stairs.

Then there was another very loud noise from upstairs and the cabinets in the hall moved. My mom and sisters ran down the stairs, too. "What's happening?" I screamed. My dad came down and pushed us all outside into the garden.

"Look," he said and pointed up at my room. A large tree was on the roof. Part of it was in my room. The windows were broken.

When I looked opposite the house, Josh Taylor was standing on the sidewalk, holding a cat and his cell phone. He was in my history class last year and I remember we exchanged phone numbers once to discuss an essay. He lived some blocks away, but was on my street to rescue his cat when he saw me reading in bed and the tree that was about to fall. That night Josh's call saved my life.

16 Complete the sentences with *can* or *can't*.

1 I _can't_ come around to see you tonight because my mom wants me to clean my room.
2 We _____ use cell phones in class – not even to go online and look for information!
3 You _____ borrow my tablet if you want.
4 _____ we look up words in the dictionary during the test?
5 I _____ learn to drive now because I'm too young.
6 My brother _____ watch TV until 11, but I _____. That's not fair!

17 Order the words to make sentences or questions.

1 leave / have / soon / you / to / do / ?
   Do you have to leave soon?
2 has / my / early / get / to / up / dad
3 to / room / don't / clean / have / my / I
4 your / day / cook / does / have / dad / to / every / ?
5 doesn't / outside / my / sleep / have / dog / to
6 chores / have / the / you / help / to / with / do / house / ?

18 Write sentences or questions with the correct form of *have to*.

1 you / get home / before 10:30 / ?
   Do you have to get home before 10:30?
2 we / not / do / Activity 4 / for homework
3 the teacher / arrive / at school / before 8:00
4 Peter / not / take out the trash / on weekends
5 your dad / take / the subway to work / ?
6 my sister / not / get up early every day

19 Circle the correct answer.

1 We _____ hand in this paper before Thursday. We have three days!
   a must not (b) don't have to c can't
2 You _____ shout at your brother. He didn't do anything.
   a must not b don't have to c can't
3 I _____ go on that website because I don't have a password.
   a must not b don't have to c can't
4 You _____ join the photography club because it's full.
   a must not b don't have to c can't
5 Olly _____ work at the supermarket next weekend. It's a holiday.
   a must not b doesn't have to c can't
6 You _____ touch that key. It deletes everything!
   a must not b don't have to c can

20 Complete the dialogue with one word in each blank.

A: Hi! Do you have ¹ _to_ work this weekend?
B: No, I ² _____. I don't have any work, so I ³ _____ do what I want! Why?
A: It's my birthday and I ⁴ _____ invite two friends to stay over! Would you like to come?
B: Cool! Yes, sure.
A: Can your sister Elise come, too?
B: No, I'm afraid she ⁵ _____. She came home last week and now she ⁶ _____ to stay home and help with the chores!
A: That's a shame. How long ⁷ _____ she have to do that for?
B: Only for a week. Anyway – I ⁸ _____ to go now. I ⁹ _____ get to my next class.

Unit 4 143

4 MY HOME, MY TOWN

21 Complete the words from the descriptions.
1. You go to this place to watch a movie:
   m o v i e   t h e a t e r
2. This is a very old building where kings and queens used to live:
   c _ _ _ _ _ _
3. Religious people usually go to this place on Sundays:
   c _ _ _ _ _
4. You can see old things at this place:
   m _ _ _ _ _
5. You go to this place to send letters and packages:
   p _ _ _   o _ _ _ _ _ _

22 Complete the sentences with the correct words.

| should | think | thanks | awful |
| advice | don't | good | why |

1. Can you give me some _advice_ about the best cell phones to buy at the moment?
2. That's a _____ idea. _____ for the advice.
3. _____ don't you talk to your teacher about your problems?
4. Where _____ I go to buy some new sneakers?
5. I _____ think you should try to fix your computer yourself.
6. What do you _____ I should wear to the party?
7. That's an _____ idea! I can't do that!

23 Choose the correct answers.
1. Where should I go on vacation?
   a. I don't think that's a good idea.
   b. Thanks for the advice.
   c. Why don't you go to France?
2. You shouldn't work so hard.
   a. That's an awful idea.
   b. Thanks for the advice.
   c. It's not your fault.
3. Can you give me some advice about my bedroom?
   a. I think you should get some new posters.
   b. That's a good idea.
   c. What should I do?
4. Why don't you take a break?
   a. I think you should relax.
   b. That's a good idea.
   c. Good for you!

24 Order the sentences to make conversations.
1. a ☐ Why don't you try the new store at the shopping mall?
   b ☐ That's a good idea. Thanks.
   c ☐ 1 I need to get a new smartphone. Where should I go to get one?
2. a ☐ That's an awful idea! She hates books!
   b ☐ You should get her a new book. I often buy books for gifts.
   c ☐ It's my sister's birthday tomorrow. What do you think I should get her?
3. a ☐ I think you should go to the Museum of Modern Art. It's great!
   b ☐ Can you give me some advice about where to go in New York?
   c ☐ Thanks for the advice. I like art museums.

25 Match the pairs of sentences. Then join the sentences with *and*, *but*, *because*, or *so*.
   a ☐ 5 During our vacation in France, we went to the beach.
   b ☐ I bought some postcards.
   c ☐ We spoke English a lot.
   d ☐ I didn't like the cheese.
   e ☐ My French friend took me to an art gallery.

1. I forgot to send them.
2. I didn't try it again!
3. It wasn't open that day.
4. My French friend needs to improve.
5. We swam in the sea.

a *During our vacation in France, we went to the beach and swam in the sea.*
b _____
c _____
d _____
e _____

SELF-ASSESSMENT

Vocabulary

1 Circle the correct answer.

0 I put a new poster on my bedroom _____.
  a window   **b wall**   c switch
1 My dad always sits in the same _____.
  a cabinet   b coffee table   c armchair
2 The cat usually sleeps _____ the table.
  a over   b between   c under
3 I need a _____ for my bedroom floor.
  a rug   b cabinet   c sink
4 Do you like our _____ new curtains?
  a clean   b comfortable   c bright
5 I can't get any water from this _____.
  a faucet   b lamp   c stove

/5

2 Circle the correct option.

0 I didn't *take* / **make** my bed this morning.
1 I *sweep* / *clean* the floor to help my mom.
2 We usually *do* / *make* the shopping on Fridays.
3 Can you *sweep* / *empty* the dishwasher?
4 My sister never *washes* / *cleans* her room.
5 Dad *made* / *took* out the trash after dinner.

/5

3 Complete the words in the sentences.

0 Our class went to the art g*allery* last week.
1 My friend works at the police d_____.
2 The new shopping m_____ is awesome.
3 There's a big meeting at city h_____.
4 I must go to the post o_____ to send these letters.
5 Why don't we get some brochures from the v_____ c_____?

/5

Grammar

4 Complete the sentences with adverbs from the adjectives in parentheses.

0 I worked really *hard* to pass this test. (hard)
1 My dad shouted _____ at the cat when it scratched the table. (angry)
2 Hester ran _____ and won the race. (good)
3 The little girl wrote her name _____ at the top of the drawing. (careful)
4 The computer downloaded the file very _____. (quick)
5 We all arrived _____ and we had to wait. (early)

/5

5 Complete the sentences with the correct form of *can*, *must*, or *have to*.

0 We *don't have to* finish this work before Friday. That's great!
1 The teacher said we _____ leave early today because we worked really hard this morning.
2 You _____ touch that dog. It's dangerous.
3 I _____ get on that website because I don't have a password.
4 My dad _____ work on Saturdays, so we do the grocery shopping on Sundays.
5 I _____ be late again! The teacher was really angry with me today.

/5

Speaking language practice

6 Order the words to make questions or sentences in the dialogue.

A: ⁰some / you / advice / give / can / me / ?
  Can you give me some advice?
B: Sure. What's the problem?
A: I'm going to London with my friend.
  ¹think / where / go / you / should / we / do / ? _____
B: ²should / to / think / I / you / go / the / British Museum _____
  It's great.
A: ³that's / don't / a / idea / think / good / I
  _____
  My friend hates museums!
B: OK! ⁴don't / to / you / gallery / why / art / go / an / ? _____
A: ⁵for / thanks / advice / the
  _____

/5

Vocabulary	/15
Grammar	/10
Speaking language practice	/5
Your total score	/30

Unit 4 145

5 TAKE CARE

1 Label the parts of the body.

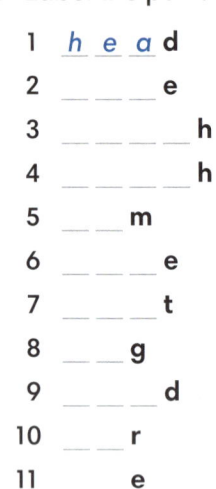

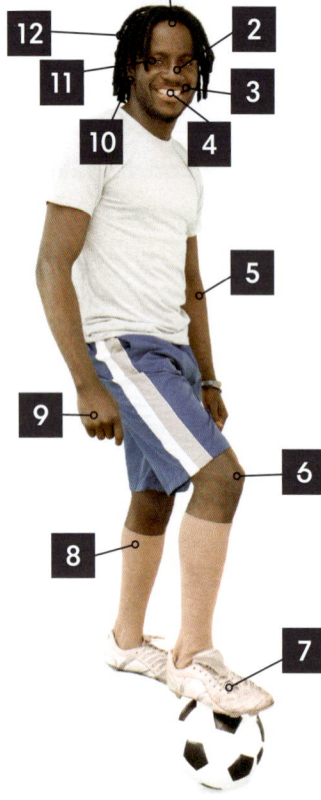

1 _h e a_ d
2 _ _ _ e
3 _ _ _ _ h
4 _ _ _ _ h
5 _ _ m
6 _ _ _ e
7 _ _ _ t
8 _ _ _ g
9 _ _ _ d
10 _ _ r
11 _ _ _ e
12 _ _ _ r

2 Circle the correct option.

1 Use your (brain) / neck and think hard!
2 My eyebrow / skin went red in the sun.
3 After the race my heart / stomach was going very fast.
4 Jack goes to the gym to get bigger bones / muscles.
5 My grandpa's hair is brown, but his ankle / beard is white.

3 Complete the sentences with the correct words.

| shoulders knee ~~toes~~ fingers |
| elbow bones |

1 These shoes are too small. They hurt my ____toes____.
2 Young children like to paint with their _____ – they don't like to use brushes.
3 My baby sister likes sitting high up on my dad's _____.
4 Drink a lot of milk and you get strong _____ that don't break.
5 I hit the desk with my arm and hurt my _____ when I fell.

4 **WORD FRIENDS** Match sentences 1–4 to pictures A–D.

1 [D] Mark hurt his back yesterday.
2 [ ] Emily cut her finger when she was cooking.
3 [ ] Jake twisted his ankle during the game.
4 [ ] Ellie broke her toe when she fell over.

5 **WORD FRIENDS** Match the parts of the sentences.

1 [e] My brother keeps
2 [ ] We never play
3 [ ] I usually go
4 [ ] My friends and I do
5 [ ] My mom takes

a tennis lessons at the club.
b basketball at school.
c yoga at the sports center.
d swimming on Saturdays.
e fit by running every day.

6 Circle the correct answer.

1 Grant has blond hair, but dark _____.
  a elbows (b) eyebrows c ears
2 Jenny twisted her _____ while she was playing volleyball.
  a bones b heart c knee
3 People who can't hear sometimes read people's _____.
  a lips b nose c teeth
4 I never _____ running before school.
  a keep b go c do
5 I don't have very big _____ in my arms.
  a skin b muscles c fingers
6 My sister and I often _____ exercises at home to music.
  a have b play c do

146 Unit 5

7 Complete the text with the correct words.

> teeth   skin   ~~play~~   broke
> muscles   hurt   foot   does   has

Tennis players often have problems when they ¹ _play_ tennis regularly. One of my friends ² _____ practice every week. She also ³ _____ lots of exercises and enters competitions nearly every weekend. She gets lots of injuries. She needs new shoes because she has bad ⁴ _____ pain – that's because she jumps up and down a lot. She also ⁵ _____ her head last month because another player hit her with a ball! When she plays in the summer her ⁶ _____ often goes very red. Last year she even ⁷ _____ a bone in her ankle because she fell over! And once someone hit the ball right in her face and she broke two ⁸ _____. She usually needs to take a warm bath after playing because all her ⁹ _____ are hurting.
You think tennis is a safe game, but it can be dangerous!

8 Match pictures 1–10 to snacks a–j.

a [8] hot dog
b [ ] sandwich
c [ ] chocolate
d [ ] yogurt
e [ ] fruit
f [ ] hamburger
g [ ] potato chips
h [ ] nuts
i [ ] salad
j [ ] cake

9 Complete the chart with the words below.

> ~~vegetable~~   ~~salad~~   banana   potato chip
> sandwich   fruit   hot dog   yogurt
> bread   food   candy bar   time   thing
> sugar   chocolate   burger

A | Countable nouns:
vegetable

B | Uncountable nouns:
salad

10 Order the words to make questions or sentences.

1 many / do / month / burgers / how / eat / you / a / ?
How many burgers do you eat a month?

2 cake / too / eat / I / much
_____

3 much / refrigerator / isn't / the / food / there / in
_____

4 you / food / salt / how / your / put / much / on / do / ?
_____

5 should / fruit / lot / a / you / eat / of
_____

6 sell / here / nuts / do / any / they / ?
_____

Unit 5

5 TAKE CARE

11 Complete the sentences with *some*, *any*, *much*, *many*, and *a lot*.

1. A: How _many_ sandwiches do you have today?
   B: I don't have _____! We didn't have _____ bread at home, so I brought _____ potato chips and fruit instead.
2. A: How _____ time did you spend on your homework?
   B: I didn't spend _____ of time on it. It was pretty easy.
3. I didn't get _____ answers right in that activity. Only two!
4. I ate too _____ food at breakfast. I feel sick!
5. You have _____ of snacks today!

12 Complete the text with the *some*, *any*, *much*, *many*, and *(a) lot*.

Healthy living?

Are people healthy today? ¹ _Some_ doctors think we eat ² _____ many unhealthy snacks. For example we eat a ³ _____ of burgers and hot dogs because they're quick to eat and they don't cost ⁴ _____ money. Schools are trying to encourage their students to eat healthy food. In some schools there aren't ⁵ _____ machines that sell snacks – not one! The students can't bring ⁶ _____ candy bars or potato chips into school! They sell a lot ⁷ _____ healthy food in the cafeteria. There is always ⁸ _____ salad and a lot of fruit and vegetables, but unfortunately not ⁹ _____ students eat them! ¹⁰ _____ students at these schools – not all – go out at lunch and buy a ¹¹ _____ of unhealthy food, like French fries from snack bars! So, ¹² _____ many snacks do you eat every day?

13 **WORD FRIENDS** Complete the sentences with the correct verbs.

have   sleep   go   get x2
~~fall~~   stay   wake

1. Sometimes I _fall_ asleep during my history class!
2. I know that I _____ dreams, but I can never remember them.
3. I usually _____ in bed until noon on Saturdays!
4. During the week I always need to _____ up at 7:30, but I need an alarm clock to _____ me up on time.
5. I like to _____ ready for bed early and then read a book for half an hour.
6. My baby sister has to _____ to bed early and she hates it.
7. If I _____ badly, I can't study very well the next day.

14 Read the emails on p. 149 and circle the best answers.

1. Tanya is writing to Ellie
   a about a letter she saw on her problem page.
   ⓑ about a sleep problem she has.
   c about some advice for another reader.
2. Tanya is worried because
   a she can't get up in the mornings.
   b she goes to bed too late in the evenings.
   c she can't go to sleep quickly at night.
3. Ellie thinks that
   a Tanya's problem is unusual.
   b Tanya's problem is normal.
   c Tanya's problem is interesting.
4. She believes the reason is that Tanya
   a works too hard.
   b argues with her parents.
   c thinks too much in bed.
5. Ellie advises Tanya to
   a have some quiet time before bed.
   b go to bed at different times.
   c see her doctor.

Email 1:

To: Ellie
From: Tanya
Subject: Help!

Hi Ellie,
Your email about sleep problems was very interesting. I have a sleep problem, too. It's a big one and I'm very worried about it. I'm a teenager. Many teenagers don't want to get up in the morning because they go to bed late at night. They sleep very well and can't wake up. My problem isn't about waking up, it's about going to sleep. I go to bed really early, but then I don't fall asleep for hours. I am so tired the next day. Help!
Tanya

Email 2:

To: Tanya
From: Ellie
Subject: Help!

Hi Tanya,
Don't worry! You're not the only one with this problem. Teenagers have a lot of things to worry about. They have a lot of tests and school work. Sometimes they have problems with friends or their parents. Maybe when you go to bed you can't stop thinking about the problems and then you can't sleep. You need to relax before bedtime. Sometimes it's a good idea to take a warm shower or listen to some music – not too loud! Don't spend a long time talking to your friends before bed – just get some peace and quiet. It's also important to have the same routine – go to bed and get up at the same time. The body likes that! Some teenagers have some herbal tea to help them fall asleep – That's a good idea. And don't worry about not sleeping – that makes it worse!
Ellie

15 Complete the sentences with the affirmative form of the Past Continuous.

| wait   watch   play   walk   sleep   ~~dance~~   do

1 In the picture, Kate _was dancing_ with Phil at his party.
2 At 5:00 this morning I _____ in my bed!
3 When you called me my parents _____ TV in the living room.
4 I _____ home from school when my dad drove past.
5 My sister _____ her guitar very loudly while I _____ my homework.
6 Sorry! We _____ for you at the park – not outside school.

16 Write the negative and question form of these sentences.

1 I was talking to Danny when you saw me.
I wasn't talking to Danny when you saw me. Was I talking to Danny when you saw me?

2 Jake was doing his homework during class.
_____
_____

3 The students were eating French fries and salad.
_____
_____

4 You were playing well in the game.
_____
_____

5 The teacher was explaining a difficult grammar point.
_____
_____

6 You were having lunch when Sammy arrived.
_____
_____

17 Match the parts of the sentences.

1 _f_ We were walking across the park
2 ☐ While I was eating my dinner
3 ☐ When I went downstairs
4 ☐ I fell asleep
5 ☐ My brother wasn't skiing
6 ☐ Jack was singing a song in the concert

a I dropped red sauce on my shirt.
b when he broke his ankle.
c Dad was cooking breakfast.
d when he fell off the stage.
e while I was reading my book.
f when it started to rain.

Unit 5   149

5 TAKE CARE

18 Complete the sentences with the Past Continuous or the Simple Past form of the verbs in parentheses.

1. We _were eating_ (eat) dinner outside when it _started_ (start) to rain.
2. The students _____ (do) an activity when the bell _____ (ring).
3. While I _____ (shop) on Saturday I _____ (meet) an old friend.
4. When I _____ (arrive) home my sister _____ (watch) a movie online.
5. I _____ (not look) when Paul _____ (fall) off his bicycle. I _____ (talk) to Marie.
6. What _____ (you/do) when I _____ (call) you last night?

19 Complete the text with the correct past forms of the verbs.

| look   go (x2)   see   not see   ~~wake~~   read |
| sit   chat (x2)   say   hurt   call   fall   ride |

When I ¹ _woke up_ yesterday my head ² _____, so I ³ _____ to the doctor. I ⁴ _____ a magazine in the waiting room when suddenly someone ⁵ _____ "Hello Pat!". I ⁶ _____ up and it was Terry Marsden. I last ⁷ _____ him five years ago! He ⁸ _____ down beside me and we ⁹ _____ for a long time. Last week he ¹⁰ _____ his horse when he ¹¹ _____ off! While we ¹² _____ the doctor ¹³ _____ out his name. I ¹⁴ _____ him later – I hope he was OK.

20 Complete the words in the sentences.

1. I'm feeling s _i_ _c_ _k_.
2. I have a h __ d __ __ __ __ __.
3. I have a s __ __ e t __ __ __ __ t.
4. I'm c __ __ __ h __ __ __ g.
5. I'm s __ __ e __ __ __ g.
6. I have a s __ __ m __ __ h __ __ e.
7. I have a food a __ __ __ __ r __ y.
8. I have a f __ __ __ __.
9. I have the f __ __ .

21 Complete the sentences with the correct words from Activity 20.

1. I ate too much and now I'm feeling _sick_.
2. I worked on my computer for a long time and now I have _____.
3. If you get the _____, you should stay in bed.
4. I can't eat or drink anything because I have a _____.
5. I shouldn't eat fish because I have a _____.
6. Your face is hot and red. I think you have a _____.

22 Circle the correct option.

1. What's the *wrong* / *matter*?
2. *What* / *How* are you feeling?
3. I have the *cold* / *flu*.
4. I feel *a headache* / *sick*.
5. My *back* / *fever* hurts.
6. Sit *on* / *down*.
7. *Have* / *Take* some water.
8. You should stay *at the hospital* / *in bed*.
9. You should *do* / *make* an appointment.
10. You should *go* / *take* to the hospital.

23 Complete the dialogues with the correct words.

| make   terrible   should   feeling   feel   ~~wrong~~ |

1. A: What's _wrong_?
   B: I _____ sick.
   A: You _____ go home.
2. A: How are you _____?
   B: I feel _____. My back hurts.
   A: You should _____ an appointment with the doctor.

24 Circle the correct answer.

1. What's _____ on outside?
   a doing   b going   c taking
2. I _____ up a cough during my trip.
   a caught   b found   c picked
3. Mom _____ up coffee because she got a lot of headaches.
   a fell   b gave   c made
4. Why don't you _____ out this website?
   a look   b find   c check
5. Bread _____ off after three or four days.
   a makes   b goes   c gives
6. Chris _____ up soccer last year.
   a took   b topped   c got

150 Unit 5

SELF-ASSESSMENT

Vocabulary

1 Complete the words from the descriptions.

0 Your food goes here: **s** t o m a c h
1 This sometimes goes red: **s** _ _ _
2 Men have this when they don't shave: **b** _ _ _ _ _
3 Your foot joins your leg here: **a** _ _ _ _ _
4 When you exercise a lot these get very strong: **m** _ _ _ _ _
5 The dentist checks these: **t** _ _ _ _

☐ /5

2 Circle the correct answer.

0 I try to eat well and ____ fit.
   a have   b do   **c keep**
1 I usually ____ to bed at 10:30 to get eight hours of sleep.
   a go   b make   c sleep
2 I got a ____ for my sister's birthday with her name on it.
   a nut   b cake   c yogurt
3 It's a good idea to eat ____ every day, even just one apple.
   a potato chips   b sandwiches   c fruit
4 Doctors say it's important to ____ regular exercise.
   a make   b do   c play
5 Would you like your chicken with ____ or French fries?
   a beef burger   b salad   c hot dog

☐ /5

3 Complete the sentences with the correct words.

| allergy   flu   sneezing   headache   ~~fever~~   throat |

0 He needs to see the doctor because he has a _fever_ – his temperature is very high.
1 I can't eat that. I have a(n) ____ to nuts.
2 Sorry, I'm ____ because I'm allergic to your cat!
3 The music at the concert was very loud and I got a(n) ____ .
4 We shouted a lot at the soccer game and now I have a sore ____ .
5 Oli has to stay in bed because he has the ____ .

☐ /5

Grammar

4 Complete the sentences with the correct words.

0 How _much_ water do you drink every day?
1 There aren't ____ students here. Only two.
2 I watched too much television last night and I didn't do ____ work! Nothing!
3 A ____ of people don't exercise and get sick.
4 Did you eat all the fruit? There ____ any left.
5 I answered ____ of the questions, but not many.

☐ /5

5 Make sentences in the Simple Past and the Past Continuous.

0 where / you / go / when / I / see / you?
   Where were you going when I saw you?
1 Hannah / read / a book / when / Gary / call
2 I / not work / when / Dave / come / to visit us
3 you / wait / at the bus stop / when / it / start / to rain / ?
4 the teacher / shout / because we / not concentrate / in class
5 you / have / dinner / when / I / call / you / ?

☐ /5

Speaking language practice

6 Complete the dialogues with one word in each blank.

1 A: How are you ⁰ _feeling_ ?
   B: My back ¹ ____ .
   A: You should go to the ² ____ .
2 A: What's ³ ____ ?
   B: I ⁴ ____ sick.
   A: Sit down and have ⁵ ____ water.

☐ /5

Vocabulary ☐ /15
Grammar ☐ /10
Speaking language practice ☐ /5
Your total score ☐ /30

6 SHOPPING AROUND

1 Unscramble the letters to write the names of types of stores that sell the things in the pictures.

1 SANNWSEDT
   newsstand
2 EROKOBOST 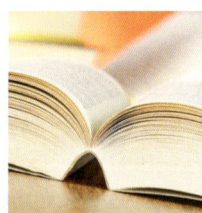
   _____
3 OHES OTRSE 
   _____
4 EMAT RAKETM 
   _____
5 OWERFL HOPS 
   _____
6 EKRABY 
   _____
7 CRERENOGREG 
   _____
8 OLGNITCH TROES 
   _____
9 GUTSORDRE 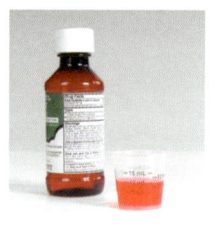
   _____

2 Complete the sentences with the correct words.

> meat market   shoe store   flower shop
> ~~bakery~~   newsstand   clothing store
> drugstore   greengrocer

1 We need some bread. Can you go to the *bakery*?
2 I bought some new jeans at the _____.
3 They sell delicious apples at the _____.
4 I want a magazine and some chocolate from the _____.
5 Please get some chicken from the _____.
6 I need some new boots. I must go to the _____.
7 I have a bad headache. Can you get me some medicine from the _____?
8 It's Mom's birthday tomorrow. Let's get her some flowers from the _____.

3 Match containers 1–8 to items a–h. Then label the pictures below.

1 [c] a loaf of   a jam
2 [ ] a bar of   b flowers
3 [ ] a jar of   c bread
4 [ ] a package of   d apples
5 [ ] a bunch of   e chocolate
6 [ ] a bottle of   f potato chips
7 [ ] a box of   g lemonade
8 [ ] a bag of   h matches

A *a loaf of bread*
B _____ 
C _____ 
D _____ 
E _____ 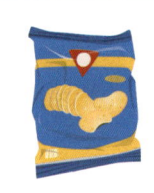
F _____ 
G _____
H _____ 

4 Circle the correct answer.

1 I need some oranges, but the _____ is closed.
  a drugstore   b shoe store
  (c) greengrocer

2 I bought three _____ of chocolate this morning.
  a cans   b bars
  c bunches

3 If you get a _____ of bread, I can make some sandwiches.
  a loaf   b package
  c box

Unit 6

4 We got these beautiful flowers at the _____.
  a bakery   b flower shop
  c meat market

5 Our _____ sells shampoo.
  a greengrocer   b clothing store
  c drugstore

5 Complete the sentences with the correct form of the adjectives in parentheses.
1 This movie theater is ___*older*___ (old) than that one.
2 These flowers are _____ (nice) than the ones at the market.
3 The phone signal is _____ (good) here than inside the house.
4 I bought _____ (expensive) bike in the store.
5 Emily is _____ (happy) person I know.
6 My _____ (bad) grade this year was in math!

6 Make three sentences for the pairs of adjectives 1–4.

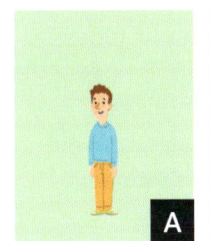

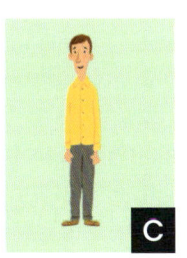

1 short/tall
  A is ___*shorter than*___ B.
  B is ___*taller than*___ A.
  C is ___*the tallest*___ person in my family.

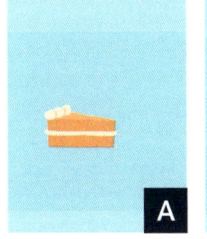

2 small/big
  A is _____ B.
  B is _____ A.
  C is _____ cake in the store.

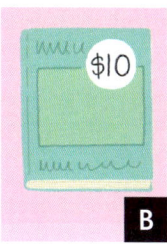

3 cheap/expensive
  A is _____ B.
  B is _____ A.
  C is _____ book in the store.

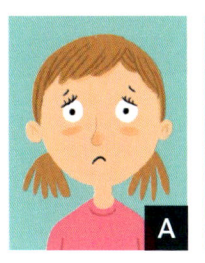

4 sad/happy
  B is _____ A.
  A is _____ B.
  C is _____ student in the class.

7 Complete the second sentence with *as … as …* so that it means the same as the first sentence.
1 I'm taller than my brother.
  My brother isn't ___*as tall as me*___.
2 It's colder in Scotland than it is here.
  It isn't _____.
3 This TV show is more interesting than the TV show last night. The TV show last night wasn't _____.
4 Your jeans were more expensive than mine. My jeans weren't _____.
5 My new bed is more comfortable than my old one. My old bed wasn't _____.
6 My sister's bedroom is messier than mine. My bedroom isn't _____.

Unit 6

6 SHOPPING AROUND

8 Complete the email with the correct forms of the adjectives in parentheses.

To: grace@hellomail.com

Hi Grace,

Finally our end-of-year tests are finished! I'm ¹ _happier_ (happy) than I was this time last year. Geography was ² _____ (easy) than before and French was ³ _____ (good), too. But IT was horrible. The test definitely wasn't as ⁴ _____ (long) as last year's, but it was ⁵ _____ (difficult). Last year I was ⁶ _____ (bad) in the class! I don't want to be that bad again! My friend Tina is ⁷ _____ (good) student in my class, but I get ⁸ _____ (high) grades than her in English! Last night I was very stressed, but now I'm ⁹ _____ (relaxed).
Love,
Katy

9 Complete the sentences with the correct words.

shoppers   shopping cart   multiplex
~~department store~~   escalator   food court
public restrooms   parking lot

1 We went to the _department store_ and bought some new clothes, some things for the kitchen, and a lamp for my bedroom.
2 The _____ wasn't working in the mall, so we had to use the stairs.
3 Dad bought so many things at the supermarket that he needed a big _____ to carry them all.
4 The _____ was nearly empty, so it was easy to find a space for the car.
5 The new shopping mall has thousands of _____ every day.
6 There's a new burger bar at the _____ where we can have lunch today.
7 The _____ at the new mall are always very clean and are like those in a hotel!
8 There are ten movies showing at the _____. I'm sure there's one you want to see!

10 Read the text. Mark the sentences ✓ (right), ✗ (wrong), or ? (doesn't say).

1 [?] Selfridges is the biggest department store in London.
2 [ ] Harry Selfridge wasn't from England.
3 [ ] Before Selfridges, people bought lots of things they did not need.
4 [ ] At Selfridges it was easier for shoppers to see things.
5 [ ] Selfridges has more windows than other stores on Oxford Street.
6 [ ] Nothing in Selfridges is very expensive.

The best department store in the world?

Oxford Street in London is well-known for its big department stores. Selfridges is one of them. It is named after Harry Selfridge, an American man who came to London with his family in 1909. He opened his new store on March 15 and it immediately became very popular. But why was it so successful? There were many reasons. At that time shoppers bought things because they needed to, not because they wanted to. Harry Selfridge wanted to change that. He wanted to make shopping more fun, more of an adventure than a chore. He wanted people to enjoy going around his department store. So he didn't keep all the items in cabinets or on shelves, he put them on counters for people to see. The shoppers could look and touch things and choose what they wanted. And Selfridge's motto was "The customer is always right!." This idea made the shopper more important than the seller.
The store was also an amazing building. It had a garden on the roof and incredible store windows. People came to Oxford Street just to look at the scenes in the windows – at Christmas Selfridge's windows are in magazines all over the world! Harry Selfridge changed shopping for everyone with his new store. It isn't the cheapest place to go shopping, but it is certainly one of the most beautiful and interesting stores in the world!

11 Complete the sentences with the correct form of *going to* and the verbs in parentheses.

1. I _'m going to call_ (call) Laura later to ask about her test.
2. We _____ (look) around the new shopping mall on Saturday morning.
3. _____ (your mother/get) a new car soon?
4. I _____ (not become) a doctor. I want to be a research scientist.

12 Complete the sentences with the correct Present Continuous form of the verbs.

1. My mom _'s starting_ (start) a new job on Monday.
2. It's my birthday on Saturday and I _____ (have) a party at my house in the evening.
3. _____ (you/fly) from JFK or Newark Airport this weekend?
4. Sorry, my mistake! We _____ (not meet) Jane at 6, but at 6:30.

13 Complete the sentences with the verbs in bold. Use *going to* or the Present Continuous.

1. My plan is to **ask** Dad to lend me some money for a new laptop.
   I _'m going to ask Dad_ to lend me some money for a new laptop.
2. The arrangement is for Leo and me to **catch** the same train tomorrow.
   Leo and I _____ the same train tomorrow.
3. I want to **take** a quick shower and then go out with Jeff.
   I _____ a quick shower and then go out with Jeff.
4. Jack's aim is to **study** hard for the next tests.
   Jack _____ hard for the next tests.
5. The arrangement is for Dan and Kevin to **arrive** at 7, not at 8!
   Dan and Kevin _____ at 8, but at 7.
6. Do you plan to **spend** a lot of money at the mall on Saturday?
   _____ you _____ a lot of money at the mall on Saturday?

14 Complete the message with *going to* or the Present Continuous form of the verbs.

play   make   ~~have~~   go   bring
check out   buy   show   do

Nicky,
I'm writing about our arrangements to go out next week. My schedule is really full!
I [1] _'m having_ a guitar lesson on Monday at 4:30 and on Tuesday I [2] _____ shopping with my grandma at 4:00. She [3] _____ my birthday gift and she wants me to choose it! I [4] _____ her around the new mall downtown. Then on Wednesday I [5] _____ tennis at lunchtime and in the evening I think Sally [6] _____ over some pictures from her vacation to show me – if she has time. How about Thursday? [7] _____ you _____ anything on Thursday after school? I really need some summer tops, so I [8] _____ some shopping websites – but I can do that any time, so let me know if you are free. OK, now I [9] _____ some sandwiches and watch some TV.
Talk to you soon
Monica

15 WORD FRIENDS Match the parts of the sentences.

1. [e] When I was a child I
2. [ ] I went shopping yesterday and I
3. [ ] My aunt has a job in Boston and she
4. [ ] Kenny was very nice and he
5. [ ] Last year my dad was careful and he
6. [ ] Last month I lent Paul some money and yesterday he
7. [ ] My sister never has much money and often

a spent a lot of money at the expensive clothing store downtown.
b borrows some from me to go shopping.
c lent me some money to buy a concert ticket.
d saved enough money to buy a new car.
e got $8 as allowance every week.
f paid me back.
g earns $2,000 a week.

6 SHOPPING AROUND

16 Circle the correct option.
1. This coat is too big. Do you have a smaller (one) / ones?
2. Do you want the cheap tickets or the expensive one / ones?
3. I love the chicken sandwiches, but I don't like the cheese one / ones.
4. This cell phone is very old. I'd like a newer one / ones.
5. My laptop isn't as big as this one / ones.

17 Complete the sentences with the correct words.

| take sale ~~help~~ size forget |

1. Can I ___help___ you?
2. These ones are on _____.
3. What _____ are you?
4. Don't _____ your change.
5. I'll _____ them.

18 Order the words to make sentences.
1. a / looking / jacket / for / I'm
   I'm looking for a jacket.
2. this / please / try / I / on / can / ?
   _____
3. is / how / much / it / ?
   _____
4. it / have / color / do / another / you / in / ?
   _____
5. sneakers / these / too / are / small
   _____

19 Match questions 1–6 to answers a–f.
1. [a] Can I help you?
2. [ ] How much are these?
3. [ ] Can I try these on, please?
4. [ ] What size are you?
5. [ ] Do you have them in a smaller size?
6. [ ] Are they the right size?

a. I'm looking for some jeans.
b. They're too big.
c. I'm sorry, we don't.
d. I'm size twelve.
e. Sure. The changing rooms are over there.
f. They're on sale. They're fifteen dollars.

20 Complete the sentences with the correct words.

| hope should Let's Maybe Help ~~going~~ Let
leaving Can Would planning can't there |

A Greeting
Hi Rita,

B The information you want the other person to know.
I'm ¹ ___going___ to the beach.
² _____ ! My computer isn't working.
I'm really busy – I ³ _____ come.
The subway is really late.

C A request, offer or invitation
⁴ _____ you like to come?
⁵ _____ you help?
⁶ _____ you could come over after school?
Please wait for me.

D Arrangements
I ⁷ _____ be outside my house at two o'clock.
⁸ _____ meet at the entrance of the park at 12:30.
We're ⁹ _____ at two o'clock.
I'm ¹⁰ _____ to be at the tennis club at 7:30.

E Ending
See you ¹¹ _____ /soon.
¹² _____ me know.
I ¹³ _____ you can come/help.
Love,

156 Unit 6

SELF-ASSESSMENT

Vocabulary

1 Write the letters to complete the words.

1 You can buy a ⁰b <u>u n c h</u> of flowers at the ¹f _____ s _____ .
2 You can buy a ²l _____ of bread at the ³b _____ .
3 You can buy a ⁴b _____ of shampoo at the ⁵d _____ .

/5

2 Complete the sentences.

0 The <u>escalator</u> wasn't working, so we used the stairs.
1 We had a lot of food to buy and our _____ was full.
2 We had a meal at the food _____ .
3 I like _____ stores because they have a lot of different things.
4 Where are the public _____ ?
5 I was the last _____ in the supermarket!

/5

3 Circle the correct words to complete the sentences.

0 My younger sister gets (an allowance) / a wallet of ten dollars a week from our parents.
1 I think you gave me the wrong money / change. I gave you twenty dollars.
2 Excuse me, how many / much are these jeans?
3 I bought this sweater at the winter sale / size and it was very cheap.
4 Did you put your money in a piggy bank / pocket when you were a child?
5 Oh, no! I left my shopper / wallet in the store. There was a lot of money in it!

/5

Grammar

4 Complete the sentences with the comparative or superlative form of the adjectives.

0 Your book is <u>more interesting</u> than this one. (interesting)
1 The new department store is _____ than the old one was. (big)
2 Toy Story 4 was the _____ movie I saw last year. (enjoyable)
3 My bed isn't _____ as my sister's. (comfortable)
4 Mom's laptop was _____ than the one in the store. (cheap)
5 Oh, no! I got the _____ grade in class. (bad)

/5

5 Make sentences with *going to* or the Present Continuous form of the verbs.

0 how much / you / spend on Sunday / ?
How much are you going to spend on Sunday?
1 my dad / look for / a new job soon
2 I / play tennis / with Erica at 2:30 today
3 when / you / arrive back / from vacation / ?
4 I / try / to do my homework / this evening
5 what time / the bus / leave ?

/5

Speaking language practice

6 Match sentences a–f to blanks 0–5.

A: Can I help you? B: ⁰ *d*
A: These ones are on sale. B: ¹ _____
A: They're forty-five dollars. B: ² _____
A: They're a thirty-eight. B: ³ _____
A: Certainly. Here's a seat. B: ⁴ _____
A: Sure, here you are. B: ⁵ Thanks. _____

a They're fine. Thanks. I'll take them.
b What size are the brown ones?
c Can I try them on?
d I'm looking for some boots.
e How much are they?
f They're too big. Do you have a smaller size?

/5

Vocabulary /15
Grammar /10
Speaking language practice /5
Your total score /30

Unit 6

7 LEARNING TO WORK

1 Match jobs 1–8 to pictures A–H.

1. [E] builder
2. [ ] artist
3. [ ] hairdresser
4. [ ] mechanic
5. [ ] firefighter
6. [ ] pilot
7. [ ] lawyer
8. [ ] nurse

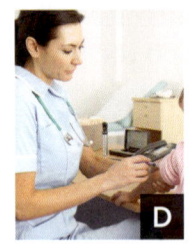

2 Match words 1–5 to words a–e to make jobs.

1. [e] police
2. [ ] tour
3. [ ] IT
4. [ ] bike
5. [ ] sales

a guide
b assistant
c courier
d specialist
e officer

3 Which jobs are the people talking about?

1. People come to me when they arrive at the hotel. I'm a(n) *receptionist*.
2. I design new buildings. I'm a(n) _____.
3. I fix cars. I'm a(n) _____.
4. I write stories for newspapers. I'm a(n) _____.
5. I paint pictures. I'm a(n) _____.
6. I work outside and I keep cows and pigs. I'm a(n) _____.
7. I cook meals for people in my restaurant. I'm a(n) _____.
8. I fly planes and helicopters. I'm a(n) _____.

4 Complete the sentences with the correct words.

farmer   police officer   ~~builder~~   electrician
gardener   pilot   tour guide   mail carrier
soldier   writer

1. My uncle is a(n) __builder__ and he helped my dad put up a wall in our yard.
2. The _____ was late this morning, so I didn't get the letter until two o'clock.
3. There's a problem with the lights in my bedroom. We need a(n) _____.
4. Melissa is a(n) _____ of famous fantasy books.
5. It takes a long time to become a(n) _____ and fly planes.
6. Someone stole my dad's car and a(n) _____ came to our house today to ask questions.
7. I'd like to be a(n) _____ and show tourists around interesting places and historic buildings.
8. A(n) _____ has a long day. They get up really early to feed their animals.
9. My brother is in the army. He's a(n) _____.
10. I want to be a(n) _____ because I can work outside and grow flowers and plants.

5 **WORD FRIENDS** Order the words to make questions or sentences.

1. to / people / from / five / work / nine / some
   Some people work from nine to five.
2. you / work / happy / at / are / ?
   _____
3. don't / indoors / work / farmers
   _____
4. wouldn't / uniform / like / a / I / wear / to
   _____
5. get / on / must / time / work / you / to
   _____
6. to / team / a / need / in / work / firefighters
   _____
7. do / have / teachers / weekend / the / on / work / to / ?
   _____
8. work / receptionists / indoors / usually
   _____
9. often / work / have / drivers / early / start / bus / to
   _____

Unit 7

6 Complete the sentences with the correct words.

> happy   team   earn   ~~wear~~   time   from
> alone   weekend

1 Firefighters have to _wear_ a uniform at work.
2 Most salesclerks work _____ nine to five.
3 Artists usually work _____ .
4 I think it's important to be _____ at work.
5 Lawyers can _____ good money.
6 I need to get up early to get to work on _____ .
7 My mom's a doctor and she often has to work on the _____ .
8 In a hospital, nurses have to work in a _____ .

7 Complete the text with the correct words.

I'm still a student, but I have a part-time ¹ _job_ . I'm a ² _____ at a restaurant in my town. I take the meals from the kitchen to the customers. I like my job. I don't earn much ³ _____ , but it's fun. It's nice to work ⁴ _____ a team and I like the ⁵ _____ a lot. He cooks great food! I have to work on the ⁶ _____ , so I can't go out a lot with my friends on Saturdays and Sundays. I also have to wear a blue and white ⁷ _____ , but that's OK! In the future, I'd like to be a ⁸ _____ like my dad and work for a newspaper, or an ⁹ _____ like my mom and design houses. I think it's important to work when you're a student. You learn lots of things, like – it's important to ¹⁰ _____ to work on time. Also it's important to be happy ¹¹ _____ work. I'm happy in my job now and I hope I can be happy in the future, too.

8 Complete the sentences with the correct words.

> ~~schedule~~   classroom   uniform
> textbook   test

1 A: Which room is geography class in?
   B: I don't know – look at the _schedule_ .
2 This _____ is good. The pictures are interesting and the activities are, too.
3 I like our school _____ . The colors are nice.
4 We're having a French _____ today and I can't remember anything!
5 I left my cell phone in the _____ . Wait for me.

9 Complete the sentences with *will* and the correct verbs.

> rain   be   work   win   ~~get~~   break

1 Helena _will get_ the best grades on the test. She's very smart.
2 It _____ on the weekend. I heard that on the radio.
3 In 2020 I _____ a teacher and I'll live in the country.
4 Be careful! You _____ the pen!
5 Our team is very good. I think we _____ the game.
6 People _____ from their homes in the future.

10 Make negative sentences and questions from the positive predictions.

1 Danny will pass the test.
   N: *Danny won't pass the test.*
   Q: *Will Danny pass the test?*
2 It will rain tomorrow.
   N: _____
   Q: _____
3 Prices will be lower in the summer.
   N: _____
   Q: _____
4 In the future classes will start at 10 a.m.
   N: _____
   Q: _____

Unit 7   159

7 LEARNING TO WORK

11 Make predictions with *will/won't*.

1 Wait here. I / not / be / long
   I won't be long.

2 you / help me / with this homework / later / ?
   _____

3 The journey is short; It / only / take / an hour
   _____

4 I / not think / Miss Jones / teach us / next semester
   _____

5 where / your family live / in Canada / ?
   _____

6 people / live longer / in the future
   _____

12 Complete the text with the correct future form of the verbs in parentheses.

So, what ¹ *will shopping be* (shopping/be) like in the future? No one knows definitely, but I think we ² _____ (do) ALL our shopping online. People ³ _____ (not need) to go out to shop. For food – our refrigerator ⁴ _____ (tell) our computers what we need. We ⁵ _____ (not have to) do anything! Robots ⁶ _____ (drive) the food to our houses and put it directly into our refrigerators and cabinets. But ⁷ _____ (robots/choose) our clothes, too? No, I don't think they ⁸ _____. We ⁹ _____ (go) online, choose our clothes and then we ¹⁰ _____ (see) a picture of ourselves in the jeans or dress on our screens and we ¹¹ _____ (decide) to buy or not to buy! Of course, we ¹² _____ (not have) any money in our wallets in the future. We ¹³ _____ (pay) for everything automatically. So, in the future there ¹⁴ _____ (not be) any salesclerks or bank clerks, just lots of IT specialists and robots.

13 Complete the sentences with the correct words.

full-time   part-time   ~~temporary~~   summer

1 My friend has a *temporary* job in the supermarket for the next six weeks, but then he'll need to find another one.

2 My mom had a _____ job when I was very young. She only worked a few hours every day.

3 I want to get a _____ job when I finish high school, before I go to college.

4 My dad works from nine to five at the bank. It's a _____ job. This is his tenth year there!

14 Circle the correct answer.

1 A secretary usually works _____ an office.
   a on
   b at
   c in

2 If you're looking _____ a job, let me know.
   a for
   b over
   c on

3 At the moment I'm _____, but I think I'll find a job soon.
   a employed
   b unemployed
   c employing

4 My brother worked _____ a server last summer and earned a lot of money.
   a like
   b by
   c as

5 Jake _____ his job in the supermarket because he never got there on time.
   a got
   b lost
   c missed

6 My grandpa worked _____ the same company for fifty years!
   a about
   b for
   c into

Unit 7

15 Read the text. Mark the sentences ✓ (right) ✗ (wrong), or ? (doesn't say).

1. ✓ The writer believes that children often want to have the same job as famous people or people they know.
2. ☐ The writer wanted to be on television.
3. ☐ The writer works on television now.
4. ☐ Boys and girls have different types of dream jobs.
5. ☐ Today's children will earn more than their parents did.
6. ☐ It isn't a good idea to have an unrealistic dream.
7. ☐ The writer thinks that people's dreams stay the same through their lives.

What was your dream?

What were your dreams and ambitions when you were a child? Are your dreams the same now? Nearly all children have a dream for the future. Sometimes they want to be like people they see on television or someone in their family. When I was a child, I wanted to be a lawyer because I admired the lawyer in a TV series! My sister wanted to be an actress!

A recent survey asked 11,000 seven-year-olds about their ambitions and the results were interesting. Most of them had definite ideas about their future careers. The most popular jobs included teacher, scientist, firefighter, and police officer. In general boys wanted jobs related to sports (a third of them wanted to become a soccer player or sportsman) and girls preferred a job helping people, like a doctor or teacher.

Experts say that today's children have greater ambitions than their parents had and this is a very good thing. People who have a dream will work harder and have fewer problems. Sometimes those dreams aren't realistic and they change. Not every seven-year-old boy will become a rich and successful soccer player! I didn't become a lawyer – and surprisingly, my sister didn't become an actress! But it is important to be ambitious. We all need to dream.

16 **WORD FRIENDS** Circle the correct option.

1. I must *learn* / (*study*) for my English test tomorrow.
2. Unfortunately, I *missed* / *failed* my math test yesterday because I didn't study.
3. We're going to *write* / *take* a history test next week.
4. We're *getting* / *finding* the results of our tests next Thursday.
5. I never *make* / *get* good grades on tests. I get too nervous.
6. The teacher sent Rob to the principal's office because he *cheated* / *failed* on a test.

17 Put *if* in the correct position in the sentences. Add commas where necessary.

1. *If* dad doesn't arrive home soon , his dinner will be cold.
2. ✗ We won't fail our tests *if* we work hard.
3. ☐ I'll be happy ☐ I get a good grade.
4. ☐ I get home too late ☐ I won't call you.
5. ☐ I won't go running ☐ it's very cold and rainy.
6. ☐ I get a summer job ☐ I'll earn lots of money.
7. ☐ you don't go to bed soon ☐ you'll be very tired tomorrow.

18 Match the parts of the sentences.

1. g If the bus is late,
2. ☐ If my dad doesn't like his new job,
3. ☐ If I don't see you after school,
4. ☐ If we get good grades,
5. ☐ If the jeans don't fit,
6. ☐ If we win the game on Saturday,
7. ☐ If you don't work hard,

a. I'll take them back to the store tomorrow.
b. we'll be the best team in town.
c. you won't get a good job.
d. I'll see you at the party.
e. our teacher will be really happy.
f. he'll find a different one.
g. I'll miss the start of the movie.

Unit 7

7 LEARNING TO WORK

19 Complete the sentences with the correct form of the verbs in parentheses.

1. If Dad ___*drives*___ (drive) us to the movies, we ___*'ll get*___ (get) there by 4:30.
2. I _____ (not buy) any tickets if you _____ (not want) to go to the concert.
3. We _____ (be) back home before lunch if we _____ (leave) now.
4. If you _____ (go) to France in May, you _____ (have) sunny weather.
5. David _____ (have to) wear a uniform if he _____ (become) a police officer.
6. If the teacher _____ (not give) us a test tomorrow, I _____ (be) very happy.
7. _____ (you/wait) for me if my train _____ (be) late?

20 Complete the dialogue with the correct form of the verbs.

| buy | not see | ~~miss~~ | not have |
| go | ask | be | give | spend |

A: The new clothing store has a sale on today! Let's go after school.
B: I have a swimming lesson after school. If I ¹___*miss*___ it, my teacher will be angry.
A: But if I ² _____ without you and get some cheap boots, you ³ _____ angry!
B: If you ⁴ _____ any more money you ⁵ _____ enough to go on vacation!
A: Ah. It's my birthday soon. If I ⁶ _____ my parents, they ⁷ _____ me money instead of a gift.
B: OK! But I can't miss swimming. If I give you some money, ⁸ _____ me a cheap black T-shirt?
A: Yeah. If I ⁹ _____ any cheap ones, I'll buy you something else.
B: No, don't! Don't buy anything then!

21 **WORD FRIENDS** Complete the sentences with the correct words.

| do (×2) | give | ~~take~~ | write |

1. Did you ___*take*___ any notes in our history class today?
2. We have to _____ a long essay for English tonight.
3. If we _____ activities 1 and 2 now, we won't need to _____ any homework tonight!
4. Tomorrow Jason is going to _____ a presentation about New York in class.

22 Match blanks 1–6 to sentences a–f.

A: Hi, Beth! The Rubies are playing in town tonight at the Grange Theater. Mike and I are going. ¹ ___*e*___
B: Oh, I'm not sure. ² ___ If I finish this history essay early, I'll come.
A: Oh, Beth. The Rubies are more important than work. ³ ___ I can help you with your homework.
B: OK, then! ⁴ ___ What time are you and Mike going?
A: ⁵ ___ I'm going to call him in a moment to confirm. Do you want to meet us there?
B: ⁶ ___ I only get home from swimming at 7:20. How about I meet you inside at 7:45?
A: OK. Let me help you with that essay now!

a I definitely won't be there by 7:30.
b I might come but I have a lot of work.
c We'll probably meet outside the Grange at about 7:30.
d They probably won't come to our town again for a long time.
e Would you like to come, too?
f Then I'll definitely come!

23 Complete the sentences with the correct prepositions.

| in | ~~at~~ (2x) | of | about |

1. I'm good ___*at*___ French.
2. I'm interested _____ languages.
3. I'm afraid _____ the dark.
4. I'm crazy _____ pop music.
5. I'm bad _____ art.

SELF-ASSESSMENT

Vocabulary

1 Complete the sentences with the correct jobs.

0 My dad is a *journalist* and he writes articles for magazines and newspapers.
1 Liz loves repairing cars. She wants to be a _____.
2 I don't want to be an _____ like my cousin. He just calculates numbers for businesses all day.
3 We need an _____ to fix these lights.
4 My brother is studying to be an _____. He wants to design modern, eco-friendly buildings.
5 The police arrested Kevin for dangerous driving. He needs a good _____ to work for him.

/5

2 Circle the correct option.

0 Some people don't want to work in /(for) a company, so they start their own business.
1 It's important to work *at / in* a team if you want to get results.
2 My brother worked *as / like* a server in the summer.
3 Nelson is bad at getting to work *in / on* time.
4 It's great to *win / earn* a lot of money, but it's more important to be happy at work.
5 When the company closed, a lot of people *were / had* unemployed.

/5

3 Complete the sentences with the correct words.

| classmates   library   playground
| principal   ~~students~~   lounge

0 My first school was small. It only had sixty *students*.
1 I'd like to speak to Miss Turner. Is she in the teacher's _____?
2 The teacher sent Tom to see the _____ because he was cheating on the test.
3 At recess, the children play in the _____.
4 Let's work in the _____. It's quieter there than in the classroom.
5 I get along with my _____. We're friends.

/5

Grammar

4 Complete the sentences with *will* and the verbs below.

| be (x2)   be able   get   travel   watch

1 In the future there ⁰ *won't be* any TVs. We ¹ *'ll watch* shows on computers.
2 After college I ² _____ a job right away. I ³ _____ for a few months.
3 Jan ⁴ _____ eighteen next Sunday. She ⁵ _____ to learn to drive!

/5

5 Circle the correct option.

1 ⁰*Does /(Will)* your brother take his driving test again if he ¹ *fails / will fail* it tomorrow?
2 If I ² *go / will go* to bed late tonight, I ³ *am / will be* tired tomorrow.
3 We ⁴ *move / will move* to the USA if my dad ⁵ *gets / will get* a new job.

/5

Speaking language practice

6 Order the words to make sentences.

0 Look at the time! be / will / late / we / definitely
   We will definitely be late.
1 probably / you / won't / I / see / later
   _____ Good luck with the test!
2 Don't leave. arrive / they / soon / might
   _____
3 you / party / come / the / definitely / to / will / ?
   _____
4 Sophie doesn't eat a lot. might / meal / want / big / she / a / not
   _____
5 Take an umbrella. rain / it / later / may
   _____

/5

Vocabulary /15
Grammar /10
Speaking language practice /5
Your total score /30

Unit 7 163

8 CLOSE TO NATURE

1 Look at pictures 1–8 and complete the names for natural features.

1 b _e a c h_
2 c _ _ _ _ _
3 l _ _ _
4 r _ _ _ _
5 f _ _ _ _ _
6 i _ _ _ _ _
7 r _ _ _ _
8 s _ _

2 Use the clues to complete the crossword.

Across
3 an area of land with lots of tropical plants and trees
4 a forest with tall trees, warm climate, and lots of rain
6 very big sea
8 where a river falls over a cliff
9 hot and dry area with no plants

Down
1 very high hill
2 a hill with a hole at the top that sometimes has fire coming from it
5 an area of grass where farmers can grow things
7 this is where the land meets the sea

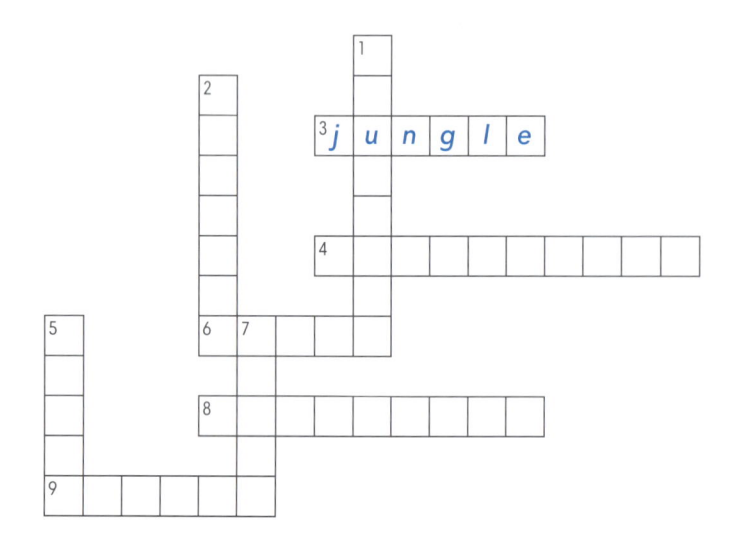

3 _j u n g l e_

3 Read the signs. Then complete the labels with the correct words.

a cliff   a desert   a beach   ~~a mountain~~   rainforest   a river   a field

1 Check the weather forecast before starting to climb.
a mountain

2 Use the bridge to cross – 300 meters away.

3 No water for the next 500 km.

4 Sun chairs here   50¢ an hour

5 NO CLIMBING. DANGER – FALLING ROCKS.

6 Help the environment – save the trees!

7 Public path, but please shut the gate – farm animals.

4 **WORD FRIENDS** Circle the correct option.

1 We went skiing (in) / up the mountains last year.
2 We saw some black cows on / in a big field.
3 My uncle has a house by / on a lake.
4 My parents would like to live in / on the coast, so they can look at the sea every day.
5 My friend lives in / on an island and has to take a boat to go to school every morning.
6 We can walk along this path and then have a picnic by / in the river.

Unit 8

5 Circle the correct answer.

1. I live about 100 kilometers from Canada's ___ city, Ottawa.
   a official   **b capital**   c national
2. I live with my parents in a small house on the south ___.
   a beach   b sea   c coast
3. Our house is in a village where the ___ is only 540 people!
   a population   b country   c border
4. It takes five minutes to get to the ___ and we often go swimming there in summer.
   a cliff   b island   c beach
5. From the window of my room I can see the farmer's ___ with black and white cows.
   a fields   b rocks   c waterfall
6. I can ride my bike along a path to a ___ where we sometimes pick flowers.
   a jungle   b forest   c desert

6 Circle the correct option.

If you're looking for somewhere to spend a vacation that is full of natural ¹borders / **features**, then come to South Carolina! It is one of the most beautiful areas in the ²capital / country. If you stay in a hotel in Harbor Town village, you can go on trips to the ³coast / rocks and see the yachts and a lighthouse. If you like walking, then this is the place for you! You can see different types of trees, follow small ⁴lakes / rivers, and try to see a wild turkey! If you go to the ⁵rainforest / sea, you can walk along the ⁶beaches / jungle and look across the water to some pretty ⁷flags / islands. The ⁸cliffs / desert along the beaches are high and can be dangerous, so don't walk too close to them. Interested in South Carolina? Check out our website …

7 Complete the sentences with the affirmative form of the Present Perfect of the verbs.

| eat win ~~sleep~~ write play see |

1. I _have slept_ in a tent.
2. My brother _____ two short stories.
3. My mother _____ Mexican food.
4. My cousins _____ basketball in the USA.
5. You _____ lots of medals.
6. Danny _____ the Eiffel Tower.

8 Order the words to make sentences or questions.

1. been / Italy / I've / to / never
   I've never been to Italy.
2. you / Japanese / ever / eaten / have / food / ?
   _____
3. seen / we / new / movie / the / horror / haven't
   _____
4. never / my / played / has / soccer / brother
   _____
5. times / how / been / have / France / you / many / to / ?
   _____

9 Complete the dialogue with the correct form of the verbs in parentheses.

A: So, you'd like to be a tour guide for our company. ¹ *Have you been* (you/be) to many countries?
B: Yes. I ² _____ (travel) a lot. I ³ _____ (be) to most European countries on vacation and I ⁴ _____ (stay) with friends in Thailand twice.
A: ⁵ _____ (you/ever/give) talks or presentations about famous sights?
B: Yes, I ⁶ _____ (do) that pretty often! At school! I'm really interested in museums and important buildings. I ⁷ _____ (also/do) some projects about famous art galleries in the world.
A: Excellent. What other experience do you have that's important for a tour guide?
B: Well, I ⁸ _____ (learn) three languages, so I now speak Spanish, Chinese, and Russian … and English, of courses. I think that will help.
A: Oh, yes.
B: And I ⁹ _____ (make) lots of friends in different countries, so I know quite a bit about different cultures.
A: Very good. I think you'll be very good for the job!

Unit 8

8 CLOSE TO NATURE

10 Circle the correct answer.

1. I know you're tired, but don't give _____. Keep running!
   a on   **b up**   c over

2. It's raining! I think we should go _____ to our hotel.
   a back   b up   c out

3. What do you do when you come _____ a word you don't know?
   a over   b at   c across

4. The bomb hit the target and it blew _____.
   a off   b up   c down

5. I need to find _____ when the movie starts.
   a in   b out   c up

11 Read the blog post and circle the correct answer.

1. Joe Simpson and Simon Yates
   a were from Peru.
   b met while they were climbing Siula Grande.
   c had the same ambition.

2. Because of the bad weather
   a they didn't get to the top of the mountain.
   b Joe had an accident.
   c Simon lost the rope.

3. On the way down the mountain Simon
   a saved Joe's life.
   b saved his own life.
   c died.

4. After Joe fell into the hole
   a he climbed back up again.
   b he found his way back to the camp.
   c he stayed there for three days.

5. Since 1985, Joe
   a has published some books.
   b has never climbed again.
   c has made a movie about his survival.

My blog

ABOUT ME | **MY POSTS** | CONTACT ME

I've seen a lot of movies about survivors, but my favorite is a true story about an English mountaineer called Joe Simpson. He climbed a very dangerous mountain, Siula Grande in Peru, in 1985 with his friend and partner Simon Yates. Joe and Simon wanted to be the first people to climb the west face of the mountain.

When they started, the weather was fine, but then it changed. The two climbers reached the top successfully, but then they had to get back down quickly because of the bad weather. Unfortunately, Joe then fell and broke his leg. Simon tried to help his friend get down the mountain. He tied him onto a long rope, but the weather got worse and he had to make a terrible decision. He had to cut the rope that was holding Joe or die.

Simon cut the rope and Joe fell into a big hole. Luckily, Joe found a way out of the hole at the bottom. It took him three days to get down the rest of the mountain. With his broken leg he could only move very slowly. He had no food or water, and when he got to the camp he was nearly dead. But he got there and he survived!

Joe wrote a book called "Touching the Void" about the experience and in 2003 director Kevin MacDonald made a movie with the same title. Since his adventure, Joe has had lots of operations on his leg. Doctors told him never to climb again. But he has! He has also written several books and given lots of presentations about climbing. In my opinion "Touching the Void" is the best movie about survival that I've ever seen.

[leave a comment]

12 Put the words in parentheses in the correct position in the sentences.

1. I've woken up. (just)
   I've just woken up.
2. I've read that book. (already)
3. We haven't studied grammar. (yet)
4. Mick has called. (just)
5. Has the teacher corrected our homework? (yet)
6. I haven't been to the beach. (yet)

13 Match the sentences in Activity 12 to sentences a–f below.

a ☐ He can't go swimming with us.
b ☐ 1 I'm really tired.
c ☐ Is it sandy?
d ☐ Do you have another one?
e ☐ We gave it to her a week ago.
f ☐ We can't do this activity.

14 Order the words to make sentences or questions.

1. the / yet / been / exhibition / have / new / to / you / ?
   Have you been to the new exhibition yet?
2. just / Chile / dad / in / vacation / booked / has / our
3. spoken / about / I / the / yet / haven't / to / concert / Bill
4. seen / we've / movie / that / already
5. just / your / I've / email / opened
6. party / she / the / invited / to / already / you / has / ?

15 Rewrite the sentences using the Present Perfect and *already*, *just*, or *yet*.

1. I spoke to Pat a few moments ago.
   I've just spoken to Pat.
2. I did my homework earlier this morning.
3. I need to clean my room.
4. Did you clean the car this morning?
5. My friend sent me a really funny video clip about five minutes ago.
6. We went to the museum yesterday.

16 Circle the correct answer.

Hello from Barbados! I've ¹___ been on a vacation like this before. It's amazing! We arrived some hours ago, but we've ²___ been to the beach and it's beautiful. Have you ever ³___ a picture of a Caribbean beach? It has beautiful white sand and the sea is a beautiful blue! And I ⁴___ ever felt so hot before – but not uncomfortable. I've ⁵___ swimming and my back ⁶___ already gotten a suntan! I've met some really nice people and we're going to have a meal with them tonight. OK, I have to go now because Dad has ⁷___ called me. We're going back to the hotel. We haven't unpacked ⁸___!

1. a ever   (b) never   c sometimes
2. a yet   b already   c ever
3. a see   b saw   c seen
4. a have   b haven't   c had
5. a gone   b go   c was
6. a have   b has   c haven't
7. a already   b yet   c just
8. a ever   b just   c yet

Unit 8

8 CLOSE TO NATURE

17 Find seven more outdoor activities in the wordsearch.

V	V	G	I	C	Y	C	L	I	N	G	C
C	L	I	B	Y	P	N	E	N	L	O	F
S	N	O	W	B	O	A	R	D	I	N	G
V	Z	K	C	B	G	S	S	Z	S	N	V
S	H	S	R	K	N	F	Z	T	I	N	C
U	E	Q	L	D	I	J	G	K	N	P	S
R	T	C	F	S	M	Y	I	R	D	Y	K
F	I	Z	H	U	M	H	Z	E	Y	I	I
I	C	I	G	N	I	K	A	D	A	K	I
N	N	U	B	C	W	R	A	G	V	W	N
G	C	J	Z	I	S	V	P	X	E	U	G
K	A	Y	A	K	I	N	G	P	D	A	A

18 Complete the sentences with the correct words.

| rock   wind-surfing   scuba   biking   ~~trekking~~ |

1 Have you ever gone pony _trekking_ ?
2 We often go mountain _____.
3 I'm going _____ diving in Egypt soon.
4 I'd love to go _____ climbing, but it's pretty dangerous.
5 I once went _____, but I kept falling into the water!

19 Complete the words from the descriptions.

1 You wear this on your head for protection:
    h e l m e t
2 You can use this to find your way when you are mountain biking: c _____
3 You wear this to keep warm in water:
    w _____
4 You use these wooden things to move a boat through water: p _____
5 You wear these on your hands for protection:
    g _____
6 You wear these to protect your eyes:
    g _____
7 You wear these on your feet when you're climbing:
    b _____

20 Circle the correct option.

1 Is *there* / *it* all right for me to walk through this field?
2 Sure – go *ahead* / *forward*.
3 *Can* / *Might* my brother borrow your life jacket?
4 Can I ask *for* / *for a* favor?
5 I'm *frightened* / *afraid* it's not possible.
6 I'm sorry, but you *couldn't* / *can't* use your cell phone here.
7 No *problem* / *worry*. That's fine.

21 Mark sentences from Activity 20 AFP (asking for permission), GP (giving permission), or RP (refusing permission).

1 _AFP_
2 _____
3 _____
4 _____
5 _____
6 _____
7 _____

22 Order the sentences to make an email.

☐ What about your trip to Hawaii? I can't wait to hear about it!

☐ However, my parents have told me to study more, so we can come back soon.

☐ You won't believe where I am right now!

☐ That's it! Paris! I have never been more excited in my life — and scared because my French is not that good.

[1] Dear Alex,

☐ I have already been to lots of cool places, but the best part was seeing the Eiffel Tower.

☐ I have spoken to some people in a restaurant and back at the hotel and I guess it was OK.

Unit 8

SELF-ASSESSMENT

Vocabulary

1 Circle the correct option.

1 On Sunday afternoon we sunbathed on the ⁰coast / **beach**.
2 We swam across the small ¹waterfall / river and walked in the ² fields / rocks.
3 We went around the ³desert / island in a boat. We saw beautiful ⁴cliffs / lakes.
4 What's the capital ⁵language / city of your country?

/5

2 Complete the sentences with the correct words.

| snowboarding   climbing   diving   fishing |
| wind-surfing   ~~trekking~~ |

0 Young people often go pony _trekking_ in the path near my home.
1 My brother fell in the river from the bridge when he went _____ last month.
2 This is a good place to go scuba _____.
3 I love winter sports. I'm not very good at skiing, but I love _____.
4 We can't go _____ today because there's no wind!
5 My dad goes rock _____ in the mountains every year.

/5

3 Complete the words in the sentences.

0 You should always wear a l i f e j a c k e t when you're in a boat.
1 We went down the river in a k_____.
2 Oh, no! I lost a p_____ in the water! We can't get back to the beach!
3 Don't forget your h_____. You can hurt your head.
4 I always wear g_____ when I'm skiing to protect my eyes.
5 I can see on the m_____ that we're close.

/5

Grammar

4 Complete the sentences with the Present Perfect form of the verbs.

| buy   drink   ~~forget~~   leave   see   write |

0 I _have_ never _forgotten_ to do my English homework. It's true!
1 My mom _____ already _____ ten emails today! She's still on the computer.
2 Jack and Pete _____ already _____ this movie five times. Let's find a different one.
3 My brother _____ already _____ all the milk. I need to get some from the store.
4 I'm afraid Helen _____ already _____ the office. You can contact her at home.
5 I _____ never _____ plastic shoes. I think they are uncomfortable.

/5

5 Complete the sentences with the Present Perfect and the words in parentheses.

0 _Have you seen_ (you/see) the new travel TV show yet?
1 We _____ (not have) dinner yet.
2 I _____ (just/speak) to Sally about the hotel arrangements.
3 Tom _____ (already/buy) our train tickets, so don't worry.
4 _____ (your mom/ever/live) in France? Her French is amazing.
5 Lara and Dan _____ (never/go) camping, but I think they'll like it.

/5

Speaking language practice

6 Complete the conversations with one word in each blank.

1 A: ⁰ _Can_ I use your goggles, please?
   B: Yes, of ¹_____ you can.
2 A: Is it OK ²_____ me to leave my bike here?
   B: Sure – ³_____ ahead.
3 A: Is it all ⁴_____ to borrow this wet suit?
   B: I'm ⁵_____, but you can't. I'm going to wear it.

/5

Vocabulary	/15
Grammar	/10
Speaking language practice	/5
Your total score	/30

Unit 8   169

SELF-ASSESSMENT ANSWER KEY

Unit 1

Activity 1
1 classical 2 photographer 3 romantic
4 cartoons 5 traditional

Activity 2
1 listening 2 taking 3 reading
4 watching 5 painting

Activity 3
1 don't 2 does 3 Does 4 doesn't 5 do

Activity 4
1 Do you want to go to the movies?
2 My friend doesn't live near me.
3 Jack speaks English and French.
4 Our teacher usually gives us lots of homework.
5 What time do you go to bed on Fridays?

Activity 5
1 're reading 2 read 3 'm sitting
4 'm trying 5 Do you want

Activity 6
1 Can 2 screening 3 sold 4 seat 5 much

Unit 2

Activity 1
1 bear 2 monkey 3 duck 4 rabbit 5 claw

Activity 2
1 shy 2 forgetful 3 impulsive
4 adventurous 5 careless

Activity 3
1 brush 2 empty 3 give 4 scratch 5 take

Activity 4
1 Were your parents at the concert on Saturday?
2 That documentary wasn't very interesting.
3 Was Tom at your party?
4 What was your favorite movie last year?
5 There weren't any monkeys at the safari park.

Activity 5
1 didn't like 2 did you live 3 moved
4 didn't work 5 was

Activity 6
1 all 2 totally 3 accident 4 could 5 angry

Unit 3

Activity 1
1 battery 2 flash drive 3 keyboard
4 drone 5 tablet

Activity 2
1 chat 2 text 3 charge 4 make
5 click

Activity 3
1 crashed 2 died 3 stopped
4 download 5 virus

Activity 4
1 left 2 didn't give
3 Did/cost 4 took 5 stole

Activity 5
1 where 2 which 3 where
4 which 5 who

Activity 6
1 all 2 At 3 after 4 later 5 end

Unit 4

Activity 1
1 c 2 c 3 a 4 c 5 a

Activity 2
1 clean 2 do 3 empty 4 cleans 5 took

Activity 3
1 department 2 mall 3 hall
4 office 5 visitor center

Activity 4
1 angrily 2 well 3 carefully 4 quickly 5 early

Activity 5
1 can 2 must not 3 can't
4 has to/must 5 must not

Activity 6
1 Where do you think we should go?
2 I think you should go to the British Museum.
3 I don't think that's a good idea.
4 Why don't you go to an art gallery?
5 Thanks for the advice.

Unit 5

Activity 1
1 skin 2 beard 3 ankle 4 muscles 5 teeth

Activity 2
1 a 2 b 3 c 4 b 5 b

Activity 3
1 allergy 2 sneezing 3 headache 4 throat 5 flu

Activity 4
1 many 2 any 3 lot 4 any 5 some

Activity 5
1 Hannah was reading a book when Gary called.
2 I wasn't working when Dave came to visit us.
3 Were you waiting at the bus stop when it started to rain?
4 The teacher shouted at us because we weren't concentrating in class.
5 Were you having dinner when I called you?

Activity 6
1 hurts 2 hospital 3 wrong 4 feel 5 some

Unit 6

Activity 1
1 flower shop 2 loaf 3 bakery
4 bottle 5 drugstore

Activity 2
1 shopping cart 2 court 3 department
4 restrooms 5 shopper

Activity 3
1 change 2 much 3 sale 4 piggy bank 5 wallet

Activity 4
2 bigger 3 most enjoyable
4 as comfortable 5 cheaper 6 worst

Activity 5
1 My dad is going to look for a new job soon.
2 I'm playing tennis with Erica at 2:30 today.
3 When are you arriving back from vacation?
4 I'm going to try to do my homework this evening.
5 What time is the bus leaving?

Activity 6
1 e 2 b 3 c 4 f 5 a

Unit 7

Activity 1
1 mechanic 2 accountant 3 electrician
4 architect 5 driver

Activity 2
1 in 2 as 3 on 4 earn 5 were

Activity 3
1 lounge 2 principal 3 playground
3 library 5 classmates

Activity 4
1 Will you stay 2 won't get / 'll travel
3 will be / 'll be able

Activity 5
1 fails 2 will 3 will be 4 will move 5 gets

Activity 6
2 I probably won't see you later.
3 They might arrive soon.
4 Will you definitely come to the party?
5 She might not want a big meal.
6 It may rain later.

Unit 8

Activity 1
1 river 2 fields 3 island 4 cliffs 5 city

Activity 2
1 fishing 2 diving 3 snowboarding
4 wind-surfing 5 climbing

Activity 3
1 kayak 2 paddle 3 helmet 4 goggles 5 map

Activity 4
1 has/written 2 have/seen 3 has/drunk
4 has/left 5 have/bought

Activity 5
1 haven't had
2 've just spoken
3 has already bought
4 Has your mom ever lived
5 have never gone

Activity 6
1 course 2 for 3 go 4 right 5 sorry

Self-assessment Answer Key

GRAMMAR TIME ANSWER KEY

Unit 1.2
Activity 1
2 We often watch American movies.
3 She is always busy.
4 I don't usually go out on Monday.
5 My sister doesn't read comic books.

Activity 2
2 gets 3 often eats 4 flies
5 studies 6 always goes

Unit 1.2
Activity 1
2 Does your favorite singer write songs?
3 Do your parents watch music videos online?
4 Do you and your friends like dancing?
5 Does your English teacher sometimes draw pictures on the board?

Activity 2
2 What time does the concert finish?
3 How often do your parents go dancing?
4 Students' own answers.
5 Students' own answers.

Unit 1.4
Activity 1
2 are you doing? 3 Are you having
4 'm not 5 'm studying
6 Is he studying 7 is 8 're driving
9 aren't reading 10 're playing
11 're getting

Activity 2
Students' own answers.

Unit 1.4
Activity 1
2 live, 'm visiting 3 's saving 4 often goes
5 doesn't speak, knows

Activity 2
Students' own answers.

Activity 3
Students' own answers.

Unit 2.2
Activity 1
2 Was 3 were 4 Were
5 were 6 were 7 Were

Activity 2
2 "Was it cold?" "Yes, it was."
3 "Were you at home?" "No, I wasn't."
4 "Was there a letter for me?" "No, there wasn't."
5 We weren't very hungry.
6 There weren't any tickets.

Activity 3
Students' own answers.

Unit 2.4
Activity 1
2 carried 3 played 4 helped
5 dropped 6 married

Activity 2
2 Did they like, didn't 3 didn't watch
4 Did you finish, did 5 dropped, stopped

Activity 3
Students' own answers.

Unit 3.2
Activity 1
2 drank 3 drove 4 ate 5 found 6 went
7 left 8 made 9 met 10 read 11 ran
12 spoke 13 took 14 wrote

Activity 2
Students' own answers.

Activity 3
Students' own answers.

Activity 4
2 hit 3 hurt 4 felt 5 sat 6 fell 7 got

Unit 3.4
Activity 1
2 who 3 that 4 where 5 that

Activity 2
2 a Steve Jobs was an inventor who changed the world.
3 d Parma ham is a type of meat that is popular in Italy.
4 c Drones are gadgets that can fly.

Activity 3
Students' own answers.

Unit 4.2
Activity 1
2 well 3 noisily 4 quietly 5 late

Activity 2
2 good, well 3 early, early
4 unkind, unkindly 5 heavily, heavy

Unit 4.4
Activity 1
2 You can't/must not use your cell phone.
3 You must/have to wait here.
4 You can't/must not talk here.

Activity 2
Students' own answers.

Activity 3
Students' own answers.

Unit 5.2
Activity 1
2 much 3 any 4 much 5 many

Activity 2
2 much 3 many 4 any 5 some 6 a lot of
7 much 8 any

Unit 5.4
Activity 1
2 wasn't dancing 3 was Sue going
4 wasn't listening 5 were you doing

Activity 2
2 was raining 3 put 4 was going
5 saw 6 was getting 7 wasn't looking
8 was going 9 rode 10 fell 11 hit
12 was wearing

Unit 6.2
Activity 1
2 easier, the easiest
3 later, the latest
4 more expensive, the most expensive
5 younger, the youngest

Activity 2
2 the happiest 3 the longest
4 the tastiest 5 the worst

Activity 3
Students' own answers.

Unit 6.4
Activity 1
Students' own answers.

Activity 2
2 is he arriving 3 is he catching
4 is Ben meeting 5 is he meeting
6 are they having

Unit 7.2
Activity 1
Students' own answers.

Activity 2
Students' own answers.

Unit 7.4
Activity 1
2 'll tell, do 3 doesn't get, won't move
4 won't pass, don't do 5 helps, 'll help
6 don't panic, 'll get 7 will you feel, don't pass
8 Will she help, ask

Activity 2
2 If we make a lot of noise, my parents will tell us to be quiet.
3 If I have a math test, I will stay home to study / invite a friend to study with me.
4 If I get tired of studying, I will play a board game.

Unit 8.2
Activity 1
2 have been 3 has traveled 4 've had
5 haven't fallen 6 has never been

Activity 2
Students' own answers.

Activity 3
Students' own answers.

Unit 8.4
Activity 1
2 've just fixed 3 's just made 4 's just cleaned
5 's just left 6 've just missed

Activity 2
2 I've already had breakfast.
3 Have you finished yet?
4 We've already finished.
5 She hasn't done her homework yet.
6 Have they gotten their final grades yet?

NOTES

NOTES

NOTES

NOTES

NOTES